French Law of Contract

French Law of Contract

Barry Nicholas

Barrister, Principal of Brasenose College
and formerly Professor of Comparative Law
in the University of Oxford

London
Butterworths
1982

England   Butterworth & Co (Publishers) Ltd
           88 Kingsway, London WC2B 6AB

Australia Butterworths Pty Ltd
           271-273 Lane Cove Road, North Ryde, NSW 2113
           Also at Melbourne, Brisbane, Adelaide and Perth

Canada   Butterworth & Co (Canada) Ltd
           2265 Midland Avenue, Scarborough, M1P 4S1, Ontario
           Butterworth & Co (Western Canada)
           409 Granville Street, Ste 856, Vancouver, BC V6C 1T2

New Zealand Butterworths of New Zealand Ltd
           33-35 Cumberland Place, Wellington

South Africa Butterworth & Co (South Africa) (Pty) Ltd
           152-154 Gale Street, Durban

United States Mason Publishing Company
of America Finch Bldg, 366 Wacouta Street, St Paul, Minn 55101
           Butterworth (Legal Publishers) Inc
           160 Roy Street, Ste 300, Seattle, Wash 98109
           Butterworth (Legal Publishers) Inc
           381 Elliot Street, Newton, Upper Falls, Mass 02164

© Butterworth & Co (Publishers) Ltd 1982

ISBN Hardcover   0 406 63096 8
     Softcover   0 406 63095 X

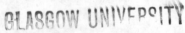
Printed in Singapore by Singapore National Printers (Pte) Limited

Preface

This book is an essay in comparative law in the sense that it attempts to set out the elements of the French law of contract as they appear to someone familiar with a Common law system, and in particular with English law. It assumes therefore that the reader is acquainted with the problems with which the law of contract has to deal in a modern western society, and that he approaches those problems with the methods and preconceptions of one whose first introduction to them was through the medium of the Common law. A comparative study of this kind should have two aims: to promote a better (and more critical) appreciation of the characteristic of one's own system, and to provide the essential keys to the understanding of the system with which the comparison is made. It should provide the keys, but not a full-scale exposition of the system itself. For this would both make the attainment of the first aim more difficult by importing an excess of detail, and also be (at least in the case of a system as accessible as the French) an unnecessary expense of labour. Comparative law, it has been well said, should enable one to use the index to a foreign law-book. This book therefore differs from a French book on the same subject[1] in leaving out both elementary matter directed to the beginner in the law and also a good deal of detail. But it differs also in other respects.

One of the important ways in which systems of law differ from one another (especially systems as divergent as the French and the English) is in their conceptual structure, and this difference must be reflected in any exposition, since the reader

1 But, as is said below (p. 19), it is not the French practice to write books on individual parts of the *droit civil*, such as the law of contract.

v

will otherwise lack an essential key. The arrangement of this book is therefore in general French, but since its purpose is to see French law through Common law eyes, that arrangement is modified not only by references throughout to corresponding Common law (and particularly English law) rules and institutions, but also by some modifications of the rigour of the arrangement itself.

A difference between this book and a French book of the classical type lies in its use of cases. The classical French textbook adheres to an abstract style of exposition and rarely leavens the abstraction by an admixture of concrete cases. This book tries, within the limits of the space available, to provide this leaven. In this it is in step with the type of French textbook which has begun to appear in the last few years. There is, however, for the readers of this book, a danger of being misled into thinking that cases play the same part in French law as they do in the Common law. One of the greatest difficulties for a Common lawyer is to get the 'feel' of his French counterpart's attitude to the authority of cases. Some attempt is made to communicate this 'feel' in the General Introduction to this book.

The subject matter, it must be emphasised, is the general principles of the law of contract. For reasons which are explained,[2] the specific contracts play a larger part in French law than in the Common law and the Common lawyer must bear in mind the importance for his French counterpart of the need to categorise an agreement as one of the specific contracts in order to determine the rules which apply to it.

But why French law and why the law of contract? A simple practical argument in favour of French law is that, though this book does not assume that the reader knows French, some acquaintance with the language is obviously an advantage in the study of a foreign system, and French is the foreign language most likely to be accessible to English-speaking lawyers. But beyond this there is the intrinsic importance of French law. For not only is it the law of France and the former French empire, but it is also the principal source of the laws of many other countries as well. The inherent virtues and the immense prestige of the Napoleonic Code led to its adoption

2 Pp. 44 f, 47, 55, below.

(or the adoption of codes based on it) not only in countries in which the Napoleonic writ once ran, but also in a number of others. The French legal family now includes Belgium, the Netherlands, Luxemburg, Italy, Spain, Portugal, Egypt, Quebec, Louisiana and countries of Latin America, as well as the francophone countries of the Third World.

The reasons for choosing the law of contract lie not only in its importance in any modern system, but also in the fact that the problems which it has to solve and the relationships which it has to regulate are the same in France as they are in England and therefore that the differences in method and approach can be seen unencumbered by differences of economic or social background. It is, moreover, a field in which lawyers are increasingly having to look beyond the confines of their own systems, particularly within the European Economic Community, and in which the movement for harmonisation and unification is likely to gain momentum. But before there can be harmonisation or unification there must first be mutual understanding.

From what has been said it will be evident that the book is directed in the first place to the student. The practitioner who needs advice on French law will of course go to an expert, but he will understand the expert's opinion the better for possessing what I have called the essential keys.

BARRY NICHOLAS
Oxford
December 1981

Contents

Table of French statutes

Table of French cases

xvii

Table of English statutes

Table of English cases etc

Table of codes and conventions

PAGE

Italy

Switzerland

Note on sources and literature

Legislation
Legislation is published in the appropriate part of the *Recueils* (see below, *Jurisprudence*). The five Codes (and other legislation on particular subjects which has been gathered together under the title of a Code, e g *Code du travail*, *Code des assurances*) are most conveniently found, together with related legislation, in the *Petits Codes Dalloz* edition.

Jurisprudence
The most commonly used reports are: *Recueil Sirey*, *Recueil Dalloz*, *Gazette du Palais* and *La Semaine Juridique* (usually referred to as *Jurisclasseur Périodique*). Sirey and Dalloz have been amalgamated (as *Recueil Dalloz Sirey*) since 1965. All these also include sections devoted to legislation and *doctrine*, the latter, in the case of Dalloz and Sirey, being indicated by the abbreviation Chr (see below).

Periodicals
A large amount of smaller scale doctrinal writing is found in the *Recueils* (above) in the form either of articles or of notes to cases. The principal review devoted to *droit civil* is the *Revue trimestrielle de droit civil* (cited as RT).

Textbooks
The characteristic work (see p. 19, below) covers the whole *droit civil*. The large-scale classical *traités* date from the nineteenth century, the most frequently cited being *Droit civil français* by Aubry and Rau in 12 vols (7th edn in course of

publication) and *Traité pratique de droit civil français* by
Planiol and Ripert (13 vols, 1952-1960). A smaller work on
the same pattern is the *Traité de droit civil* by G Ripert
and J Boulanger (4 vols, 1956-1959), based on the earlier
Traité élémentaire by Planiol and Ripert. It is cited here as
Ripert/Boulanger, references being to vol 2, unless otherwise
indicated.

A more modern (but already dating) work is *Droit civil* by G
Marty and P Raynaud (3 vols in 5, 1962-   ) (cited as Marty/
Raynaud, references, unless otherwise indicated, being to
vol 2(1)). It is distinguished by its lucid, concise and pene-
trating examination of doctrinal problems. A more discursive
approach, together with selected readings, is provided by
Leçons de droit civil by H, L and J Mazeaud (4 vols in 9,
current editions by de Juglart or Breton, 1967-   ). (Cited as
Mazeaud/Mazeaud, references, unless otherwise, being to vol
2(1).)

The modern student's textbook is best represented by:

- J Carbonnier *Droit civil* (4 vols, regularly re-edited), particularly valuable for its concise appendices to each section,
  dealing with historical, social and political aspects and with
  jurisprudence (vol 4, on *Obligations*, is cited simply as
  Carbonnier).
- A Weill and F Terré *Droit civil* (4 vols, unnumbered) is on a
  larger scale and with greater emphasis on *jurisprudence*.
  (The volume on *Obligations* is cited simply as Weill/Terré.)
- J Ghestin with others *Traité de droit civil* (2 vols so far
  published, 1977, 1980) is on a still larger scale and deals in a
  lively way with all aspects, particularly *jurisprudence* and
  modern legislative interventions. (The volume on *Les obligations - Le contrat* is cited simply as Ghestin *Contrat*.)

A useful work, left unfinished by its author's death is *Droit
civil* by Starck. The volume on *Obligations* (1972) is cited
simply as Starck.

A large scale modern work on liability in delict and contract
is *Traité théorique et pratique de la responsabilité civile délictuelle et contractuelle* by H and L Mazeaud (3 vols in 4; 6th
edn of vols 1 and 2 by Tunc); cited as Mazeaud/Tunc.

Encyclopaedias
There are two loose-leaf encyclopaedias dealing with civil law: *Encyclopédie Dalloz - Droit civil*, arranged alphabetically by subject, and, on a much larger scale, *Jurisclasseur Civil*, following the arrangement of the *Code civil* (cited as J-Cl Civ).

Source-book
A Source-book on French Law by Kahn-Freund, Lévy and Rudden (2nd edn, 1979) provides a valuable collection of materials (in French; principally doctrinal writings and cases) on the French legal system and its methods and on the law of contract, together with introductory and connecting matter (and questions designed to provoke thought) by the authors. (Cited as *Source-book*.)

Abbreviations

a Citations of cases

These follow the usual French convention, giving the court, the date of the decision and the reference to the relevant *Recueil* (see above). Decisions of the *Cour de cassation* are indicated by Cass, followed by either civ, indicating one of the three *chambres civiles* (see p. 8, n. 9, below) or com, crim or soc, indicating the *chambre commerciale*, *criminelle* or *sociale*; in cases before 1947 Cass req indicates the *chambre des requêtes* (which acted as a filter for the other chambers, its decisions being reasoned only when they were for rejection of the *pourvoi*). *Cours d'appel* are indicated by the place in which they sit (e g Paris or Lyon) and lower courts by self-explanatory abbreviations.

The *Recueils* are indicated as follows:

S	Sirey
D	Dalloz
Gaz Pal	Gazette du Palais
JCP	Jurisclasseur Périodique
	(or Semaine Jurisdique)

followed in each case by the year. The prefix D may, according to the period concerned, be followed by a letter indicating the part concerned, DA referring to the part entitled *Analytique*, DC to the part entitled *Critique* and DH to the part entitled *Hebdomadaire*. The last figure in the reference is always the page number, but between this and the year there may, again according to the period concerned, be an indication of the relevant section of the volume. In older volumes of S or D the figures 1, 2, and 3 denote respectively the sections containing decisions of the *Cour de cassation*, other civil courts and administrative courts; in current volumes of D the abbreviation Somm denotes the section containing *Sommaires*. As indicated above, Chr denotes the part entitled *Chronique*, which contains doctrinal articles. In Gaz Pal the figures 1 and 2 refer to the half-yearly volumes.

b Citations of literature
i *French textbooks*
The following abbreviations are explained above (Sources and literature):

Carbonnier
Ghestin
Marty/Raynaud
Mazeaud/Mazeaud
Mazeaud/Tunc
Ripert/Boulanger
Starck
Weill/Terré

ii *Others*

Amos & Walton	*Amos & Walton's Introduction to French Law* (2nd edn) by F H Lawson, A E Anton and L Neville Brown (1963)
Nicholas *Roman Law*	B Nicholas *Introduction to Roman Law* (1962)
Source-book	See above (Sources and literature)
Treitel *Contract*	G H Treitel *The Law of Contract* (5th edn, 1979)
Zweigert/Kötz	K Zweigert and H Kötz *An Introduction to Comparative Law* (2 vols, translated by Tony Weir, 1977)

c Other abbreviations

al	*alinéa* (a clause within an article of a Code or *loi*)
Cc	*Code civil*
C com	*Code de commerce*
CE	*Conseil d'Etat*
RT	*Revue trimestrielle de droit civil*

Chapter one
General introduction

1 Common law and Civil law[1]

French law belongs to that family of legal systems to which we attach the name of 'Civil law'. This family embraces the systems of continental Europe (or at least western Europe), and also of Latin America and many other countries which derive their legal systems from continental Europe. The name is often criticised, especially by Civil lawyers themselves, because it refers to only one element in the tradition which unites those systems, and also because it ignores the differences which distinguish one from another. (In much the same way in ordinary life a stranger sees the resemblances between members of a family, while they themselves are more aware of their individuality.) But the usage is inveterate among Common lawyers, and the name, if properly understood, does point to some important characteristics which the systems have in common and which are foreign to the Common law.

The origin of the name is clear. To the Romans the term *ius civile* had meant, at its widest, the law of a particular state, or, more narrowly, the law of Rome herself. It was in accordance with this usage that Justinian's compilation of Roman law came to be known, after its rediscovery in the eleventh century, as the *Corpus Iuris Civilis*. And 'Civil law' thereafter meant the rediscovered Roman law. As this law was 'received' by the

---

1 F H Lawson *A Common Lawyer Looks at the Civil Law*; J H Merryman *The Civil Law Tradition*. For more precise categorisations see Zweigert/Kötz vol 1; R David, J E C Brierley *Major Legal Systems in the World To-day*.

1

emergent states and cities of continental Europe as a *ius commune*,[2] or common law, which was applied in default of, or to a varying extent in substitution for, the local law, it was natural that the English, whose courts had stood apart from this reception, should see in this common factor the identifying mark of the legal systems of the continent. Nor did they habitually make any distinction between this contemporary Civil law and the historical law of Rome. Blackstone, for example, calls it 'the imperial law'.[3]

During the last two hundred years, however, the justification for thus seeing the laws of the continent as predominantly Roman law in a modern context has diminished. The most important influence in this dwindling of the Roman element has been the movement for codification, the first great achievement of which was the enactment of Napoleon's *Code civil* in 1804. The codes which thereafter spread over Europe were important (in this context) in two ways. First, they cut the law off from its Roman roots: the *Corpus Iuris Civilis* could no longer be cited as direct authority. If Roman rules were still applied, this was because they were embodied in the relevant code, and not (except as a matter of history) because they were to be found in the *Corpus Iuris*. Moreover, as Roman law disappeared from the courts, it took on a different appearance in the lecture room. The interest shifted from the task of interpreting the *Corpus Iuris* as a practical system to that of unearthing the classical law. For that law lay buried beneath both the editorial work of Justinian and the heavy layer of interpretation and harmonisation which had been elaborated by centuries of activity in the universities of Europe. 'Civil law' (or *ius commune*) was now seen to be not the same as Roman law.

This does not mean that there are no common elements in, say, French and German law which justify our still speaking of them as 'Civil law systems', but they are Civil law in a different sense. They belong to the Civil law because their methods of thought, their attitudes to law and its sources, derive from the centuries in which the *ius commune*, Romanistic but not Roman, was created out of the materials in the *Corpus Iuris*. And those methods and attitudes are different, as we shall see,

2 Nicholas *Roman Law* pp. 45 ff.
3 *Commentaries* (1st edn) p. 5.

from those of the English Common law, which was nurtured in a quite other environment.

The Roman element, therefore, has dwindled since the coming of the codes. Its importance was indeed never as exclusive as the English use of the name 'Civil law' suggested. Apart from Canon law (which was Roman in spirit and, like Roman law, universal), there were everywhere two other elements: customary law and legislation. But these varied from one legal system to another, or even, in the case of customary law, from one local area to another, and it was natural for the Common lawyer to emphasise the universal element. Moreover the non-Roman elements were mainly to be found in those areas of the law (the law of the family and of inheritance) which are everywhere most likely to be affected by differences of culture and of what one now calls 'policy'. The contribution of Roman law, on the other hand, was strongest in the parts which have, at least until recently, been most exclusively the handiwork of lawyers: the law of obligations (and especially the law of contract, which is the concern of this book), the law of property, and the general conceptual framework of the whole system. The advent of the codes, however (and this was the second way in which they diminished the Roman character of the systems to which they applied), unified and systematised the customary element, while the spirit of the times and the complexity of modern life has everywhere produced an ever-swelling volume of legislation only loosely related to the traditional Roman framework.

It is this framework which provides a link between the Common lawyer's use of 'Civil law' and the meaning which French lawyers give to *droit civil*. In its widest sense this denotes the whole of private law. In practice, however, as a glance at any of the many works published under this title will show, the term refers primarily and usually to the contents of the *Code civil*. And the *Code civil* is concerned with the central and traditional parts of the private law: the law of persons (or family law), the law of property and of succession, and the law of obligations. This is the heart of the private law, the trunk of the tree from which grow the more particular branches. All other parts (and, as has just been said, they are now both extensive and important) pre-suppose the *droit civil*. And the *droit civil* in this sense goes back to Justinian's Institutes, which

provide the framework of the *Corpus Iuris* and therefore of the
'Civil law' in the Common lawyer's sense, even though (it must
be said again) the substance which is now attached to some
parts of this framework is anything but Roman. The framework, however, though it is to be found in varying forms in all
'Civil law' systems, is not, from the point of view of the Common lawyer, the most important of the differentiating characteristics of those systems. We should now look more closely at
those differences of method and attitude to which reference
has already been made.

2 Characteristics of French law

The differences of method and attitude which have now to be
identified derive, we have said, from the *ius commune*. For
though important elements of French law come, as we have
seen, from canon law, customary law and legislation, the Common lawyer finds the principal differentiating characteristics
of the system in the inheritance from this *ius commune*.

The heart of the matter is that the *ius commune* is a law of
the book, elaborated in the universities, whereas the Common
law is a law of the case, created by the courts. The *ius commune*, in theory at least, sprang fully formed from the *Corpus
Iuris Civilis*, the function of the universities being that of interpretation. The Common law, on the other hand, is in a state of
continuous creation and by its nature is never complete.
Again, the *ius commune* was seen as universally valid,
regardless of time or place. It was a set of rules for the conduct
of life in society – rules which might or might not be applied in
any particular court or jurisdiction. (Hence it is still true today
that in the universities of the continent law is studied by large
numbers who will never go into practice.) The Common law,
by contrast, is concerned to provide solutions to individual
disputes, not to propound universal precepts; and it is
expressed, in its traditional form, in terms of actions or remedies rather than of substantive rules. In so far as nowadays it
does think in terms of rules, those rules are seen as a generalisation from the solutions of individual disputes, whereas for the
Civil lawyer the rules logically precede the solutions. In short,

for the Common law the beginning is the case, whereas for the *ius commune* the beginning is the book.

With the advent of the codes the character of the book changes, but the conception of law remains the same. The beginning is now the code or codes, not the *Corpus Iuris*, but the primacy of the written law remains. Law is still seen as a system, complete and intellectually coherent, composed of substantive rules. And the creative function is still that of interpretation, a function exercised in the first place by the universities. The decisions of the courts are, in conventional theory, merely an application of the enacted law. Some of these features need further examination in the particular context of French law.

a Primacy of legislation

In the conventional French analysis there are only two sources of law: legislation and custom. The latter is only interstitial and in the present context can be ignored. Law is primarily and characteristically a body of rules enacted by the state, to be found in the codes and, in ever-increasing measure, in legislation supplementary to the codes. The Common lawyer's approach is quite different. For him law has characteristically been the unwritten law found in the decisions of the courts. It is true, of course, that legislation is the primary source in the sense that in case of conflict it will prevail, but it has traditionally been regarded as an inroad on or suspension of the Common law, which will revive when the legislation is repealed.

This difference is reflected in a difference in the approach of the two systems to the interpretation of legislation (and, as a corollary, a difference in the style of drafting).[4] The English courts, seeing legislation as an inroad on the basic unwritten law, interpret it restrictively, so as to minimise the inroad. This attitude would make no sense for the French lawyer for whom the basic law is itself legislation. In the period of the *ius commune*, when lawyers had to adapt the unchanging texts of the *Corpus Iuris* to the changing needs of society and to find a

---

4 See, however, the observations of Lord Wilberforce in *James Buchanan & Co Ltd v Babco Forwarding and Shipping (UK) Ltd* [1978] AC 141 at 153.

harmony in the rich disordance of these texts, they necessarily adopted a very free and creative method of interpretation. The method remains, and it is indeed in accord with the relatively subordinate position which is allotted to the judiciary by the French version of the separation of powers.[5] Legislation is a manifestation of the will of the state and the function of the judiciary as an organ of the state is to give effect to that will.

This function is pre-supposed by the simplicity and brevity of French legistative drafting. The English draftsman tries to make his text 'judge-proof' by anticipating every eventuality, and he often in consequence produces a complex and technical formulation which only a lawyer can interpret. The French draftsman, by contrast, can rely on the collaboration of the courts, and his text is therefore often limited to quite broad propositions. That this is true of the *Code civil* is well-known (and it is a source of pride and confidence to the Frenchman that his law is presented in a simple and intelligible form) but even the necessarily more complex legislation of modern times leaves much to be filled in by interpretation.

b Character of the codes

If legislation is the characteristic form of law in France and the codes are the characteristic form of legislation, the *Code civil* is the characteristic code. The Napoleonic codification consisted of five codes, but the term *Code Napoléon* was reserved for the *Code civil* alone.[6] And with justice. For the *Code civil* is the centre-piece to which the great influence of the whole codification is attributable.

A code in the strict sense is a systematic and complete statement of a body of law. In this sense the *Corpus Iuris Civilis* of Justinian is not a code. For though it is complete, it is not in any recognisable way systematic. The *Code civil* is systematic, though its system (which echoes, without entirely reproducing, that of the Institutes of Gaius and Justinian) is, as a piece of analysis, easily criticised; and it is a complete statement of the law governing relations between individuals (except in so far as these are governed by the *Code de commerce*) as that law was understood in 1804. We have seen, however, that even then the

5 See further p. 22, below.
6 It has not been used since the end of the Second Empire.

simplicity and brevity of its drafting left much to be supplied
by interpretation, and it is now not complete in any sense. For
the increasing complexity of modern life has called forth a
large body of additional legislation. Some of this can be said
merely to amplify the provisions of the Code, but by far the
greater part is concerned with matters quite outside the area of
the traditional *droit civil*. Codification, moreover, creates an
expectation that all law will be presented in a systematic form,
and a good deal of the additional legislation has itself been
reduced to the form of subordinate codes. In England, by contrast, even in those areas of the law which are largely the creation of legislation, a systematic statement of the whole body of
the law is not undertaken. At most, as in the Companies Act
1948, a consolidation of existing legislation is enacted, but this
leaves the essential Common law foundations unstated; and
when such a consolidation comes to be amended, as in the
Companies Act 1967, no attempt is made to build the new
legislation into the old. A codifying statute is a rarity, and the
few which have been enacted deal in fact with areas of the law
which were almost entirely judge-made.[7]

c The courts and the position of the judiciary

Before embarking on the (to an English lawyer) rather elusive
subject of the authority of case law, we must look briefly at the
French court system.[8] This is a system with three tiers, as in
England, but beyond this the similarities are few.

In the lower two tiers the courts, as well as being more
numerous than in this country, are markedly decentralised. In
the first tier we may ignore the 475 *tribunaux d'instance*,
which may be said very roughly to correspond to the English
county courts, in that their jurisdiction is limited to relatively
minor suits. But there are also 175 *tribunaux de grande
instance*, exercising an unlimited jurisdiction. There is
nothing to correspond to the concentration of major civil
litigation in London: the only cases tried in Paris are those
which originate in Paris. Similarly, in the second tier there are
29 *cours d' appel*, each hearing appeals from the *tribunaux* of

7 Bills of Exchange Act 1882, Partnership Act 1890, Sale of Goods Act 1893
(repealed and re-enacted 1979), Marine Insurance Act 1906.
8 *Source-book* pp. 275 ff.

one or more *départements*. (Each *tribunal de grande instance* and each *cour d' appel* will be composed of several chambers or divisions.)

There is, moreover, a difference beteen a French *appel* and an English appeal. A *cour d' appel* conducts a re-examination of the whole case, and can substitute its view of either facts or law for that of the original court. It is true that the English Court of Appeal is empowered to do the same, but in practice it will not interfere with the trial court's view of the primary facts (i e what was said or done), though it may feel free to substitute its own view of the secondary facts, (i e the interpretation to be put on the primary facts). The reason for this difference lies in the difference between the English and the French trial. In England the facts are in principle established by oral evidence elicited by the adversarial process in a single continuous hearing. A repetition of this hearing is impracticable, and for the Court of Appeal to rely on the written record alone would be inconsistent with the firmly held judicial belief in the importance of seeing and hearing the witnesses. In France, on the other hand, the facts are in principle established in a written *dossier* compiled by a predominantly investigatory process by the court itself, and a review of the *dossier* does not present the same difficulty.

The only court with jurisdiction over the whole country is the *Cour de cassation* (composed of five chambers for civil cases[9] and one for criminal).[10] This is a court of error, in the sense that the only basis for recourse to it (*pourvoi en cassation*) is that the judgment of the court below reveals a *violation de la loi*, i e an incorrect foundation in law. (The court below must be a court from which there is no appeal. It will usually be a *cour d' appel*, but may be an inferior court if in the particular case no appeal is allowed, e g because the amount in issue is too small.) If the *Cour de cassation* finds the *pourvoi* justified, it does not substitute its own judgment, as a *cour d' appel* does, but, as its name indicates, it merely quashes the decision. The case is then remitted for further consideration, not to the original court but to another court of equal jurisdiction. If this

9 Three *chambres civiles*, a *chambre sociale* and a *chambre commerciale*.
10 If the *jurisprudence* of different chambers is in conflict or if the point in issue is particularly important, the case is heard by a *chambre mixte*.

court nevertheless takes the same view of the law as the original court, the matter is referred to the *Assemblée plénière* of the *Cour de cassation*, on which all chambers are represented. The *Assemblée plénière* is empowered to enter a final judgment if the issues are the same as in the original hearing. If they are not, or the *Assemblée* thinks it lacks the information necessary for a judgment, it remits the matter to a third court, which is bound by the view of the law taken by the *Assemblée*.

The *Cour de cassation* differs greatly from the House of Lords.[11] Its primary function is to secure a uniform interpretation of the law. In England this unifying function is usually discharged by the Court of Appeal itself, leaving to the House of Lords the function of resolving legal issues of public importance and, in general, guiding the development of the law. This function does indeed also belong to the *Cour de cassation*, but its discharge is hampered by the primacy of the unifying function. For that function requires – or is seen as requiring – that there should be unrestricted access to the *Cour de cassation* for every litigant who wishes to argue a point of law. Any filter such as that provided by the need, before an appeal can be launched in the House of Lords, to obtain leave from the Court of Appeal (or the Appeals Committee of the House of Lords) is ruled out. This absence of a filter, combined with the much larger volume of cases before the French courts, means that the *Cour de cassation* is swamped and cannot find time for the unhurried thought and debate which difficult issues call for. (The five civil chambers decide well over 6,000 cases a year, compared with about 50 in the House of Lords.) It also means that the court is numerically very large (its judicial personnel amount to 120) and lacks the unity which a small court like the House of Lords can achieve.

With the exception of the *tribunaux d' instance*, all courts are 'collegial'. By this is meant not only that they consist of a bench of at least three judges (at least seven in the *Cour de cassation*), but also that they act as a body, giving only a single judgment. Dissenting opinions are unknown, and even the existence of dissent is not revealed. Moreover the laconic form

11 For a survey of supreme courts see the special issue of Rev int droit comp 30 (1978) 5 ff, esp. the *synthèse* by Tunc.

of the judgment (discussed below)[12] offers none of the opportunity for the expression of individual views which is afforded
by its discursive English counterpart. The leading English
judges are public figures whose judgments and attitudes are
the subject of discussion in the press and elsewhere, but the
French judge is typically anonymous. He is, as Montesquieu
put it,[13] the mouthpiece of the law.

There are two departures from this principle of anonymity:
the *rapport* of the member of the court to whom the case is
remitted for initial consideration, and the *conclusions* of the
representative of the *ministère public*.

The predominantly written character of French procedure
makes it possible (and the pressure of business, especially in the
Cour de cassation, would in any case make it necessary) for the
initial consideration of each case to be assigned to only one
member of the court (or chamber). He presents a *rapport*,
which examines the state of the law, including the case law,
and the arguments before the court, and discusses wider considerations of what we would call 'policy'. It reads in fact rather
like an English judgment (except that it is directed to convincing the court rather than the parties or their representatives) and it contrasts markedly with the impersonal and
unargumentative style of the formal judgment. The *rapport* is
then in principle discussed, and the judgment which is proposed is accepted, rejected or amended, by the full bench, but
it is clear that in practice, at least in the *Cour de cassation*, the
volume of cases to be dealt with precludes substantial discussion or amendment in all but a small minority of cases.

The *ministère public*[14] has no counterpart in Common law
jurisdictions. The judicial profession (*magistrature*) is divided
into two branches: the judiciary in the ordinary sense, i e those
who sit on the bench (*magistrature assise*) and the *ministère
public*, whose function is to represent before the court the
public interest (*magistrature debout*, since they stand to
address the court). There is no rigid division between the two
branches: a *magistrat* may pass from one to the other in the
course of his career. The *ministère public*, representatives of

12 P. 12.
13 *L'Esprit des lois* xi.vi.
14 Or *parquet*. See generally *Source-book* pp. 286 ff.

which are attached to each court from the *tribunaux de grande instance* upwards,[15] has several functions (including the conduct of the prosecution in criminal cases), but we are here concerned with the representations (*conclusions*) made to the civil courts about the cases before them. The representative of the *ministère public* has the right to place before the court his *conclusions* as to how the case before it should be decided. He does so as the representative of the public interest, but this is not to be understood in a broad sense as the interest of society at large, as contrasted with the interests of the individual litigants. The interest which he represents is rather the interest of the state in the correct functioning of the legal system, seen as a public service. (It is for this reason that in cases before the *Cour de cassation* the *ministère public* not only may, but must submit *conclusions*. For every recourse to that court necessarily, as we have seen, alleges a *violation de la loi*.) The *conclusions* are therefore similar in content to the *rapport*, though the style may be more rhetorical and more vigorously argued (reflecting the difference in standpoint of the speaker). Both are expressions of the speaker's own views.

The *conclusions* or the *rapport* are occasionally published along with the judgment itself. The publication of the *conclusions* is not, of course, a breach of the principle of collegiality, since the author is not a member of the court, but the publication of the *rapport* – especially when, as is sometimes the case, the court has rejected the recommendation made – is tantamount to such a breach. But both give an insight into the working of judicial minds and the possible or probable reasoning behind the decision. This, and often the elegance and vigour of their argumentation, make the reader regret that they are not published more often and that such talent is otherwise confined in the strait-jacket of the formal judgment.

A more surprising breach of the principle of collegiality occurs when a member of the court writes a note on the case – even on occasion a note criticising the decision.

15 In the *Cour de cassation* there is a *procureur-général* (who ranks in the judicial hierarchy next after the *Premier président* of that court) and seventeen *avocats-généraux*; in each *Cour d'appel* there is a *procureur-général*, one or more *avocats-généraux* and one or more *substituts du procureur-général*; and in each *tribunal de grande instance* there is a *procureur de la République* with one or more *substituts*.

d Authority of case law[16]

The courts of the *ancien régime* (the *parlements*) were one of
the main objects of the hostility of the Revolution, not least
because of their pretensions to a law-making function. The
Constituent Assembly of 1790 took care that the new courts
should be confined to the narrowly judicial function of
applying the law in suits between private individuals (or, in
criminal matters, between the state and the individual). They
were to have no jurisdiction over the administration,[17] and in
exercising their proper function they were not to lay down
general rules. They were even required to refer any matter of
interpretation to the legislature. This was of course quite
impracticable and remained a dead letter, but the prohibition
against laying down general rules when deciding individual
cases was repeated in article 5 of the *Code civil*.[18]

This attempt to prevent the growth of case law was under-
mined, however, by another requirement laid down by the
Assembly. The *parlements* had not given reasons for their decisions, but now, in order to ensure that the courts did not
exceed their powers, every decision was to be 'motivated'. The
form of judgment which the courts adopted to meet this
requirement (and which survives without significant change
today) does not set out, as an English judgment does, the process
of argument by which the decision was reached – this would
have been inconsistent with the ruling mechanistic view of the
judicial process; but equally it does not simply state the
legislative text upon which the decision was based – the
generality of many provisions in the Codes would have defeated
the original purpose of the requirement of 'motivation'. The
form adopted states a principle from which, by syllogistic
reasoning applied to the facts, the decision can be logically
derived. The principle is presented as self-evident and is in
theory, in the normal case, derived from a text or texts which
are cited at the beginning of the judgment. But it is of course

16 *Source-book* pp. 116 ff. For a selection from the large literature see
Source-book pp. 539 f. On the history see J P Dawson *Oracles of the Law*
ch V.
17 See further p. 22, below.
18 'The Judges are forbidden to make pronouncements of a general and
normative kind (*prononcer par voie de disposition générale et réglement-
aire*) on the cases brought before them.'

in the act of derivation that the creative power of the judiciary resides, and the result of requiring that act to be recorded was inevitably the evolution of what is in substance a vast body of judge-made law.

It was not, however, until late in the nineteenth century that the literature of the law began seriously to take cognizance of this development. This delay reflects the dominance in the thought of the period of the positivist view of law as the expression of the will of the state (a view which accords, as we have seen, with the doctrine of the separation of powers and which is still to be found in French textbooks). The persistence of the mechanistic view of the role of the courts was also, however, encouraged by the form of the judgment, which, by making no reference to the arguments which have led the court to adopt the governing principle (even when the court is in fact reversing a previously established principle), conceals the creative process.[19]

No-one, in any event, now disputes that the decisions of the courts (*la jurisprudence*) must play a large part in any attempt to state the law. To go no further, what we should call the law of torts, which is stated in the *Code civil* in only five articles, is very largely a creation of the courts,[20] and the law of unjustified enrichment derives from a decision of the *Cour de cassation* in 1892 which did not even purport to be based on a text.[1] The writers regularly, and increasingly, take account of *jurisprudence*; no practitioner would fail to deal with it in presenting a case; and though the judgments (with some exceptions in the lower courts) continue to make no reference to it, it is fully examined in the *conclusions* of the representative of the *ministère public* and in the *rapport*.

The constitutional theory that *jurisprudence* cannot be a legal source is, however, normally maintained.[2] Theory and practice may be reconciled by drawing a distinction between a source (in law) and an authority (in fact).[3] It is an obvious and important fact that courts do follow previous decisions, and

19 For a trenchant criticism of this form see Touffait and Tunc RT (1974) 487 ff.
20 See p. 29, below.
1 See Nicholas (1962) 36 Tulane L Rev 605, 622 ff.
2 An exception is Starck *Droit Civil - Introduction* ss. 119 ff.
3 Carbonnier *Droit civil* (13th edn) vol 1, s. 31.

statements of what the law is necessarily take account of this fact. But it is nevertheless a fact and not a rule; no court is legally required to follow any previous decision. There is no system of binding precedent, though there is a practice which produces similar results. This may look like splitting hairs to preserve a principle, but the distinction between rule and fact does have practical consequences, and the results, though similar, are not identical.

The practical consequences lie partly in the way in which judgments are formulated and partly in the attitude of judges. The former is indeed something of a technicality. A court may not cite as the justification for its decision a previous decision, or line of decisions, even of the *Cour de cassation*. If it does so, the decision will be quashed for lack of legal foundation. Conversely, if the *Cour de cassation* wishes to quash a decision as being in conflict with its own *jurisprudence*, and every lawyer knows that this is what it is doing, it will nonetheless state as the foundation for its decision not the *jurisprudence*, but the text or legal principle of which the *jurisprudence* is ostensibly an interpretation.[4]

As far as the attitude of judges is concerned, the consequences of the distinction between rule and fact are not merely technical. To say that an English judge of first instance is bound by decisions of the Court of Appeal is not merely to say that he will in fact follow these decisions, or that even if he does not, his decision will be overturned on appeal; it is an assertion both that the judge accepts that he must follow those decisions and that, if he were not to do so, even on good grounds, he would be subject to criticism by the profession.[5] The French judges accept that they ought usually to follow decisions of the *Cour de cassation*, if only because stability and predictability are important in the law, but their legal duty is to apply the

4 There are other practical consequences. For example, a *Cour d'appel*, wishing to help litigants in a particular type of case, gave a direction as to practice and procedure; this was quashed by the *Cour de cassation* on the intervention of the *Procureur-général* (Civ 22.10.1957, D 1957.772). Another *Cour d'appel*, having to deal with a case involving a standard-form contract in common use in its area, included in the *motifs* a general statement about the meaning of a clause in this contract; the decision was quashed (Civ 16.6.1955, RT (1955)696). See Sinay D 1958 Chr 85.
5 Cf Hart *Concept of Law* pp. 54 ff.

law and if they are convinced that a decision of the *Cour de cassation* does not represent the law, they will ignore it; and they will not incur the same criticism as would an English judge. Resistance of this kind to decisions of the *Cour de cassation* is not very uncommon and may, if maintained, particularly by several *Cours d'appel*, presage a change (*revirement*). For what is true of the lower courts is true also of the *Cour de cassation*, and there has never been any suggestion that that court is bound by its own decisions. It is usually said, however, that there is one court — the *Assemblée plénière* – which has such authority that no other court would think of going against it.

There is , then, no rule of binding precedent, but there is a well-established practice that lower courts will normally follow the *jurisprudence* of the *Cour de cassation*. This leaves open, of course, the question of what constitutes a *jurisprudence*. It has often been said that the important difference in practice between the English and the French systems of precedent is that in England a simple decision is sufficient, whereas in France authority attaches to what is called a *jurisprudence constante*, i e to a concordant series of decisions. But it is easy to point to single decisions which marked a new departure – and were immediately recognised as doing so. The significant distinction is rather between an *arrêt de principe* and an *arrêt d'espèce*, i e between a judgment which is intended to establish a principle (either because the case law has been uncertain or conflicting or because the court has decided to alter its previous jurisprudence) and one which, as an English lawyer might say, is to be confined to its own facts. This is not to suggest that all decisions are capable of being labelled as one or the other. The great majority of the vast number of *arrêts* rendered every year by the *Cour de cassation* are unremarkable decisions which merely augment an already well-established *jurisprudence constante* on the matter in issue. It is to the small residue of cases which do not fit into this category that the distinction applies. It is not, of course, a distinction which declares itself on the face of the *arrêt*, and its application is a matter of art as much as of science, but the reader of the French reports will acquire a part of the skill if he remembers that in a literary form as laconic as that of the French judgment, particularly as it is practised in the *Cour de cassation*, no word is wasted and none is unconsidered. For example, the formulation of the principle which constitutes the major premise of the judgment will often be repeated unaltered through dozens or hundreds of cases, while the critical reader wonders at the increasingly forced interpretation of either the principle or the facts which is necessary in order to complete the syllogism, until finally a small alteration is made which so adjusts the principle that the forced interpretation is no longer necessary. This is one example of an *arrêt de principe*.[6]

There remains a very considerable difference in the methods by which in the two systems the principle established by a decision is identified. In the example just given the alert reader will notice the change in formulation, but may well be left in doubt as to what it portends. The judgment itself will give him no assistance. If he is fortunate, this may be one of the rare cases in which the *conclusions* or the *rapport* are published. Otherwise he must interpret the change in the light of the *doctrine* on the subject, which will have discussed the difficulties presented by the previous cases. An attempt at such an interpretation will often be appended as a *note* to the report.

In an English judgment, on the other hand, the principle of the case is not encapsulated in a single carefully pruned and polished sentence. The decision of the case typically evolves from an examination of the previous cases and a discussion of how far the pattern set by those cases needs to be adapted to accommodate the new fact situation. The characteristic English intellectual device of 'distinguishing' is unknown in France, both because the form of the judgment provides no opportunity for it and because, at least in the *Cour de cassation*, the facts play a subordinate role, and may indeed be so elliptically stated as to be unintelligible without a reference to the decision of the court below. The reason for this is in part that the *Cour de cassation* is, as we have seen, concerned only with an examination of the proposition of law relied on by the court below, and in part that the courts as a whole still think of the judical process as one of applying to the facts before them a rule established a priori.[7] The cases are illustrations of prin-

6 For a discussion see Ghestin and Goubeaux *Traité de droit civil – Introduction générale* ss. 465 ff.
7 Cf Zweigert/Kötz vol 1, p. 267.

ciples rather than the material from which principles are drawn.

This attitude to facts lends considerable importance to the distinction between fact and law. The *Cour de cassation* cannot interfere with the finding of fact made by the court which tried the case (and this, on the French view of the nature of an appeal, includes the *cour d'appel*). Facts are within the *pouvoir souverain du juge du fond* (unless his interpretation of the primary facts is so unreasonable that it can be said to have 'denatured' them).[8] From this it follows that the wider the area of what is categorised as fact, the more restricted will be the unifying power of the *Cour de cassation*. The view of cases as illustrations, which is an aspect of the tendency of a 'law of the book' to formulate broad rules, leaves a large area to fact. In the Common law, by contrast, since the law evolves from the cases, there is a constant tendency for fact to harden into law. Case-made rules are by their nature narrow. From time to time an act of judicial generalisation, or perhaps the intervention of the legislature, will produce a broad rule or principle, but the process of producing small rules out of facts will then resume.

In general therefore the area of fact is wider in French law than in English. This means, of course, that the operation of the law is less predictable, that the discretion of the court is more extensive. We shall find instances of this in the law of contract, but two may be mentioned here. The English law of offer and acceptance embraces a number of detailed rules evolved from the cases. In French law, by contrast, there is only one broad rule – that there must be agreement.[9] Whether there is agreement or not, and when and where the agreement occurred, is a matter of fact. This at least is the position in strict theory, but the inconvenience of such a lack of certainty and predictability has led, as we shall see, to some stretching of the area of law.

Again, the *Code civil* lays down the broad rule that a mistake makes an agreement null if it concerns the 'substance' of the object to which the agreement relates.[10] What constitutes 'substance' is a question of fact outside the control of

8 See p. 47, below.
9 Art 1108 Cc.
10 Art 1110 Cc.

the *Cour de cassation*, and since the form of the judgment
given by the trial court does not require it to justify or explain
its interpretation of the word, or to relate that interpretation to
the interpretations implicit in other decisions of the same or
other courts, there is here a very wide area open to judicial
discretion. The French judge, supposedly confined and controlled by a clear written law, often in fact has a much freer
hand than the English judge.

e Functions of *doctrine*

By *doctrine* is meant the whole body of writing about the law
by those learned in it. As its name indicates, it originated in the
teaching of the universities and it is still to a very large extent
the work of academic writers. As we have seen, the *ius commune* was created in the universities out of the materials in
the *Corpus Iuris*, and it was to the universities that the
courts looked for an authoritative interpretation of that
law. Any system of law, if it is to be capable of growth and
adaptation, must have, in addition to a body of rules, a web of
principles from which those rules derive. These principles can
never be exhaustively defined or finally fixed. They derive
from a continuing debate. In classical Roman law this debate
was conducted by the jurists; in medieval England it was to be
heard in the courts (and its content was much more technical).
In Europe of the *ius commune* the debate was conducted in the
universities and in the literature which emanated from them.
If one is to find its equivalent in the Common law, at any rate
before the beginnings of academic writing in the last two
decades of the nineteenth century, one must look in the
judgments of the courts. The argumentative form of the
English judgment provides, in the hands of the great judges,
something of that web of principles to which we have referred.
The English judgment fulfils in fact two functions. In its *ratio
decidendi* it constitutes a source of law; in its discursive
element it provides a part of what is supplied in French law by
doctrine. The part which it cannot provide is large-scale
systematic exposition, and it is only in the course of the last 100
years that this gap has gradually been filled, as it always has
been in France, by academic writing. There remains a marked,

though diminishing, difference in the authority which is attached to such writing in the two systems. In France *doctrine* has inherited the authority enjoyed by the universities in the period of the *ius commune*, an authority which is augmented by the relatively subordinate position which is, as we have seen, accorded to the judiciary in the constitutional scheme. The positions are reversed in England, though the standing accorded to academic writing by the courts (and its influence on their decisions) has risen considerably in recent decades.

The typical product of French *doctrine* is the large-scale treatise or the student's manual. It is in accord with the French conception of law as a system that these works usually embrace the entire *droit civil*, or the entire *droit commercial*, or at least a large and coherent part of it, such as the law of obligations. The English practice of writing books, such as this one, on the law of contract by itself is unknown, since, as we shall see, the law of contract can only be properly understood as part of the law of obligations. In those areas outside the traditional *droit civil* which constitute appendages to it, the pattern is more like that with which we are familiar.

In addition to the treatises and manuals, there are also specialised monographs (often academic theses) and articles, but the peculiar contribution of French *doctrine* has been the *note* appended to a case and providing an explanation of and commentary on it. This has provided a bridge between traditional *doctrine* and the courts. On the one hand it has brought into the mainstream of the law the rich contribution of *jurisprudence* which would otherwise have been locked up in the cramped clauses of the judgments, and on the other hand it has brought the courts into touch with the critical and creative debate of which we have already spoken.

It should be said that not all *notes* are the work of academic writers. They may also be contributed by practitioners or by judges – even on occasion, as we have already remarked, by a judge who took part in the decision.

f Conceptualism and pragmatism
It is sometimes said that the Civil law is excessively conceptual or 'logical' or 'formalist', whereas the Common law is

pragmatic and concrete. (A similar contrast is made, within the Common law between English law and American law.)[11] This observation seems to bear two different meanings.

(i) It can mean that the Civil law will apply a given principle or concept 'logically' even though the practical consequences are unjust or inconvenient, whereas the Common law will abandon a principle if its consequences are unacceptable. More precisely[12] this is a contrast not between logic and the lack of it, but between an approach which treats principles as having an immutable meaning (or at least is unwilling to re-examine the established interpretation in the light of its consequences), and one which acknowledges that meanings and interpretations change with circumstances. In other words it is a contrast between an approach which speculates as to the correct conceptual analysis of a situation or relationship without adverting to the consequences which flow from that analysis (or without considering what policy may account for the attribution of those consequences to that analysis) and an approach which acknowledges that principles and concepts are shorthand for practical consequences. For the realist or anti-formalist cannot dispense with concepts without abandoning the element in law which ensures that like is treated alike; he can only insist that concepts be seen in the context of their consequences.

As far as French *jurisprudence* is concerned, this Common lawyer's view is encouraged by the form of the judgment, which gives no place to a consideration of practical consequences or of questions of 'policy'. It appears to treat principles as frozen in a single interpretation, whereas the English judgment makes plain the process by which convenience prevails over 'logic', or, more precisely, by which the previously accepted principle or interpretation is distinguished from one which can accommodate the argument from convenience. We have seen, however, that the form of the judgment does not correctly record the process by which the decision is reached.

As far as *doctrine* is concerned, the criticism was certainly well-founded in the nineteenth century, when the survival of eighteenth century natural law ideas, combined with an exclu-

11 Atiyah *The Rise and Fall of Freedom of Contract* pp. 388 ff, 660 ff.
12 Hart 11 Georgia L Rev (1971) 969 ff.

sive concentration on deriving the law from an examination of the words of the Code, did produce an attitude like that characterised above. Nor was this attitude confined to France. It was to be found even more markedly in German writing. And this in turn dominated the work of the contemporary English analytical jurists and the early English academic text-books. It probably survived longest in Italy, where the isolation of doctrinal writing from the decisions of the courts and a general lack of interest in the application of principles to facts is still noticeable.[13]

Present-day *doctrine*, particularly the more recent works, is much more practically orientated than it used to be, but it can still sometimes appear to the English lawyer to be examining a closed system. To some extent this is a mistaken impression, attributable to the different status of case law. As we have seen, the English lawyer, because he is constantly returning to the cases, is visibly rooting his principles and concepts in prac-tical situations, whereas the French lawyer looks for his prin-ciples and concepts primarily in the Code and legislation. That these principles and concepts are not reconcilable with *jurisprudence* is not, as it would be in England, a reason for abandoning them outright, though it is one ground for criti-cising them. And to say that a principle is not rooted in the cases does not mean that it takes no account of practical con-siderations. What is true is that the emphasis in doctrinal writings is placed more on rational coherence and less on prac-tical consequences than it is either in Common law writing or, usually, in the *rapports* or *conclusions* presented to the courts.

(ii) This brings us to the second sense which can be borne by the observation which we are discussing. In this second sense the observation refers to the fact, which we have already noted, that the French *droit civil* is, ostensibly at least, a complete and coherent system, each part of which is capable of being related to every other part. As we can see from the many cross-references which editions of the *Code civil* provide, a French lawyer takes it for granted that one article can be interpreted in the light of another in a quite different part of the Code or in some subsequent legislation. This view of the law as a single,

---

13 Cf Cappelletti, Merryman and Perillo *The Italian Legal System* pp. 171 ff.

intellectually coherent system is common to all Civil law systems (it is carried to a far higher degree of generality by German law than by French) but it does not come readily to the mind of the Common lawyer. This is not, however, a matter of the presence or absence of logic or concepts, but of the scale on which each system thinks. English law thinks in pigeon-holes and rarely seeks to relate one pigeon-hole to another. It is for this reason that it is uncomfortable when it has to deal, for example, with the borderland between contract and tort. This relative lack of large-scale concepts reflects, of course, the primacy of the judge over the academic lawyer in the development of English law.

3 The divisions of French law[14]

In all legal systems the content of the law is divided into categories. Many of these divisions serve merely to facilitate exposition; others also have a practical significance within the legal system. In French law the most important divisions of the latter kind which are relevant to the law of contract are those between public law and private law and between civil law and commercial law.

a Public law and private law
In English law this distinction is purely expository (as indeed it is in Roman law, where it originated). In France it is of fundamental practical importance.

i *Nature of the distinction*
We have seen[15] that the Constituent Assembly of 1790 laid down that the courts were to have no jurisdiction over the administration. Article 13 of the *loi* of 16–24 August 1790 lays down that:

> The judicial functions are distinct from the administrative functions and shall always remain separate from them: the judges shall not, on pain of forfeiture of office, interfere in any way whatsoever with the activities of the administrative bodies.

14 *Source-book* pp. 315 ff.
15 P. 12, above.

This expresses the principle of the separation of the administrative and judicial authorities, which is an aspect of the separation of powers as it is understood in France.

The *loi* of 16–24 August 1790, which has been maintained through all the many subsequent constitutional changes, embodies the idea, inherited from the *ancien régime*, of an executive with an inherent power to act – a *pouvoir d'action d'office*. The executive has the power to take what steps are necessary to ensure good government, even if these steps infringe the rights of the individual. This power exists except in so far as it has been taken away by the legislature (or the constitution). In the United Kingdom, by contrast, the executive has no power over the individual except such as has been given to it by the legislature. (The royal prerogative, if it had not been curbed by the Revolution of 1688, would, one may imagine, have given us an executive of the French kind.) Moreover, in this country the executive is subject to the jurisdiction of the courts, both in the sense that if it acts illegally it is, in general, exposed to the same remedies as any other defendant, and in the sense that its acts or failures to act can be controlled by the prerogative remedies. In France all this is excluded by the *loi* of 1790.

The French executive therefore disposes of considerable inherent powers and the courts have no jurisdiction over the exercise of those powers. If there were nothing else to be said, France would be a police state.[16] But in fact in the course of the nineteenth century there evolved a system of judicial control which, in the contradiction which it embodies between appearance and reality and in its lack of foundation in legislative texts, would look more at home in an English than in a French context. The prohibition of the *loi* of 1790 is observed. The executive is free from the jurisdiction of the ordinary courts (the courts of the *ordre judiciaire*), but it is subject to the control of a central organ of the executive itself (the *Conseil d'Etat*) which, in this capacity, functions in almost every way like a court. In short, the executive can be 'interfered with' by a court, but it is a court within the executive itself. The *Conseil d'Etat* has been supplemented by a system of inferior administrative courts, so that now there are two

16 Waline *Droit administratif* (9th edn) s. 22 (*Source-book* p. 206).

separate judicial hierachies, one for public law and the other for private.

Nor are these courts concerned only with judicial review of administrative action, which in France is expressed in the power to annul (*juridiction d'annulation*). Since all acts of the executive are in principle outside the jurisdiction of the ordinary courts, public law embraces all aspects of redress for administrative wrongdoing, whether the wrong be a breach of contract or what would in civil law be a delict or quasi-delict. This is the subject matter of the *pleine juridiction*. The law which the administrative courts apply is almost entirely case law, to be found in the decisions of the *Conseil d'Etat*, around which there has grown up a very large literature.

There is thus a fundamental division between public and private law, or, more narrowly and more precisely, between administrative law and private law. For public law embraces also constitutional law, which lies outside the jurisdiction of the administrative courts, and it is with the division of jurisdiction that we are concerned. There are indeed occasions when a civil or a criminal court will have to apply administrative law (notably when a person charged in a criminal court with an offence created by an administrative regulation wishes to contest the legality of the regulation), or when an administrative court will have to take cognizance of private law, but in general the two systems are distinct. Matters of administrative law are for the *Conseil d'Etat* and its subordinate courts, matters of private law for the courts of the *ordre judiciaire*. This clear division is reflected also in the teaching and literature of the law: a French jurist is either a *publiciste* or a *privatiste*.

ii *When is a contract governed by public law?*
In this book we are concerned with the private law of contract, but it is important to know that this law does not govern all contracts. To determine whether a contract belongs to the public law can be a matter of some complexity, but at the risk of some over-simplification it can be said that there are two main conditions which such a contract must usually satisfy.

(a) One of the parties must be a public body or at least a body providing a public service.[17] Where the contract is made with a minister or the prefect of a *département* or the mayor of

17 Vedel *Droit administratif* (5th edn) p. 239.

a *commune* there is no difficulty, but in recent decades there has grown up in France, as in England, a wide range of other entities,[18] from public utilities to bodies with a variety of social and cultural purposes, and the precise limits of the category are the subject of controversy.

(b) Not every contract made by a public body is governed by public law. For such a contract to be a *contrat administratif* one or both of the following conditions must also be satisfied:[19]

(i) The object of the contract must be the entire performance by the private party of a public service, as opposed to merely the making of a contribution to its performance. In the case which established this principle[20] the private party had agreed to provide the catering at a reception centre run by the defendant ministry. This was held to be a *contrat administratif*. It would have been otherwise if the contract had been merely for the supply of the raw materials.

(ii) The contract must contain provisions which would not usually be found in a private contract of a similar kind. Examples of such *clauses exorbitantes de droit commun* are terms which empower the administration, but not the private party, to vary or rescind the contract. For reasons which will appear, provisions such as these are normal in public contracts, but they would obviously be surprising in other contexts.

Contracts between public bodies of a commercial or industrial character and the users or consumers of their products belong to the private law, even if they contain *clauses exorbitantes*.

iii *What are the rules applicable to such contracts?*
We have seen that administrative law is almost entirely based on the decisions of the *Conseil d'Etat*. In the sphere of contract this case law largely follows the law of *Code civil* and the ordinary courts, though with special rules to take account, for example, of the need for public contracts to be duly authorised. The most important differentiating features derive from the overriding purpose of all administrative law, which is to ensure the supremacy of the public interest. The rights of the

18 Vedel pp. 729 ff.
19 Vedel pp. 230 ff.
20 Bertin CE 20.4.1956, D 1956.433, S 1956.34.

private contracting party, even if they are embodied in the terms of the contract, may not stand in the way of the public interest. The administration must, however, compensate the private party for any loss which he suffers by the overriding of his rights. In the contractual context the most important power of which the administration disposes is that of unilaterally modifying or abrogating the contract if this is necessary to protect the public interest (and the power to do so will in fact often be expressly stated in the contract). We shall see that this power is the foundation of the doctrine of *imprévision*.[1]

Finally, it is a characteristic of the whole of administrative law that the administration has the privilege of *exécution d'office*. It can take what steps are necessary to enforce or supervise the contract, without invoking the assistance of the administrative courts. The administration is never the plaintiff.

iv *Conflicts of jurisdiction*

It is obvious that a division of jurisdiction as fundamental and complex as this (and there are comparable problems of definition in areas other than that of contracts) will give rise to conflicts. The ultimate arbiter of such conflicts is the *Tribunal des conflits*, composed of four judges from the *Conseil d'Etat* and four from the *Cour de cassation*. A tied vote is resolved by the Minister of Justice.

b Civil law and commercial law

In English the term 'commercial law', in so far as it is used at all, is used, like 'public law', for convenience of exposition.[2] It embraces an ill-defined group of subjects which are thought to be particularly important for business, but no practical consequences flow from the classification. In France, however, a commercial transaction is governed, to some extent at least, by special rules, to be found in the *Code de Commerce* and related legislation, and falls within the jurisdiction, at first instance, of special *tribunaux de commerce* consisting exclusively of unpaid lay judges.

A rare instance of commercial law in this sense in England is

1 Pp. 202 ff, below.
2 *Source-book* pp. 255 ff.

found in section 14 of the Sale of Goods Act 1979. The liability for defects established by the section is confined to cases in which 'it is in the course of the seller's business' to supply goods of the description in question (subsection 1) or in which the seller 'deals in goods of that description' (subsection 2). Translated into the terms used by French *doctrine*, these subsections lay down that a sale is (for this limited purpose) 'commercial' if the seller is a merchant (*commerçant*). This is the 'subjective' criterion for determining whether a transaction is governed by commercial law or not. The *Code de commerce* applies primarily the 'objective' criterion of the type of transaction involved. Not all contracts of sale of goods, for example, are commercial, but only those in which goods are bought for re-sale or hire. The Code lays down a list of such *actes de commerce*.[3] This objective criterion is modified, however, by the subjective in various ways. For example, a transaction which would not otherwise be an *acte de commerce* is subject to commercial law if it is entered into by a *commerçant* (defined as one who makes it his habitual occupation to conclude *actes de commerce*) and if it is accessory (*un acte accessoire*) to his commercial activities. The contract of employment of a shop-assistant is therefore governed by commercial law, whereas that of the shop-keeper's domestic servant is not.

The result of this and other modifications of the objective criterion is that the distinction between commercial law and civil law cannot be expressed in any simple proposition. Moreover, the influence of commercial law on civil law since 1804 has been such that the practical consequences of the distinction, apart from the peculiar composition and simplified procedure of the *tribunaux de commerce*, are now relatively few.[4] We need notice only two: oral evidence is admitted more freely in commercial cases; and the law of bankruptcy applies only to *commerçants*. It can be argued therefore that the maintenance of the distinction cannot be justified. Italy, for example, which based its original codification on the French, abandoned the distinction when it enacted a new Civil Code in 1942.

3 Art 632; *Source-book* p. 259.
4 The bulk of the *Code de commerce* and the legislation associated with it is concerned with specific transactions (e g negotiable instruments, charter-parties, bankruptcy).

Chapter two
Introduction to the law of contract

1 The place of contract in the Civil Code

a The concept of obligation

For the French lawyer, as we have said, any institution is to be seen in its place in the structure of the law as a whole. From this point of view contract is one of the sources from which obligations derive, and obligations are one of the component elements of the *patrimoine*. These terms need further elucidation.

The *patrimoine* is the totality of an individual's economic assets and liabilities, i e those rights and duties which are capable of valuation in money terms. The nearest analogy in English law is the rather imprecise notion of the 'estate' of a deceased person. The *patrimoine* consists of property (*biens*) and obligations. *Biens* are rights *in rem* (*droits réels*), obligations are rights *in personam* (*droits personnels*) and the duties correlative to such rights. The *patrimoine* is thought of in terms of a balance sheet, the assets constituting the *actif* and the liabilities the *passif*. *Biens* occur, of course, only in the *actif*, but obligations may appear on either side. For obligation, in spite of what the word suggests, is a two-sided concept. In the *passif* it is a debt (*dette*), in the *actif* it is a credit (*créance*). If *A* owes *B* 100 francs, an obligation exists between them, which will appear in the *passif* of *A*'s *patrimoine* as a debt and in the *actif* of *B*'s as a credit. *A* is a *débiteur* and *B* a *créditeur*. We must note, however, that these terms are not confined, as they are in normal parlance in both French and English, to money debts. The content or object of an obligation may be any act or forbearance, and the duty to

28

perform that act or forbearance is a *dette*. In the same way the term *paiement* extends to the performance of any obligation, whatever its content.

It is thus in the *patrimoine* that property and obligation meet and merge.[1] And obligation itself is the meeting-point of other concepts. For contract is only one of the sources of obligations. The *Code civil* distinguishes[2] between obligations which arise from agreement and those which do not. The latter category is further divided[3] into those which derive from an act of the person obliged and those which derive purely from the authority of *la loi*. The latter is a residual category of little importance, which accommodates, for example, the relationship between neighbouring owners. The former embraces delict, quasi-delict and quasi-contract. Quasi-contract covers very roughly what is commonly placed under the same heading in English law.[4] Delict and quasi-delict are usually treated as a single category. For both are, unlike contract, unlawful acts causing damage to another; they differ only in that a delict is an intentional act, whereas a quasi-delict is unintentional (i e negligent).[5] The law of delictual and quasi-delictual obligations therefore corresponds to the law of tort in so far as the latter is concerned with compensation for damage wrongfully caused. It must, however, be emphasised that, unlike the law of tort, the law of delict and quasi-delict is based on a single principle of the utmost generality. The relevant chapter of the *Code civil* (which comprises in all only five articles) begins:

> **Art 1382** Any human act (*fait*) whatever which causes damage (*dommage*) to another obliges the person by whose fault the damage has occurred to make it good.
> **Art 1383** Everyone is liable for the damage which he has caused, not only by his act (*fait*), but also by his negligence or his imprudence.

1 An obligation is an incorporeal thing; the chose in action provides an analogy in the Common law, but one which, in the absence of a law of obligations, has remained undeveloped.
2 The distinction is implicit in arts 1101 and 1370.
3 Art 1370.
4 But English law has no counterpart to *gestion d'affaires* (art 1372 ff Cc); see Amos and Walton pp. 192 ff.
5 This use of the word (which is found also in Scots law) provides a trap for those who are familiar with its meaning in Roman law. For the historical development see Stein (1955) 4 ICLQ 356.

In principle therefore any fault which causes (and this word of course bears a lot of weight in so general a principle) damage is actionable and no distinction will be made in what follows between delict and quasi-delict.

The fact that contract and delict both create an obligation has two consequences which may catch the attention of an English lawyer. There is a greater unity of treatment of consequential matters, such as assignment and discharge of the obligation, which are dealt with in English books, if at all, under the heading of contract only. And, where it is clear that an obligation exists under one heading or the other, there is sometimes a tendency in French courts to blur or ignore the distinction between the two.[6] This is made all the easier by the existence of another unifying factor: that liability under both headings is based on fault.

b Liability for fault

The content of a contractual obligation, we have said, is the performance of what has been undertaken, whereas the content of a delictual obligation is the payment of compensation, i e damages. But it is obvious that there is here a logical imbalance: like is not being compared with like. If A contracts with B to take him for a drive in the country and on the way is involved, by his own fault, in an accident in which both B and X, a stranger, are injured, the equivalent of A's obligation to compensate X is not, as it should be, A's obligation to convey B carefully, but A's liability to compensate B for his failure to perform that obligation. French writers in fact usually at this point abandon the analysis in terms of obligation and resort to one in terms of liability (*responsabilité*).

The most prominent common factor of *responsabilité contractuelle* and *responsabilité délictuelle* is the requirement of fault.[7] That fault should be necessary for the latter will not surprise a Common lawyer, even if he rejects it as a basis for liability in tort in his own law, but it plays no part in our thinking about contract. The Common law has traditionally

6 And yet paradoxically French law in principle will not allow an action in delict where the alleged fault arises from the performance of a contractual obligation (so-called rule of *non-cumul*). See further p. 53, below.

7 There is, however, no express reference to it in the contractual provisions of the *Code civil*.

thought of contractual obligations as in principle absolute, though subject to modification in modern times by the doctrine of supervening impossibility or frustration. And yet the results at which the two systems arrive are not radically different. The explanation is that here, as elsewhere, the Common law resorts to construction of the contract where French law resorts to a rule. Where the French contracting party is liable for fault, his English counterpart is usually liable for breach of an implied term to use due care. To this we shall return. Here we need only remark that the blurring of the line between *responsabilité contractuelle* and *responsabilité délictuelle*, which we have already noticed, is made easier by the fact that both are based on the fault of the debtor.

c The theory of the autonomy of the will

The treatment of contract in the *Code civil* echoes the philosophy of the eighteenth century. The starting-point is the freedom of the individual, which can be curtailed only by free will, either in the original social contract or, within society, by individual acts of will. The characteristic source of obligation is therefore contract; non-contractual obligations are justifiable only to the extent that they are necessary for the protection of the freedom of others. And since a contractual obligation can exist, on this view, only if the other party has willed it, the content of the obligation must also be determined by his will. This approach is summed up in article 1134 al 1 Cc, which declares the contracting parties to be law-givers for themselves: 'Agreements legally formed have the character of *loi* for those who have made them'.

The theory of the autonomy of the will was reinforced both by the economic doctrine of *laissez-faire* and by the moral argument that the individual must be the best judge of his own interest and therefore that the outcome of the meeting of two wills must necessarily be a just balance of both interests. The theory was taken for granted as the foundation of contractual doctrine in all Civil law countries in the nineteenth century. Its principal practical consequences were these:[8]

   (i) Individuals must be free to make a contract or not to make one.

8 Cf *Source-book* p. 319.

(ii) They must be free, subject only to restrictions necessary in the public interest, to make any agreement that they wished. The law must not, as Roman law had done, limit them to certain types of contract.[9] But the rigorous application of this principle would be inconvenient. For the parties to a routine transaction, such as sale, could not be expected on each occasion to state expressly every term of their contract. The advantage of the list of typical contracts which French law had inherited from Roman law was that the normal incidents of each type (such as the seller's liability for defects or the passing of risk) were governed by rules of law (as they still are in the *Code civil*). Convenience and principle have usually been reconciled by a distinction between rules which merely fill gaps left by the parties (*lois supplétives*) and which therefore do not apply if the parties' intention is to exclude them, and those which concern the public interest and cannot therefore be excluded (*lois impératives*).[10] Except in the relatively few cases where a rule is expressly declared to fall into one category or the other, classification is made by the courts. In the *Code civil* itself most of the rules in the contractual sphere are *lois supplétives*, and the principal public interest protected by the small number of articles which lay down *lois impératives* could be subsumed under the principle of freedom of contract itself (e g the rules governing capacity to contract or defects in consent).[11] In English law there is no such express distinction, but we arrive at much the same result by another route. We start from the principle that rules of law cannot be excluded, but we express what are in substance *lois supplétives*, not in the language of rules, but as implied terms (or otherwise in a way which links them to the intention of the parties). They are therefore necessarily capable of being excluded[12] (*expressum facit cessare tacitum*). Thus, what is in substance a *loi supplétive* setting out the seller's duty in regard to latent defects is expressed as an implied term[13] ('. . . an implied

---

9 See p. 39, below.
10 *Source-book* pp. 238 ff. In spite of the use of the word *loi*, not all these rules are statutory.
11 Modern legislation, however, has added others which restrict that freedom; see pp. 135 ff, 226 ff, below.
12 Sale of Goods Act 1979, s. 55.
13 Ibid, s. 14.

condition that the goods shall be reasonably fit . . .') and the rules as to the passing of risk are expressed as presumptions as to the intention of the parties,[14] whereas the rules as to the passing of title[15] (which are *lois impératives*, because the interests of third parties are involved) are stated in the plain language of rules.

(iii) If *lois supplétives* do not fill all the gaps left by the parties, the court may not supply what is missing. Here (as with the corresponding English principle that 'the court will not make a contract for the parties') there is obviously a difficult line to draw between filling a gap and interpreting the intentions of the parties, but, to take a simple example from the contract of sale, if the parties have not fixed the price (or made provision for it to be fixed),[16] the court will not fix it for them.

(iv) Since the theory of the autonomy of the will postulates, as we have seen, that a contract necessarily achieves a fair balance of the parties' interests, the court may not intervene to adjust that balance. (The contract may, of course, be affected by fraud, or mistake or duress, but in that event the initial consent will have been defective and the contract will be null.)

It will be plain to an English lawyer that, although the language in which the theory of the autonomy of the will is expressed is unfamiliar, the substance of what is set out above is to be found in the English law of contract as it was built up by the nineteenth century judges and made systematic by the textbooks of Pollock and Anson. Nor is it a mere chance, of course, that this classical English theory of contract should thus correspond closely with the French (which, as we have said, does not in this respect differ radically from that of other Civil law countries). For the philosophical, moral and economic pre-suppositions were the same on both sides of the channel, and there was direct influence as well, both on the courts, and, far more, on the writers. The English courts do not seem to have been influenced by the *Code civil* or by contemporary French law, but there are references to Pothier (who lay behind this part, in particular, of the Code). Both Pollock and Anson (and through them all subsequent expositors of the law

14 Ibid, s. 18, s. 20.
15 Ibid, ss. 21-26.
16 See p. 109, below.

of contract) and also the writers of works on analytical jurisprudence were greatly influenced in their analysis of the law by Savigny, who himself was a powerful influence on the legal thought not only of Germany but of all Civil law countries.

It is clear therefore that the analysis of contract in terms of a free *consensus ad idem* of the parties is common to both French and English law. Where the two systems differ, as we shall see, is partly in the intellectual rigour with which the analysis is carried through to detailed consequences, and partly in the way that *consensus* is understood: as a subjective meeting of two minds or as the objective appearance of agreement. English law usually favours the latter approach, as being the more practical and the more conducive to the certainty which commercial convenience demands, whereas French law inclines to the former, though sometimes with a corrective which yields much the same practical result as the objective approach.

Both in France and in England, however, it has long been clear that, on the one hand, the pre-suppositions upon which the analysis rests are no longer acceptable, at least in their crude form, and, on the other hand, that the practical consequences which flow from it, and which are set out above, no longer entirely correspond to the actual law in either country. This is familiar in England and is true also in France.[17]

The freedom to contract or not to contract has been so greatly restricted in both countries by statute (e g compulsory third-party insurance of motorists, landlord and tenant legislation) or by economic circumstances (e g monopolies or standard-form contracts) as to be, in some instances, meaningless.

The freedom to determine the content of one's contract has been radically affected by the great expansion in the number and scope of *lois impératives* (or their analogues in England), many of them designed to correct the consequences of inequality of bargaining power. Recent examples in England are found in the Hire Purchase Act 1965, the Supply of Goods (Implied Terms) Act 1973 and, most extensively, in the Unfair Contract Terms Act 1977. There are comparable instances in France.

17 Cheshire and Fifoot *Law of Contract* (10th edn) pp. 17 ff; Atiyah *Introduction to the Law of Contract* (3rd edn) pp. 13 ff; Mazeaud/Mazeaud ss. 118 ff; Ghestin *Contrat* ss. 53 ff. And see pp. 135 ff, below.

Such legislation necessarily also enlarges the power of the courts to intervene in the execution of contracts.

It can, however, reasonably be said that while all this requires the analysis in terms of agreement to be qualified, it does not invalidate it.[18] And no thoroughgoing substitute has indeed been proposed.

d *Acte juridique* and *fait juridique*

The classification of obligations in the *Code civil* is obviously imperfect. Quasi-contract has no unity; there is no sense in dividing delict from quasi-delict (and, as we have seen, this is not in practice done); and to isolate a handful of obligations as arising from *la loi* is absurd, since the same can be said of all the institutions in the Code. Various other schemes have been proposed. Among them we may notice that which is founded on the German concept of the 'act in the law'[19] or juridical act (*Rechtsgeschäft, acte juridique*), a concept which plays a central and very elaborate part in the German Civil Code. The French theory is less ambitious, but it attempts to provide a framework which will both accommodate more rationally what is in the Code and also allow for developments beyond the Code. Like the theory of *autonomie de la volonté* it is based on the will, but attains a greater degree of generalisation. According to this theory every change, of whatever kind, in a person's legal position is produced by either an *acte juridique* or a *fait juridique*. The analysis is therefore not confined to the law of obligations. An *acte juridique* is a voluntary act which is intended to produce (and does produce) legal effects. It may be either unilateral or bilateral. An *acte juridique bilatéral* is a *convention* (an agreement with legal effects) and most *conventions* are contracts. The most familiar instance of an *acte juridique unilatéral* is a will (*testament*), but the Code includes a number of others, such as the act of renouncing an inheritance or the act of recognising a natural child and thereby conferring rights upon it.

Legal effects may also be produced by a *fait juridique*. This may be a purely external event, such as a death (which will, for

18 Treitel *Contract* pp. 5 f.
19 See e g Holland *Jurisprudence* (12th edn) pp. 117 ff; Pollock *Contracts* (12th edn) ch 1.

example, create rights in those designated by will or by the rules of intestacy) or a stroke of lightning which founds a claim under an insurance policy; but more importantly it may be a voluntary act which produces legal effects, but was not intended to do so. All delictual and quasi-delictual obligations, for example, are the result of *faits juridiques*.

The practical consequences of the distinction are that *actes juridiques*, since they depend for their legal effect on the intention of the actor, will in principle be invalidated by a defect in that intention, whereas *faits* will not; and that *actes juridiques* in general have to be proved by writing, whereas *faits juridiques* can be proved by any method.

The theory is sound in so far as it analyses the contents of the Code in a more intelligible way than the Code itself does, but it has a wider relevance. We have said that there are scattered instances in the Code in which legal consequences flow from what can be analysed as a unilateral juridical act. If this analysis can be generalised, it will provide a satisfactory theoretical basis for decisions of the courts which have attached legal consequences to analytically comparable acts. These acts, which are further discussed below, are (a) firm offers, (b) offers to the public, (c) offers of rewards. They are among the instances, referred to above, in which an 'injurious reliance' is difficult to accommodate within the established theory of contract. If I can confer rights on a natural child by recognising it, it can be argued that I should be able, for example, to confer rights on an offeree by indicating an intention to hold the offer open for a period.

e *Convention* and contract

We have seen that in the arrangement of the *Code civil* contract appears as one of the sources of obligations. But it is also presented as a member of a larger class (to which we have already referred) of *conventions*, the difference between the two being that whereas contracts create obligations, *conventions* may create either obligations or some other legal consequence, such as the transfer or extinction of an obligation. All contracts are *conventions*, but not all *conventions* are contracts. The terminology of the distinction is confusing, because there is no third word to identify those *conventions* which are not contracts. Moreover, the Code itself is not consistent in its use of the two terms, and the general principles governing both types of *convention* are the same.

f Preliminary classifications of contract

The treatment of contracts in the Code opens with a group of preliminary distinctions:

i *Synallagmatic (or bilateral) and unilateral contracts*

A synallagmatic or bilateral contract is one which creates reciprocal obligations, each party having both rights and duties. A contract of sale, for example, is synallagmatic. A unilateral contract, on the other hand, creates only rights in one party and only duties in the other. An agreement to make a gift, for example, is a unilateral contract.

The distinction has a number of practical consequences.[20] Thus, the characteristic feature of synallagmatic contracts is that they create reciprocal or interdependent obligations. This characteristic is reflected in the *cause* of these contracts, which is different from that appropriate to unilateral contracts. From this follow also differences in the effects of the contracts (risk, *exceptio non adimpleti contractus*) and in the availability of the remedy of *résolution*. There is also a difference in the evidentiary requirements for the two types of contract.

The distinction presents several pitfalls for the Common lawyer. The first is that he is so imbued with the idea of consideration that he finds it difficult to adapt his thinking to a system which knows nothing of it (and this is true, of course, of all Civil law systems). To this we return below.[1] The second pitfall is that the French lawyer distinguishes more easily than the Common lawyer does between a unilateral contract (which is, like all contracts, an agreement) and a unilateral promise or *pollicitation*. A promise is not a contract unless it has been converted into an agreement by an acceptance (i e an act of will) by the other party. To this also we return.[2]

The third pitfall is that the Common lawyer's understanding of the term 'unilateral contract' is quite different from the one

20 These are considered in more detail at the appropriate places below.
  1 Pp. 42 ff, 138 ff.
  2 Pp. 63 ff.

which we are examining. For him it denotes a 'contract on executed consideration', i e a promise in return for an act. In French law this can be a contract only if, once again, there is an agreement; and if there is an agreement, the contract which results will be bilateral and not unilateral. For example, an offer of a reward, which is one of the typical starting-points of a unilateral contract in the Common law sense, will become a contract in the analysis of French law, not by the performance of the act which is to be rewarded, even if it is performed in awareness of the offer, but only if that awareness can be construed also as an acceptance of the offer. This construction can easily appear forced and artificial. By contrast, the English analysis is in terms of consideration rather than of agreement: the performance of the act is the consideration for the promise of the reward, just as in an executory contract the making of the counter-promise is seen as the consideration. This approach via consideration enables English law to escape from the full rigour of the need to find an agreement.

We should note also an ambiguity in the English use of the term 'bilateral contract'.[3] It is sometimes used in the French sense, but it can also (and with greater consistency in view of the English meaning of 'unilateral' in this context) mean a wholly executory contract, i e a contract on executory consideration. As we have seen, a contract is bilateral (or synallagmatic) in the French sense whether or not one party has at a given moment performed his side of the agreement.

Finally, we should remark that the distinction between bilateral and unilateral contracts is not the same as that between bilateral and unilateral juridical acts. All contracts are necessarily bilateral acts. It is possible, for example, to analyse the promise of a reward (which, as we have seen, fits into a contractual analysis only with difficulty) as a unilateral juridical act whereby the promisor by his own will binds himself to pay the reward if the act to be rewarded is done, but this is not a contractual analysis.

The distinction between synallagmatic and unilateral contracts presents difficulties also for the French lawyer. It will be useful now to examine these difficulties in what would otherwise be disproportionate detail, because this will help

3 Cf the remarks of Diplock LJ in *United Dominions Trust (Commercial) Ltd v Eagle Aircraft Services Ltd* [1968] 1 WLR 74 at 82.

the Common lawyer to get the flavour of the French way of thinking, and in particular will enable him to appreciate the greater emphasis which, as we have already seen, French law places on the need for agreement.

(a) *Real contracts*　Roman law[4] (which provided the basis on which later commentators erected the distinction which we are discussing) did not have a unitary conception of contract based on agreement. It recognised only certain specific contracts (together with a form, the *stipulatio*, which, like the English seal, could be used to validate any agreement). These specific contracts were of two types, either consensual or real. The consensual contracts (sale, hire, partnership, mandate) were of the familiar bilateral kind, based on agreement. The real contracts, of which the simplest example is a loan of money or other thing intended for consumption (Roman *mutuum*, French *prêt de consommation*) represented a different principle.

In the Roman view the real contracts came into existence when the thing (*res*) was delivered to the borrower, who then came under an obligation to return it (or, in a loan for consumption, its equivalent) at the appointed time. In terms of the distinction which we are discussing this is a unilateral contract, the borrower having a duty (to return the money) and the lender a correlative right, but not vice-versa. Until the delivery of the thing there is no contract, because even if there was an agreement which preceded the delivery, as will usually be the case, this agreement cannot in Roman law be a contract because it is not one of the four 'consensual' contracts (and is not clothed in the form of the *stipulatio*).

Essentially the same analysis can be applied to the other real contracts, viz loan for use (*prêt à usage* or *commodat*), deposit (*dépôt*) and pledge (*gage*).[5] These are, from the English point of view, bailments and it is precisely because they are, in French terms, unilateral contracts and therefore, according to the usual English view, lack consideration, that they present a difficulty of analysis in English law.

The difficulty which they present in French law is different. The Code preserves the specific contracts of Roman law within

4 Nicholas *Roman Law* pp. 159 ff.
5 On the *don manuel* see p. 141, below.

its unitary system of contract, the rules of the specific contracts being related by *doctrine* to the unitary consensual principle, as we have seen, by way of the concept of the *loi supplétive*. In the case of the consensual contracts this presents no difficulty, since they can be seen as an application of the unitary principle. But the real contracts, as the Romans saw them (and it is clear that this is how the draftsmen of the Code also saw them), cannot easily be so regarded. They come into existence not by the making of the agreement, but by the delivery of the thing. Until then the borrower (to take the example of a loan) is under no obligation. And yet the Roman corollary, that the preceding agreement is without effect, is no longer correct. The promise of a loan is valid in French law in the same way as any other unilateral promise. (It is, in banking terms, the opening of a credit in favour of a customer.)

The conservative view, adopted by the courts, is that the real contracts retain their traditional character: they are unilateral, and they come into existence only when the thing is delivered. The preceding agreement is independent and it is also unilateral; it is an agreement that the prospective transferor shall lend etc.

The more radical view is that the real contracts are an anachronism in a unitary system based on consent, and that the transaction can be realistically expressed as a single synallagmatic contract in which the lender, for example, undertakes to lend and the borrower to return. This analysis is accepted by a great preponderance of *doctrine*, but it is not without difficulty and the Common lawyer needs to see clearly where the difficulty lies. For, as we have already said, his thought is so coloured by the idea of consideration that he may read it into other systems.

We have seen that the principal characteristic of synallagmatic contracts is that the obligations of the parties are reciprocal. Since it is usually true that where there is consideration there is also reciprocity of obligation (e g in a contract of sale), the Common lawyer may assume that where there is no consideration (as in the example which we are considering, of a gratuitous loan) there is also no reciprocity. But this is not so. The requirement of reciprocity is satisfied if the obligations are interdependent; it is not also necessary that one should be the price of the other. The difficulty in analysing a gratuitous and executory agreement for a loan as a synallagmatic contract does not lie in any lack of reciprocity: the obligation to lend and the obligation to return are plainly reciprocal. The difficulty lies in the fact that the obligations are not concurrent. In a contract of sale, for example, the obligations of buyer and seller are not only reciprocal but also, in principle, concurrent;[6] but it would obviously be absurd to say, in the case of a loan, that the borrower's obligation to return is concurrent with the lender's obligation to deliver. *Doctrine* meets this difficulty, rather artificially, by construing the borrower's obligation as conditional on his receiving the thing.

(b) *Imperfectly bilateral contracts* We said that all real contracts were susceptible of the same analysis as the loan for consumption and that all were, on that (conservative) analysis, unilateral. There is, however, one difference. If a loan for consumption is regarded as unilateral at all, it is necessarily and always unilateral: there can never be a duty on the lender. But in the other contracts, although there is necessarily and immediately a duty only on the recipient, there may subsequently and contingently be a duty on the transferor. In a gratuitous contract of deposit, for example, the depositor will be bound to compensate the depositee if the latter incurs expense or suffers damage as a result of keeping the thing. This duty is contingent on there being such expense or damage. The term which the commentators on Roman law applied to such contracts was 'imperfectly bilateral'.

How are these contracts, which are (on the analysis which we are now assuming) initially unilateral, but potentially bilateral, to be classified? The practical relevance of this question (which has given rise to much doctrinal debate) is that if they are classified as bilateral, the consequences listed above[7] will follow, and in particular the party contingently entitled (in the example, the depositee) will have the protection of the *exceptio non adimpleti contractus* and the remedy of *résolution*. The Code is not explicit, but neither it nor the *jurisprudence* is

6 Cf Sale of Goods Act 1979, s. 28.
7 P. 37.

consistent with a strictly unilateral analysis, i e with a denial of all the listed consequences.[8] This partially bilateral solution is sometimes justified analytically on the ground that in imperfectly bilateral contracts the obligations are reciprocal but not interdependent. The (contingent) obligation of the lender to compensate the borrower is not interdependent with the (immediate) obligation of the borrower to return the thing on demand. For the borrower did not enter into his obligation to return the thing *in order to* obtain his right to compensation.[9] In a sale, on the other hand, to take the example of a fully bilateral contract, the buyer can be said to enter into his obligation to pay the price in order to obtain his right to the delivery of the thing.

ii *Onerous and gratuitous contracts*

The distinction between synallagmatic and unilateral contracts looks to the character of the obligations created; the present distinction looks to the purpose pursued by the party obliged. In a *contrat à titre onéreux* he confers an advantage (i e a right) on the other party with the intention of obtaining a reciprocal advantage for himself; in a *contrat à titre gratuit* he confers the advantage with the intention of obtaining no such advantage, i e he has an *intention libérale*.[10] The two distinctions very largely coincide: all synallagmatic contracts are *à titre onéreux*, and most unilateral contracts are *à titre gratuit*; but, if real contracts are regarded as unilateral, a loan of money will be either *à titre onéreux* or *à titre gratuit* according as the borrower does or does not undertake to pay interest.

A further distinction is made within the category of *contrats à titre gratuit* between those which are intended to transfer value from one patrimony to another (the most obvious

8 See Marty/Raynaud pp. 52 f.
9 See Mazeaud/Mazeaud p. 80.
10 This at least is the way in which the distinction is usually formulated. It rests on the definition in art 1105 Cc of a *contrat à titre gratuit* (or *de bienfaisance* in the terminology of the Code; see the next paragraph in the text) in terms of the intention of one party 'to confer a purely gratuitous advantage on the other'. Art 1106, however, defines a *contrat à titre onéreux* as one which 'requires each party to convey or do something'. The two definitions are not in harmony. See p. 142, below.

example being an agreement for a gift – a *donation*), and those which relate only to the performance of a gratuitous service and which are therefore not seen as effecting a transfer of value between the patrimonies.[11] The terminology is not altogether settled. Contracts for gratuitous services are usually referred to as either *contrats de bienfaisance* or *contrats désintéressés*, but the Code applies the term *contrats de bienfaisance* to the wider category which is here (and generally) called *contrats à titre gratuit*.

A number of practical consequences attach to these distinctions, of which the principal are the following. (a) There is a clear policy in the *Code civil* to protect the patrimony (seen as an asset handed down from one generation of the family to another) from the generosity of its present owner. The policy is put into effect mainly in the law relating to succession on death,[12] but it accounts also for the related requirement of public written form for *donations*[13] (which are also taxed more heavily than transfers *à titre onéreux*). (b) A *contrat à titre gratuit* entered into by an insolvent debtor can be attacked by his creditors (by the *action Paulienne*)[14] without proof that the beneficiary knew of the debtor's insolvency, whereas this proof is required where the contract is *à titre onéreux*. (c) The liability of the debtor in a *contrat à titre gratuit* is lightened in several respects (e g a donor, unlike a vendor, is not liable for eviction or for defects; the standard of care required of a gratuitous depositee or mandatory is diminished; and withdrawal from the contract is in some cases easier).[15] (d) Mistake as to the identity of the other party is, as we shall see,[16] a ground for nullity only if that identity is the 'principal cause' of the contract. This requirement is always satisfied in the case of *contrats à titre gratuit*, but only exceptionally in those *à titre onéreux*.

11 As a proposition of economics this is obviously naive. For the historical origin see J P Dawson *Gifts and Promises* (1980) pp. 14 ff, 66 ff.
12 See pp. 133, 140, below.
13 The distinction which we are considering applies not only to contracts, but to all juridical acts.
14 See p. 187, below.
15 Arts 1625, 1927, 1928, 1992 Cc.
16 Pp. 92 ff, below.

iii *Commutative and aleatory contracts*

This is a distinction within the category of contracts *à titre onéreux*. A contract is aleatory when the extent of one party's performance depends on some future uncertain event and the other party's performance does not vary correspondingly.[17] (A sale of next year's crop at so much per ton is not therefore aleatory.) A wager is the simplest form of aleatory contract, but it has a very limited legal effect.[18] Since, outside games and wagers, the only practical consequence of a contract's being aleatory is that the remedy of rescission for *lésion*[19] (i e gross disproportion between the performances required of the parties) is not available, and since the scope of that remedy is limited to contracts of sale, the most significant practical example is the contract by which a party (usually elderly or disabled) sells land to another and receives as the price a life annuity (*rente viagère*).[20] Since what the buyer has to pay depends on how long the seller lives, it is usually held that there can be no remedy for *lésion*. (The place of the annuity may be taken by a promise to provide board, lodging and care. The arrangement is then referred to as a *bail à nourriture*. Since the 'price' is not expressed in money, it cannot be a sale and the question of *lésion* cannot therefore arise. It can, however, pose a question as to the existence of a *cause*.)[1]

iv *Nominate and innominate contracts*

We have seen that the *Code civil* embodies the Roman inheritance of a list of specific or named contracts (*contrats nommés*), but that it also accepts, as a consequence of the principle of the autonomy of the will, that the parties are free to make other contracts (*contrats innomés*).[2] The significance of the distinction is that the standard incidents of *contrats*

---

17 On the inconsistency between the definition of a commutative contract in art 1104 Cc and the definition of an aleatory contract in art 1964 see Ghestin *Contrat* s. 559.
18 Art 1965 Cc. In English terms it is (broadly) unenforceable, but not void.
19 See pp. 131 ff, below.
20 See p. 115, below.
 1 See ibid.
 2 The name comes from the late Roman law (see Nicholas *Roman Law* pp. 189 ff), but it should be noted that the innominate contract of French law is not confined to agreements which have been executed on one side.

nommés are, in the absence of contrary intention, laid down by *lois supplétives*,[3] whereas the content of a *contrat innomé* derives in principle directly from the intention of the parties. The first step in interpreting a contract is therefore to 'qualify' or characterise it, i e to determine whether it falls within the limits of one or other of the nominate contracts (and this is a question of law subject to the control of the *Cour de cassation*). Of course, the parties to what the court concludes to be an innominate contract will often have left some or all of its terms unexpressed. The court may well then decide that the contract is akin to one or other of the nominate contracts or that it embodies elements of several of them (a contract for board and lodging in a hotel provides an example) and will interpret it accordingly.

2 Interpretation of contracts

a General

In the preceding pages and in particular in the last paragraph of the preceding section we have touched on matters of interpretation. We may now try to pull the threads together. In accordance with classical doctrine French law, like English law, takes as its starting-point the common intention of the parties,[4] but, as every lawyer knows, this is of little assistance. For the cases in which difficulties arise are precisely those in which the intention of the parties is not clear or in which they have simply failed to provide for the matter in issue at all. Where the intention is not clear, the question is one of interpretation in the strict sense, and interpretation is a matter of fact which lies outside the control of the *Cour de cassation*. It is in consequence difficult to go beyond generalities in assessing the attitudes of the courts. For although the judgments of the lower courts are less starkly laconic than those of the *Cour de cassation*, they nevertheless rarely throw much light on the processes by which the judges arrive at their interpretation. The *Code civil* has nine brief articles on the subject,[5] which hardly venture outside the commonplace and which are in any

3 See pp. 40 f, above.
4 Arts 1134, 1156 Cc.
5 Arts 1156-1164.

case regarded as *lois supplétives* and therefore themselves beyond the control of the *Cour de cassation*. From the point of view of the Common lawyer the most noticeable feature of the French approach to the interpretation of contracts is its greater subjectivity. We shall find that where the Common law, in the interests of commercial convenience and the security of transactions, looks to the external appearance of consent, French law, with more concern for theoretical consistency, often takes account of the true state of mind of one of the parties. It is for this reason that the category of 'defects of consent', and in particular of mistake and *dol par réticence*,[6] plays a more important part in French law than it does in the Common law.[7] In the same way, the requirement of good faith, though explicitly mentioned by the Code only in connexion with the performance of contracts,[8] is introduced into the context of their formation under cover of the requirement of a genuine consent. For, it is held, there cannot be a genuine consent if one party is aware of the other's mistake, even if only to the extent of passively acquiescing in it. The absence of a parol evidence rule leads in the same direction.

An inconvenient consequence of the principle that the interpretation of a contract is a matter of fact is that in a world of standard form contracts each court is free to interpret each contract as if it were unique. There are standard terms, but strictly speaking no standard interpretation. In a decision of 1907, for example, the *Cour de cassation*[9] refused to intervene where a standard clause which had been drafted and recommended by the Chamber of Notaries of Paris had been differently interpreted by the *Cours d'appel* of Paris and of Lyons. The *procureur-général* urged the court in the public interest to be bold and to give a ruling, but the court stuck to the principle of the *pouvoir souverain*. Standard terms have of course multiplied enormously since then and the *Cour de cassation* has on occasion treated them tacitly as if they were

6 See pp. 80 ff, 88 ff, 98 ff, below.
7 See pp. 106 ff, below.
8 Art 1134 al 3.
9 Cass civ 28.1.1907, S 1912.1.22; Gaz Pal 1907.1.228; cf Cass civ 18.11. 1930, Gaz Pal 1930.2.940 (a case in which the same term in two closely related contracts was differently interpreted).

rules of law,[10] but it has done so without any concession of principle. Even widely adopted terms such as those in the York-Antwerp Rules are not within the control of the *Cour de cassation*.

One ultimate limit is, however, set to the *pouvoir souverain*. It must not 'denature' a provision which is 'clear and precise' (*clause claire et précise*).[11] The basis of the intervention by the *Cour de cassation* in such a case is that a *clause claire et précise* can need no interpretation and therefore any intervention by the court below must be a contravention of that *loi* which, according to art 1134 Cc,[12] is constituted by the agreement of the parties. This much is clear, but the instrument which is thus given to the *Cour de cassation* is obviously very imprecise and unpredictable.[13] All that can be said is that the court uses it sparingly.

b Rules and terms[14]

The differences of approach between the two systems are more marked where the parties have failed to provide for the matter in issue at all. As we have remarked above,[15] French law inherits from Roman law a set of typical contracts or *contrats nommés*, the standard incidents of which are laid down in the *Code civil* in the form of *lois supplétives*. The first step for a French court is therefore to 'qualify' or characterise the agreements before it. If it falls within the definition of one of the *contrats nommés*, its content will be largely determined by the appropriate *lois supplétives*. Even if it is 'qualified' as a *contrat innomé*, its incidents will often be determined by reference to that one (or more) of the *contrats nommés* to which it is most analogous. The French starting-point is that the incidents of a contract are fixed by law, subject to the parties' power to vary them. By contrast, the starting-point for a Common law court is the implied term. Where French law

10 E g Cass civ 3.6.1930, 14.1.1931, DP 1931.1.5 concl Matter, note Savatier; Cass civ 18.3.1942, S 1943.1.13 note Houin; DA 1942.89; *Source-book* p. 106.
11 Cass com 15.5.1950, D 1950.773.
12 See p. 31, above.
13 Ivainer D 1976 Chr 153.
14 Nicholas (1974) 48 Tulane L Rev 946 ff.
15 Pp. 39 f.

began with the Roman system of typical contracts and super-
imposed on it the unitary consensual principle that any agreement is a contract, English law reversed the process. In so far as
it thinks in terms of typical contracts, it has derived them from
the general principle of contract through the device of the
implied term. The primary question is, in principle, not: 'Into
what type of contract did the parties enter?', but 'To what
terms did the parties agree?' Fact hardens into law, however,
and what begins as a reasonable implication becomes, in
effect, a legal presumption and eventually perhaps a legal
fiction, as in the extreme case exemplified by section 6 (1) of
the Unfair Contract Terms Act 1977, which declares void any
attempt by the seller in a consumer sale to exclude the implied
terms as to title, description and quality. (In French terms,
what was a *loi supplétive* is declared to be a *loi impérative*.)[16]

In the case of sale of goods and of partnership English law
has codified the implied terms. Elsewhere the extent to which
the process of the hardening of fact into law has gone may be
debated, but as a technical device the implied term is one of
the differentiating characteristics of the Common law. It is
criticised as artificial, but the approach is ineradicable (it is
retained even in the otherwise innovatory Uniform Commercial
Code (USA)). Faced with a problem in contract, the Common
lawyer is as likely as not to try to solve it with an implied term.
But the Civil lawyer will probably resort to a rule, whether
it is a broad and fundamental precept such as the German
requirement of good faith,[17] or one derived from the nature of
obligation or of contract in general, as with the French
requirement of an *objet*,[18] or, finally, one derived from the
nature of the contract in question.

c *Obligations de moyens, de résultat, de garantie*
An important instance of this last category is to be found in the
distinction between an *obligation de moyens* and an *obligation
de résultat*. We have seen that French law (following Roman
law) bases contractual liability, as it also bases delictual
liability, on fault, whereas the Common law has traditionally

16 For the French approach to 'clauses abusives' see pp. 136 f, 229, below.
17 See p. 147, below.
18 See pp. 108 ff, below.

thought of contractual obligations as in principle absolute and therefore ostensibly finds no place for fault in contractual liability. In practical consequence, indeed, the difference in this respect between the two systems is largely illusory in that what French law expresses in terms of a rule is embodied by English law in an implied term, but whereas the English approach is fragmentary and turns ostensibly on the interpretation of the individual contract,[19] French law applies a broad rule and proceeds, once again, by categorising the agreement in question. The court asks, not, as an English court ostensibly does, what terms the parties must be taken to have intended, but what was the 'nature' of the contract into which they have entered.

The distinction with which we are concerned was proposed by Demogue[20] and rapidly found favour with the courts and with most of the writers. He identified two types of contract. In one the debtor is bound to no more than the exercise of reasonable care. His obligation is to take the measures which a *bon père de famille* (the French reasonable man) would take to achieve the purpose of the contract, and this therefore Demogue called an *obligation de moyens*. The example always given is that of the doctor who is bound to take reasonable steps to cure his patient, but who is not liable if, in spite of such steps, no cure is achieved. The second type of contract is that in which the debtor's obligation is not simply to show due diligence, but to achieve the result which he has promised (*obligation de résultat*). Thus it had been settled long before Demogue wrote that in a contract of transport the obligation of the transporter was to carry the person or the goods safe and sound to the destination.[1] Similarly it has been held that a restaurateur, though he is under only an *obligation de moyens*

19 See Treitel *Contract* pp. 634 ff.
20 *Traité des obligations* (1925) vol 5, s. 1237, vol 6, s. 599.
1 Cass civ 21.11.1911, S 1912.1.73 note Lyon-Caen; D 1913.1.249 note Sarrut; *Source-book* p. 172. As far as the transport of persons is concerned (for which contrast *Readhead v Midland Rly Co* (1869) LR 4 QB 379) the rule has given rise to difficulty (a) in determining what constitutes transport (roundabouts or 'dodgem cars' at a fair, ski-lifts, an outing on horse-back; as to which see text, below), (b) in determining when transport begins and ends, since the obligation to persons entering on premises, e g a railway station, is normally *de moyens*; cf p. 51, n. 5, below. See Starck ss. 1781 ff.

in regard to the 'gustatory and digestive quality' of his food, is under an *obligation de résultat*, as far as his customer's health is concerned, to leave him safe and sound at the end of the meal.[2] The *obligation de résultat* is not, however, absolute. The debtor can escape liability by showing that his failure to produce the result promised is due to a cause beyond his control (*cause étrangère*).[3] The essential difference between the two types of obligation lies therefore in the burden of proof. In both cases the burden of showing that the debtor has not performed his obligation lies, as usual, on the creditor, but since in an *obligation de moyens* the failure to take care is an essential element in the non-performance, the burden of proof of fault lies on the creditor, whereas in an *obligation de résultat* the creditor has only to show that the result has not been achieved and it is then for the debtor to show a *cause étrangère*. (It has been argued[4] that he should need only to show that he has used all reasonable care, but the *jurisprudence* has continued to insist on his showing a *cause étrangère*. The practical difference lies in the case where the cause is unknown.)

Demogue's distinction is usually accepted as removing an apparent contradiction between article 1137 and article 1147 Cc:

1136   The obligation of *donner* imports that of delivering the thing and looking after it until delivery, on pain of the payment of damages to the creditor.
1137   The obligation of looking after the thing . . . requires the person obliged to exercise the care of a *bon père de famille*.
1147   The debtor is condemned, where this is appropriate, to the payment of damages, whether for the non-performance of the obligation or for delay in its performance, whenever he does not show that the non-performance results from a *cause étrangère* which cannot be imputed to him, even though there is no bad faith on his part.

Article 1137 makes liability depend on proof of fault, whereas article 1147 makes exemption from liability depend on proof of a *cause étrangére*. The literal approach, which a

2 Poitiers 16.12.1970, Gaz Pal 1971.264.
3 See pp. 193 ff, below.
4 Tunc RT (1945) 235; Mazeaud/Tunc ss. 661 ff.

Common law court might perhaps be tempted to adopt, would treat article 1147 as the rule and article 1137 as confined to cases of an obligation to look after a thing, but French statutory interpretation, particularly when applied to a Code, expects internal consistency and the literal approach yields none. Why should looking after a thing entail a different duty of care from looking after a business? For Demogue the two articles are exactly appropriate to his two types of obligation (though the wording is imperfect, since article 1137 has to apply to other obligations in addition to that of looking after a thing, and article 1147 has to be less universal then it seems).

Whether or not Demogue's distinction does provide a satisfactory reconciliation of the two articles, the two categories are now universally accepted (though terminology, whether of *doctrine* or of *jurisprudence*, sometimes varies, the *obligation de moyens* being sometimes called an *obligation de prudence et de diligence* and the *obligation de résultat* an *obligation déterminée*). They are not, however, free of difficulty. On the one hand they are deceptively simple, and on the other hand they leave open the question of how one determines whether in any given situation the obligation is of one kind or the other.

The two categories are deceptively simple, in the first place, in that any particular contract may generate both. The *restaurateur* provides, as we have seen, a simple example: he is under an *obligation de moyens* in regard to the safety of his premises[5] or the 'gustatory quality' of his food, but under the an *obligation de résultat* to ensure that the food is not poisonous. Or a doctor is under an *obligation de moyens* in regard to the success of his treatment, but may be under an *obligation de résultat* in regard to the safety of equipment which he uses.[6] The second way in which the two categories are deceptively simple is that there are some contractual relationships to which the *Code civil* attaches obligations which do not fit precisely into either category. For example, the obligation of a tenant of an immovable in regard to dilapidations straddles the two categories: he is liable unless

5 See Cass civ 17.3.1947, D 1947.1.269; *Source-book* p. 426; Cass civ 11.2.1975, D 1975.512 note Le Tourneau; JCP 1975.II.18179 note Viney; *Source-book* p.427.
6 Starck ss. 1769 ff; Cass civ 4.2.1959, D 1959.153.

he can show that he has not been at fault.[7] And his obligation in regard to fire is an enlargement of the *obligation de résultat*: he is liable unless he shows a *cause étrangère* or a defect in construction.[8]

A more important difficulty is that of determining the basis for the incidence of one or the other type of obligation. It might be thought that this would be a pure question of fact, since ostensibly we are concerned with a matter of interpretation. It is clear, however, that this is a matter of law over which the *Cour de cassation* exercises control in the same way as it controls the 'qualification' of a contract as sale, hire etc. The character of the obligation depends on the 'nature' of the contract,[9] and that is treated as a matter of law. In spite of a multitude of cases,[10] however, the *jurisprudence* offers no clear principle. The criterion which is most commonly accepted by *doctrine* and of which traces can perhaps be seen in the cases,[11] is that of the aleatory or otherwise character of the debtor's undertaking. If the promised performance can in the ordinary course of events be expected to be achieved, the obligation is *de résultat*. When one travels by train one does not think of one's arrival as an aleatory or speculative matter, but in the case of a surgical operation one accepts that the element of uncertainty is greater. Similarly, if one hires a horse for a gallop one accepts that there is an element of risk of injury.[12] Moreover in this case the active participation of the creditor increases the *aléa* for the debtor.[13] But the criterion of *aléa* is a very imprecise one, which leaves a good deal that is unpredictable. One would agree, for example, that the manager of a football team[14] or a water-diviner[15] does not

7 Art 1732 Cc. The same meaning has been given to art 1789 (hire of services) Cass civ 16.12.1924, DP 1925.1.21.
8 Art 1733 Cc; cf arts 1772, 1773.
9 As e g in Cass civ 4.2.1959, n. 6, above.
10 Discussed by Le Tourneau J-Cl Civ arts 1136–1145, fasc II, ss. 60 ff.
11 Cass civ 16.1.1951, D 1951.292; Cass civ 6.6.1961, D 1961.772.
12 Cass civ 16.3.1970, D 1970.421 note Rodière; Gaz Pal 1970.1.363; *Source-book* p. 428.
13 Cf Cass civ 8.10.1968, S 1969.157 note Mazeaud; Gaz Pal 1968.2.361; Starck s. 1805.
14 Trib Lille 18.4.1977, D 1978.361.
15 Montpellier 16.1.1951, D 1951.283.

promise success, and perhaps that the owner of a racecourse undertakes only an *obligation de moyens* in regard to injuries caused by a horse which runs off the course,[16] but one would hardly then expect the promoter of a 'dodgem' track to be burdened with an *obligation de résultat* towards his customers[17] and one would not think that the use of bleach by a hairdresser would entail an *aléa* of personal injury to the client.[18] This last example brings one, moreover, to the difficult borderline with delictual liability. The development by the court of art 1384 al 1 Cc has created the equivalent of an *obligation de résultat* in quasi-delict in regard to things under the control (*sous la garde*) of the defendant. Since French law does not allow a delictual action if a remedy is available in contract,[19] there is no direct conflict, but if the contracting party were to die as a result of the use of the bleach it is well settled that his successors (*ayants cause*)[20] could sue in their own name in delict and the hairdresser would then certainly be liable under 1384 al 1. There is therefore a certain pressure to extend the contractual *obligation de résultat* in such cases.[1]

The distinction between the two types of obligation is therefore far from precise (it is in areas such as this that one is most aware of the shortcomings of the unargued French style of *arrêt*), but the Common law method can also be criticised, not only on the familiar ground of its artificiality – that the parties usually have no intention in the matter at all – but also because it has led to a lack of explicit discussion[2] of what, as a matter of policy, the duties of the parties ought to be, and to a lack of understanding of where, in substance, the place of fault in contractual liability is.

It should be noticed that the Common law has no parallel to the *obligation de résultat*. The traditional contractual liability in the Common law was strict or absolute,[3] in the sense that no defence at all was available (until the developments which

16 Cass civ 12.7.1954, D 1954.659.
17 Cass civ 11.2.1975, p. 51, n. 5, above.
18 Cass civ 4.10.1967, JCP 1968.II.15698.
19 The rule of *non-cumul* (p. 30, n. 6, above).
20 See pp. 167 ff, below.
 1 So also in the case of a doctor's liability for his equipment, n. 6, above.
 2 Treitel *Contract* pp. 634 ff. is an exception.
 3 See pp. 193 ff, below.

flowed from *Taylor v Caldwell*).[4] The parallel to this in French law is the *obligation de garantie*.[5] This occurs in a number of contexts. In a contract of lease or hire, for example, the lessor guarantees both quiet possession and the absence of such defects as make the thing unusable.[6] And in a contract of sale the seller guarantees the buyer against eviction and against latent defects.[7] In all cases of *garantie* the debtor is strictly liable, regardless of fault or of the existence of a cause *étrangère*. In the case of latent defects in the thing sold, however, the innocent seller's liability is limited. The buyer has the choice of returning the goods and reclaiming the price or of retaining the goods and claiming a reduction of the price.[8] In addition he is entitled to the 'expenses occasioned by the sale' (which the courts have interpreted to include – to use a Common law term – all reliance damages). The seller who is in bad faith (to whom the *Cour de cassation* by an act of judicial legislation has assimilated the professional seller, on the ostensible ground that he is expected to be aware of defects) is liable for all the buyer's consequential loss.

d Style of drafting[9]

As we have remarked above[10] in relation to legislation, interpretation and the style of what is interpreted are linked in a circular relationship. The usually broad and simple style of French legislation would be unworkable if submitted to the restrictive interpretation habitual in English courts and conversely the style of English legislation reflects (or is reflected in) the style of interpretation. The same can be said of the drafting of contracts. If one leaves aside some specialised contracts,[11] it is very broadly true that French contracts are shorter and simpler than their English counterparts. And this difference derives from the other differences which we have

4 (1863) 3 B & S 826.
5 Mazeaud/Tunc s. 103–8.
6 Arts 1726, 1727, 1721, Cc.
7 See further p. 79, below.
8 These special remedies have a Roman orgin; Nicholas *Roman Law* p. 181.
9 I am grateful for the advice of my former pupil David Cox, Assistant General Counsel, Monsanto Europe SA.
10 P. 5.
11 Such as commercial leases (*baux commerciaux*).

just been discussing. The French draftsman works within a framework provided by the Civil code, a framework both of general rules and of the particular rules appropriate to the specific contracts. Just as the judge begins by 'qualifying' the contract before him, so also the draftsman begins by asking himself the same question and then proceeds in the knowledge that the main incidents of the contract are provided for and that he need concentrate only on those points which are of particular concern to the parties. By contrast the English draftsman, traditionally at least, has seen himself as drafting afresh each time an entire contract and has therefore felt compelled to make provision for every foreseeable point. Of course, he nowadays no longer in fact starts with a blank sheet: there are many statutory restraints on freedom of contract, sale of goods is in effect codified and there is an increasing number of implied terms established by the courts. But the habit of comprehensive drafting remains (and the implied terms established by the courts in any event lack the systematic framework which might encourage a draftsman to take advantage of them). Even though he knows that not everything that he puts in his contract is necessary, the English lawyer will usually prefer to be on the safe side and to aim for completeness. And this in turn no doubt affects the attitude with which the judge approaches the task of interpretation.

More widely the attitude of lawyers in the two countries perhaps reflects a difference which we have already noted in their perception of what law is. For the French lawyer (and for Civil lawyers in general) law is in principle a complete and intellectually coherent system which, explicity or implicitly, embodies the rules necessary for life in society. The Common law, on the other hand, is seen as never complete, but always in the process of becoming, and the draftsman's function therefore necessarily involves an element of prediction or anticipation. The wise draftsman reduces this element to a minimum.

Chapter three
Formation of contract[1]

A Consent

1 Formal and evidential requirements

It should follow from the doctrine of the autonomy of the will[2]
that an agreement into which the parties have freely entered is
a binding contract. And this is indeed the starting-point of
French law;[3] but some contracts are subjected to a requirement of writing. This requirement may be either formal or
evidential (*ad sollemnitatem* or *ad probationem* in the traditional terminology).

(a) Where the requirement is formal, the absence of the
writing will make the contract void. The form is necessary for
validity, as is a seal for the validity in English law of a lease for
more than three years. The parallel with the seal must not,
however, be pressed too far. In the case of the lease, the seal
is a requirement of form which is additional to the ordinary
requirements of substance (agreement and consideration); the
function of the written form in French law is the same. But in
the case of a gratuitous promise under seal the function of the
seal is different. For there it replaces one of the ordinary
requirements of substance (viz consideration). There is no

1 For an exhaustive comparative examination see Schlesinger (ed) *Formation of Contracts* 2 vols (New York, 1968). Any conclusion as to a 'common
  core of legal systems' must, however, be seen in the light of the influence
  on English and American writers in the nineteenth century of German
  doctrine; see pp. 33 f, above.
2 Pp. 31 ff, above.
3 Art 1108 Cc.

parallel to this function in French law. The form is always an additional requirement.

The writing required in the most important cases is an *acte notarié*, i e a document drawn up by a notary.[4] In the field of contract this is necessary for a *donation*, a *convention matrimoniale* (i e a contract regulating the property relations of prospective spouses) and a mortgage (*hypothèque conventionelle*).[5] In other cases a signed document (*acte sous seing privé*) is sufficient. The only instance of this in the Code[6] is an agreement fixing a rate of interest different from that laid down by law.

In these cases the requirement of form both promotes certainty and has a cautionary effect.[7] It promotes certainty in that it makes precise the content of the contract and the moment when it takes effect; and it is cautionary in that it encourages the parties to reflect before they commit themselves. But forms can serve other purposes. In particular, they may be intended to ensure publicity or, especially in recent legislation, to protect the weaker party.

Publicity may be required for two reasons. The first is the familiar one of making known to third parties the existence of real rights. Most contracts relating to immovables are therefore required to be registered.[8] But the absence of this *publicité foncière* does not affect the validity of the contract between the parties; it merely makes the contract ineffective (*inopposable*) against third parties. There are, in other words, no rights *in rem*.

The second reason for requiring publicity in modern French law is to ensure that the transaction is visible to the tax authorities. This fiscal use of the requirement of form has become prominent in recent years. An example is provided by the rule[9] that an agreement for an option to buy an immovable

4 See *Source-book* pp. 291 f.
5 Arts 937, 1394, 2127 Cc; cf art 1250 al 2. On *donations* see pp. 140 ff, below. Many other transactions, though not required to be notarised, are in practice drawn up by notaries.
6 Art 1907.
7 Cf Treitel *Contract* p. 116.
8 Weill/Terré s. 120.
9 *Loi* of 19.12.1963 (No 63-1241).

or a business (*promesse unilatérale de vente*)[10] must be registered or notarially executed. The rule arose out of the practice whereby middlemen assigned such options at a profit which, in the absence of publicity, could escape taxation. Here, and in other similar cases, the invalidity is total.

French law, like English law, has also in recent years resorted to the protective use of formality. Various types of contractual clause, for example, which may work to the disadvantage of the weaker party must be printed in some especially prominent way.[11]

(b) In other cases the requirement of writing is only evidential, in the sense that if the transaction has to be proved, the party seeking to do so must adduce written evidence. Thus, the *Code civil*[12] provides that if the sum or value involved is over 50 francs, there must be a notarial act or a signed document. This requirement is qualified, however, in a number of ways. It does not in general apply to contracts governed by commercial law.[13] And there is an exception for cases where it was 'impossible' to obtain written evidence.[14] This has been liberally construed to include the 'moral impossibility' of asking for a written document (in transactions within the family, for example, or in fairs and markets where written contracts are not customary). A wider exception is provided by the rule[15] which admits oral evidence whenever there exists 'a beginning of written proof', which is defined as any written act emanating from the defendant which makes it probable that the fact alleged is true.

2 Offer and acceptance

Subject to what has just been said, French law sees a contract as an agreement, and it shares with English law (and indeed all other Western systems) the analysis of that agreement in terms

10 Pp. 63 ff, below.
11 E g the last *alinéa* of art 9 of the *loi* of 13.7.1930 on certain clauses in insurance policies; cf Cass civ 18.3.1942, S 1943.1.13 note Houin, *Sourcebook* p. 106. For English parallels see Treitel *Contract* p. 116.
12 Arts 1325, 1326.
13 Art 109 C com; Amos and Walton p. 344.
14 Art 1348 Cc.
15 Art 1347 Cc. See Weill/Terré *Droit civil - Introduction générale* s. 447.

of offer and acceptance. The practical results of that analysis quite often, however, diverge from those found in English law, and where this is so it is usually because French law, as has been remarked above,[16] adopts a more subjective approach.

a Fact or law?

The broadest difference, however, is one which we have already noticed.[17] We have seen that in French law in general the area of fact as opposed to law is wider than in English law, and that this is particularly noticeable in matters of offer and acceptance. Neither the Code nor any other text lays down any rules on the matter. The only legal requirement is that there should be an agreement. Whether there is or is not an agreement is a matter of fact which (leaving aside questions of defective consent) is wholly within the *pouvoir souverain du juge du fond*: it escapes the control of the *Cour de cassation*. All that that court can do is to say whether or not the court below, in exercising its *pouvoir souverain*, has so far misinterpreted the facts as to 'denature' them.[18] There are none of the detailed rules on offer and acceptance which have evolved in English law. This at least is in principle the position, but in practice there is more certainty and predictability than the statement of principle might lead one to expect. For on the one hand the *Cour de cassation* is not always as forbearing as principle requires, and on the other hand, as we shall see under the particular headings which follow, there are some matters on which a fair uniformity of practice has developed.

The difficulty of adhering strictly to the principle that the whole matter is one of fact is well illustrated by a decision of the *Cour de cassation*.[19] The facts were simple. Braquet had advertised for sale in the local newspaper a plot of land at a price of 25,000 francs. Maltzkorn, having seen the advertisement, told Braquet, at a time when the land was still unsold,

16 P. 34.
17 P. 17, above.
18 Cf p. 47, above. For examples see Cass req 20.2.1905, S 1905.1.508; *Source-book* p. 322; Cass civ 28.11.1968, JCP 1969.II.1597, Gaz Pal 1969.1.95, *Source-book* p. 324; Cass civ 2.2.1932, S 1932.1.68, Gaz Pal 1932.1.702, *Source-book* p. 340; Cass civ 21.12.1960, D 1961. 417 note Malaurie, *Source-book* p. 345.
19 Cass civ 28.11.1968, see preceding note.

that he accepted his offer, but Braquet contended that he was not bound. In English terms, he contended that the advertisement was not an offer but an invitation to treat. The court below gave judgment for Braquet, declaring that 'an offer in the press of a thing which can only be acquired by one person cannot be assimilated to an offer made to a determinate person; it constitutes only an invitation to anyone who may be interested, and cannot therefore bind its author to a person who makes an acceptance'. The *Cour de cassation* quashed this decision as disclosing no foundation in law (*base légale*), in that the court had relied on a general proposition of law (*motif d'ordre général*) and had pointed to no facts from which it could have inferred that the advertisement was only an invitation to treat. The text which the *Cour de cassation* cited as the basis of its judgment was article 1589 Cc, which expresses in the particular context of the contract of sale the principle that a contract is constituted by the agreement of the parties. In short, if the court below had been content to say that, on the particular facts, there had been no agreement, the *Cour de cassation* would have had no ground for intervening (short of declaring that those facts had been 'denatured'). Where the court below had gone wrong was in relying on a non-existent rule of law about public offers.[20] And yet the *Cour de cassation* itself, at the beginning of its *arrêt*, falls into exactly the same error. It declares that 'an offer made to the public binds the offeror in regard to the first accepter in the same way as an offer to a particular person'.

b Offer or invitation to treat?

It is obvious that where two parties enter into negotiations, the question whether a particular statement by one of them is an offer or merely an invitation to treat must always be one of fact. But there are certain commonly recurrent situations, involving communications made to the public or to an indeterminate number of persons (e g advertisements, catalogues, displays of goods for sale) in which English law has evolved rules of law which at least prima facie determine the matter.[1]

---

20 And in propounding such a rule in breach of art 5 Cc (p. 12, above).
 1 Treitel *Contract* pp. 8 ff.

We have just seen that the *Cour de cassation* also has laid down a rule for such 'public offers'. But the rule is different. In English law Braquet's advertisement would have constituted only an invitation to treat. Nor is the decision of the *Cour de cassation* an isolated one (though the case law is not abundant).[2] It can indeed be said that in general where French law sees a 'public offer', English law sees only an invitation to treat. It is clear, for example, that the display of goods in a shop window constitutes an offer,[3] and this applies a fortiori to such a display in a self-service supermarket. Thus,[4] when a bottle of lemonade exploded at the cash-desk, but before it had been checked out, the Paris Court of Appeal, in a decision which was upheld by the *Cour de cassation*, ruled that in a self-service shop 'the sale is complete when the customer, having chosen from the shelf an article offered for sale at a posted price which he accepts, places it in the basket which is provided and which he is bound to use until the goods are checked out at the cash-desk'.[5] The customer, who had been injured by the explosion, was entitled to sue the supermarket in contract.[6]

The French approach to this and other variants of the public offer is based on the dogmatic argument from consensus. Since the seller has a continuing intention to sell what is on the shelves or, in the case of a shop-window or a catalogue, what he advertises, and since the buyer intends to buy when he puts the

2 See Bonassies in Schlesinger (ed) *Formation of Contracts* vol 1, pp. 356 ff, 662 ff.
3 Provided that the price is indicated (since the offer must be capable of being converted into a contract by acceptance, and there can be no sale without a determined or determinable price; see p. 33, above and p. 109, below).
4 Paris 14.12.1961, JCP 1962.II.12547 note Savatier, Gaz Pal 1962.1.135, and Cass civ 20.10.1964, D 1965.62, *Source-book* pp. 325, 326.
5 In this instance the *Cour de cassation* ignores the statement of a general rule and treats the *Cour d'appel* as simply exercising its *pouvoir souverain*.
6 The customer had also entered a claim (a) against the supermarket in delict (arts 1382, 1383, 1384 Cc), but this was excluded by the rule of *non-cumul* (p. 30, n. 6, above), (b) against the manufacturer in delict (arts 1382, 1383 Cc), but the court held that there was no fault. The supermarket had also invoked against the manufacturer the *garantie* against latent defects (p. 80, below), but the court held that there was no defect, the damage being due to the supermarket's fault in allowing the bottle to become too warm.

thing in the basket or sends off his order, it must be at this moment that the contract is formed. The reasons which English law gives for delaying the formation of the contract by construing the seller's act of placing the goods on the shelf or sending out the catalogue as merely an invitation to treat, are for the most part reasons of convenience[7] (e g that the seller by advertisement may not have enough stock, that the buyer in a supermarket may change his mind), though they can, with some artificiality, be accommodated within the theory of consensus. But not all the arguments of convenience favour the English approach.[8] In the case of the exploding lemonade bottle an English court would no doubt have held that the contract could not come into existence until the lemonade was checked out[9] and therefore that the action must be in tort. And yet it can be said to be undesirable that the nature of the action (and therefore the plaintiff's success or failure where negligence by the seller cannot be proved) should depend on the precise moment when the explosion occurred. In other situations, however, the French approach may be inconvenient. In another self-service sale,[10] where a woman walked out without paying for goods which she had picked up and was in consequence convicted of theft, it was argued in the *chambre criminelle* of the *Cour de cassation* that since she owned the goods as soon as she picked them up, she was not guilty of theft, but had merely failed to pay for goods which already belonged to her. The argument was rejected, but on no convincing ground of principle. As is often the case, arguments of convenience lead to mutually inconsistent answers in different contexts (in this case the contexts of contract, tort and crime).[11]

7 Criticised by Treitel *Contract* pp. 9 f.
8 See the passage quoted from *Sancho-Lopez v Felco Food Corpn* 211 NY 2d 953 in Schlesinger (ed) *Formation of Contracts* p. 337; *contra* Tunc RT (1962) 306. (*Source-book* p. 327.)
9 *Pharmaceutical Society of Great Britain v Boots Cash Chemists (Southern) Ltd* [1953] 1 QB 401.
10 Cass crim 14.3.1958, D 1958.513; Schlesinger (ed) *Formation of Contracts* p. 365.
11 Cf *Fisher v Bell* [1961] 1 QB 394, reversed as to the actual decision by Restriction of Offensive Weapons Act 1961, s. 1.

c Offer or unilateral promise?

In English law an offer, even if expressed to be irrevocable (or 'firm') for a certain period, may be freely revoked until it has been accepted, unless the offeree, by giving consideration for its being kept open, has 'purchased an option'. In French law offers may not be freely revoked, though the basis and limits of this restriction on revocation are, as we shall see, debatable. Moreover, since a contract requires for its creation merely an agreement, rather than a promise supported by consideration, the distinction between an offer (*offre* or *pollicitation*) and an option (*promesse unilatérale de contrat*) rests on no more than acceptance. A 'firm offer' can be seen as two offers, the principal offer (to sell, for example) and a collateral offer to keep the principal offer open for a period. Once the collateral offer has been accepted (and this is obviously an exiguous requirement) it becomes a unilateral contract and is enforceable as such. The distinction, on the one hand, between such a *promesse* and an offer, and, on the other hand, between such a *promesse* and a pre-contract which binds both parties (*promesse synallagmatique de contrat*) has acquired added importance from the recently enacted requirement noticed above, that certain *promesses unilatérales de vente* must on pain of nullity be registered or notarially executed. It is therefore crucial to know whether a given act in the preliminaries to the sale of an immovable or a business is an offer or a pre-contract, and, if the latter, whether it binds only the prospective seller or both parties.[12]

In what follows we are concerned only with an offer, as opposed to a unilateral promise.

d Revocation of offer

If the offeror changes his mind before the offeree has decided to accept, the conclusion to be drawn from the consensual principle should be that there is no contract. For there has been no moment at which the minds of the parties were at one. And it should make no difference whether the offeree is aware of the offeror's change of mind or not. The question posed in

---

12 Cass com 9.11.1971, D 1972.63; 24.4.1972, JCP 1972.II.17144. See Weill/Terré s. 108 and esp. p. 114, n. 1.

the English case of *Dickinson v Dodds*[13] should therefore present no difficulty. And this is in fact the view taken by the preponderance of *doctrine* and by the courts (subject to the qualification that, for practical reasons of proof, the change of mind must in some way be manifested). In a case which came before the *Cour d'appel* of Montpellier, Isler had offered to sell a chalet to Chastan, but a few days later, when Chastan, having by agreement made an inspection, sent a telegram of acceptance, Isler contended that there could be no contract because he had by then already sold to another buyer. The court, upheld by the *Cour de cassation*,[14] rejected this contention, the ground for the rejection being that the court did not believe that Isler had already sold to the other buyer and therefore that there had been no revocation. Nothing was made of the point, which in an English court would have disposed of Isler's contention, that the alleged revocation was not known to Chastan when he sent his acceptance.

This purely consensual approach may seem at first sight to be contradicted by the rule applied by the courts that the offeror must keep his offer open for the period indicated in that offer or, if there is no period indicated, for such period as is necessary to enable the offeree to consider and reply to it (*délai raisonnable*). Thus, in the case just considered, the *Cour de cassation*, before concluding that the court below was justified in finding that there had been no revocation, declared that

> while an offer may in principle be revoked as long as it has not been accepted, the position is different where the offeror has expressly or impliedly undertaken not to revoke before a certain time; and in the present case the judgment of the court below notes that . . . Isler, having tacitly obliged himself to keep his offer open [until after Chastan had made his inspection], could not have revoked the offer [on the day alleged] without committing 'a fault of a kind which would entail liability on his part'.

Statements such as this in the *jurisprudence* pose the question of the basis of the offeror's liability.[15] Granted that we

13 (1876) 2 ChD 463.
14 Cass civ 17.12.1958, D 1959.33, *Source-book* p. 328. See Schlesinger (ed) *Formation of Contracts* p. 815 for other cases.
15 See Ghestin *Contrat* ss. 210 ff; Schmidt RT (1974) pp. 46 ff.

are here concerned with an offer and not with a unilateral promise, the basis, at least where no period has been mentioned in the offer, cannot, except by a fiction, be found in contract. For most writers therefore the liability rests either on an obligation deriving from the unilateral juridical act which is, on this view, constituted by the making of the offer, or on a delictual obligation deriving from the offeror's premature revocation. If one leaves aside the wider difficulty of accepting that liability can ever be founded on a unilateral juridical act, the significant difference between the two approaches is that the former denies effect to the revocation, while the latter acknowledges that the revocation is effective, but declares it to be wrongful. In the terms familiar to English analytical jurists, the former approach denies that the offeror has any power to revoke, while the latter accepts that he has such a power but asserts that he is under a (delictual) duty not to exercise it. This difference should also entail a difference in the measure of damages (contractual or expectation-based in the one case and delictual or reliance-based in the other).[16]

Each approach can be found in, or read into, the words used by the courts. In the passage quoted above, for example, the *Cour de cassation*, when it speaks of an undertaking not to revoke, seems to be using the language of the unilateral juridical act, but since the decision eventually rests on the finding that there was in fact no revocation, nothing turns on the matter. And there seems to be no case in which a clearly contractual remedy has been given. On the other hand, the language of fault which the *Cour de cassation* uses in the passage quoted above is consistent with a basis in delict, and in an old but well-known decision of the *Cour d'appel* of Bordeaux[17] the remedy is clearly delictual. Jahn, the director of the theatre at The Hague, sent two telegrams to Madame Charry, a well-known singer with whom he was already in

16 But since the assessment of damages lies within the *pouvoir souverain* of the trial court (see p. 226, below), it may be difficult to discover what measure has been applied. An order for specific performance is not a distinguishing mark, since it may be made in a delictual as well as in a contractual action (Mazeaud/Tunc ss. 120, 2303–2315).

17 Bordeaux 17.1.1870, S 1870.2.219, *Source-book* p. 330; Bonassies in Schlesinger (ed) *Formation of Contracts* pp. 770, 771, cites also Cass civ 8.10.1958.

negotiation, offering her an engagement. The first telegram was reply-paid, indicating the urgency of the matter. Having had no reply by the evening of the day after the despatch of his first telegram, Jahn took steps to engage another singer. His telegrams to Madame Charry, however, had been delayed and did not reach her until the following day. She then promptly sent a telegram of acceptance.

The court of first instance had held that there was a contract and had awarded Madame Charry 20,000 francs, that being the sum fixed in the proposed agreement as a penalty for breach. The *Cour d'appel*, however, ruled that there was no contract because there had been no moment at which the intention to offer and the intention to accept had co-existed. But since, as the court held, the delay in delivery of the telegrams was attributable to the fault of Jahn, he was liable for the failure of the contract on the existence of which Madame Charry had relied, and for the damage which she had suffered in consequence of that reliance. She was entitled therefore, not to the contractual figure of 20,000 francs, but to the amount of damage which she had actually suffered, which was assessed at 4,000 francs.

While it is clear that in this case the liability is delictual, the court goes no further towards explaining its precise foundation than to say that 'justice as well as law' requires the offeror to pay compensation. And the writers have difficulty in providing an entirely satisfactory explanation for the liability of the offeror in cases such as this. As we shall see,[18] the courts on occasion give damages for breaking off negotiations even before the stage of offer has been reached, and there the liability is plainly based on some element of culpability in the defendant's conduct. But liability for premature revocation of an offer does not rest on any special feature of the offeror's conduct. And simply to say that revocation before a reasonable time has elapsed is *ipso facto* wrongful is to evade the problem. A widely accepted explanation is in terms of the theory of abuse of rights, a theory which, though it has found no acceptance in England, has a wide range of application in French law.[19] The offeror's right to revoke must not be

18 Under (f), below.
19 Starck ss. 299 ff.

exercised so as to defeat the reasonable expectations of the offeree, or, according to another and more abstract formulation, it must not be exercised except in accordance with the social purpose for which the law accords such freedom.

e Lapse of offer

Both English law and French law accept that an offer will lapse with the passage of time, but the principle is more prominent in French law[20] and the period is perhaps shorter. The reason for this is no doubt that a system which imposes liability for revocation before a reasonable time has passed necessarily places more emphasis on the principle of lapse after such a time than does a system which places no restriction on revocation before acceptance.[1] Thus a French court may speak of the need for acceptance to be made 'within the *délai moral* necessary for examining and replying to the offer'[2] or may reject an acceptance as not having been made '*en temps utile*'.[3]

f Pre-contractual fault[4]

We have seen that the liability of the offeror for premature revocation is, at least on one view, delictual, either on the ordinary principle of fault or more specifically on that of abuse of right. It can be said that the law of delict is brought in to correct the subjective view of consensus which prevails in French law and which treats a manifested, even if uncommunicated, revocation as effective, whereas the less subjective approach of English law makes the requirement of communication do the work done in French law by the law of delict.[5] But it cannot do all of the work. Where the subject matter is complex, the offeree may in reliance on the offer incur considerable expense in examining it and yet English law

20 The only reported English case seems to be *Ramsgate Victoria Hotel Co Ltd v Montefiore* (1866) LR 1 Ex 109. See also *Manchester Diocesan Council for Education v Commercial and General Investments Ltd* [1970] 1 WLR 241 at 248, per Buckley J.
1 Except the requirement that the offeree must have notice of the revocation.
2 Cass req 27.6.1894, S 1898.1.434, *Source-book* p. 327.
3 Paris 12.6.1869, S 1869.2.287, *Source-book* p. 340.
4 Cf Kessler and Fine (1964) 77 Harvard L Rev 401 ff.
5 On the difference in the measure of damages see p. 65, n. 16, above.

allows the offeror to revoke with impunity, provided only that the offeree has notice of the revocation. That his conduct does not conform to the standard of fair commercial practice is irrelevant. French law, on the other hand, in effect requires him to observe those standards. But if French law imposes liability in this immediately pre-contractual stage, should it not protect the reliance interest of the parties in earlier stages of the negotiations also?

This is the general question which was answered for nineteenth century German law by Ihering's theory of fault in the formulation of contract (*culpa in contrahendo*).[6] In modern German law liability is based on the broad requirement of good faith found in the Civil Code and developed by the courts.[7] The *Code civil*, however, while it calls for good faith in the performance of contracts,[8] has no such provision in relation to their formation. But in recent years there has been a tendency on the part of both *jurisprudence* and *doctrine* to import, in reliance on the general principle of delictual liability, a requirement of good faith or honesty and fair dealing into the pre-contractual negotiations. This tendency was consecrated in a decision of the *chambre commerciale* of the *Cour de cassation* in 1972.[9] The defendant was the exclusive distributor in France of machines made by an American firm, X. The plaintiff entered into negotiations with the defendant and eventually, after going to America to see the various types of machine which X could supply, asked the defendant for certain complementary information to enable him to make a choice. The defendant made no reply and (as the plaintiff later discovered) withheld an estimate sent by X. Two weeks later the defendant signed a contract to supply a machine to a competitor of the plaintiff's, with a clause in which the defendant undertook not to supply another machine in the same area for forty-two months. The court below found that there had been a wrongful breaking-off of negotiations and held the defendant liable in delict. This decision was

6 Cf Kessler and Fine (1964) 77 Harvard L Rev 401–403.
7 See p. 147, below. Liability is still in contract because there is no general principle of delictual liability for fault to correspond to the French art 1382 Cc.
8 See pp. 147 f, below.
9 Cass com 20.3.1972, JCP 1973.II.17543 note Schmidt.

upheld by the *Cour de cassation*, which noted that the defendant had deliberately withheld the estimate and kept the plaintiff in the dark, and had broken off the negotiations when they were in an advanced stage, in a 'brutal and unilateral way', in the knowledge that the plaintiff had incurred considerable expense. The defendant had therefore 'broken the rules of good faith in commercial relations'.

This decision arrogates to the courts a very wide discretion to police the conduct of businessmen and is one of many illustrations of the truth that, because French law thinks in large categories rather than in detailed instances, the French judge often exercises a much wider power than his Common law counterpart. But there are dangers in this wide power, as had been recognised three years earlier by the *Cour d'appel* of Pau, when it refused, in a less extreme case, to impose liability for breaking off negotiations.[10] The court recognised that 'certain obligations of honesty and fair dealing (*rectitude et loyauté*) rest on the parties in the conduct of negotiations, but fault *in contrahendo* must be obvious and beyond dispute'. Otherwise there would be grave interference with freedom of contract and the security of commercial transactions.

It would seem, indeed, from the paucity of reported cases, that pre-contractual liability of this kind is rarely invoked,[11] but even in as 'obvious' a case as that of 1972 an English court would shrink from the interference involved. For even in the performance of contracts English law does not recognise a general obligation of good faith.[12]

g Acceptance

i *Is communication necessary?*
It would be in accord with what we have seen so far of the French attitude to consensus if it were sufficient that the offeree should decide to accept, or rather, for practical reasons of proof, should manifest this decision. For at that moment the two wills are at one, and communication of the acceptance can add nothing. And this (commonly called the theory of

10 Pau 14.1.69, D 1969.716.
11 Cf Ghestin *Contrat* s. 228; Durry RT (1972) p. 779.
12 But for the USA see Uniform Commercial Code §1-203.

émission) has indeed been the predominant view of the writers. But others have argued that what is needed is not merely the co-existence of two wills, but mutual awareness of such co-existence, i e the communication of the acceptance (theory of *information*). This is, of course, a familiar problem in the English literature also, and we know that in fact the requirement of communication is no guarantee of mutual awareness, since either party may have changed his mind in the interval between dispatch and receipt of the communication. And there are obvious practical objections to giving effect to an uncommunicated acceptance. As far as the *jurisprudence* is concerned, decisions can be adduced to support either view, but their interpretation is uncertain for two reasons. In the first place, the *Cour de cassation*, for the reasons explained above, has usually treated the question as one of fact and has contented itself with saying that a decision which accords with one theory or the other is within the *pouvoir souverain* of the court below.[13] And in the second place, in any particular case the offer may be interpreted as having required that acceptance be communicated.

ii *Contracts by correspondence*

The context in which problems have arisen in practice has, of course, as in English law, usually been that of contracts by correspondence. In this context the theory of *émission* becomes the theory of *expédition*: the acceptance is effective when it is sent off (i e the English rule for postal acceptances). And the theory of *information* becomes the theory of *réception* (e g the arrival of the letter from the post office). As has just been explained, the courts have not clearly adopted either theory, and in recent years some writers, while acknowledging that it is unsatisfactory to have no rule, have argued that it is also unsatisfactory to attempt to derive from an abstract theory the same answer for the several different questions which may arise.[14] It seemed indeed that the courts were beginning to adopt this approach and were tending to apply the theory of *émission* to the question *where* the contract was formed and

13 See pp. 58 ff, above and cases cited there; Starck ss. 1268 f.
14 Ghestin *Contrat* ss. 251 ff, Starck ss. 1270 ff; cf Treitel *Contract* pp. 18 ff.

the theory of *réception* to the question *when*.[15] The answer to the former question determined which court had jurisdiction and it could be argued that in contracts of employment, for example, the acceptance usually comes from the employee and that in such cases the theory of *émission* would ensure that litigation took place in his local court and not in that of his employer, which, if the employer was a large company, might well be in some distant place. This development has, however, been cut short by the new *Code de procédure civile*,[16] which expressly excludes the place of formation of a contract as a criterion for determining local jurisdiction.

As for the question *when* an acceptance is effective, it is argued[17] that in practical terms this embraces several questions and that the same answer may not be appropriate to all of them. The most familiar are those arising from the revocation of offer or of acceptance. (i) Will an acceptance, once posted, prevail over a revocation of the offer which is made after the moment of posting but before that of the receipt of the acceptance?[18] (ii) Will an acceptance, once posted, prevail over a revocation of that acceptance which is received (e g by telegram) before the acceptance itself is received by the offeror? The traditional approach required the answer to both questions to be derived from the same 'theory', and therefore if the theory of *émission*, for example, were adopted, the answer to both would be in the negative. It is currently argued, however, that practical considerations may call for different answers. A recent international convention on the sale of goods,[19] for example, answers the first question in the negative (*émission*) and the second in the positive (*réception*). Other questions relate to the effects of the contract (when does the property or the risk pass?) or the effect on the contract of legislation enacted while the contract was being made. Here also it is argued that the blanket application of a 'theory' may produce inconvenient results. So far, however, although it is generally agreed that it is unsatisfactory to leave all such

15 E g Cass civ 21.12.1960, D 1961.417 note Malaurie, *Source-book* p. 345.
16 Art 46.
17 See n. 14, above.
18 Cf Treitel *Contract* p. 23.
19 Vienna Convention on Contracts for the International Sale of Goods 1980, arts 16, 18, 22.

questions to be answered as matters of fact, it is impossible to state a clear set of answers to all of them.

iii *Acceptance by silence*

We have seen[20] that for some purposes it is more important in French law than it is in English to be able to establish the existence of an agreement. It is therefore not surprising that there is also a greater readiness to find on the facts of a particular case[21] an exception to the prima facie rule that silence does not constitute acceptance. In general, however, the treatment does not differ significantly from that of English law. The only idea which will strike the English lawyer as novel is that an offer made exclusively in the interest of the offeree is presumed to be accepted by him. For such an offer would in any event fall foul of the doctrine of consideration. The idea first made its appearance in a case before the *Cour de cassation* in 1938,[1] the facts of which will remind the English lawyer of the *High Trees* case.[2] A landlord told his tenants that he would reduce their outstanding rents to a specified figure. Having failed to obtain payment even of this reduced figure, he brought an action for the full original amount. The question for the court below was whether the offer of the reduction had been accepted so as to constitute a *convention*. The court decided that it was, and the *Chambre des requêtes* acknowledged that

> it is open to the judges of fact, in their sovereign appreciation of the facts and the intention of the parties, and when the offer has been made in the exclusive interest of the addressee, to decide that the addressee's silence implies acceptance.

This reference to the idea, being made merely as an incident of a refusal to interfere with the *pouvoir souverain* in matters of fact, could not be regarded as a considered acceptance of it, and it did not re-appear in the *Cour de cassation* for another thirty years,[3] but then it was laid down as a general proposi-

20 P. 63, above; and see pp. 139, 180, below.
21 Starck ss. 1131 ff.
 1 Cass req 29.3.1938, S 1938.1.380, DP 1939.1.5, Gaz Pal 1938.2.32, *Source-book* p. 334.
 2 *Central London Property Trust Ltd v High Trees House Ltd* [1947] 1 KB 130.
 3 Cass civ 1.2.1969, D 1970.422 note Puech, JCP 1970.II.16445 note Aubert, *Source-book* p. 335.

tion. As a result of a collision between a car and a motor-cycle, the motor-cyclist lay unconscious on the road. The motor-cycle caught fire and a passer-by, in attempting to put out the flames, was injured. The court below had found that the passer-by had intervened in virtue of a contract between himself and the motor-cyclist. The *pourvoi* objected that the court had not pointed to any acceptance by the motor-cyclist of the plaintiff's offer of assistance. The *Cour de cassation* ruled that there was no need for it to point to any express acceptance, since 'the addressee of an offer which is made in his exclusive interest is presumed to have accepted it'.

This is clearly an *arrêt de principe* and the principle is therefore established, though its application in both casses can be criticised.[4] In the first it can be said that the landlord made his offer in order to obtain a settlement of the debt and not solely to confer a benefit on the tenants, and in the second case the construction of the act of the passer-by as an offer is very artificial.[5]

B Defects of consent

1 Introductory

The doctrine of the autonomy of the will requires that the agreement which constitutes a contract should have been freely made. Article 1109 of the *Code civil* accordingly declares that

> There is no valid consent if the consent has been given only by mistake, or if it has been extorted by violence or induced by fraud.

These are the three classical *vices du consentement* (*erreur*, *violence* and *dol*). We know from the experience of English

4 Ghestin *Contrat* s. 298, Starck s. 1139.
5 The plaintiff might perhaps have founded his action on *gestion d'affaires* (arts 1372 ff Cc; Amos and Walton pp. 192 ff) either against the motor-cyclist or against the driver of the car, if the latter was at fault and therefore under a duty to repair the damage, a duty which the plaintiff could be said to have discharged. The *Code pénal*, art 63 al 2, imposes a duty of assistance on persons in the position of the plaintiff and this could be said to negative either the existence of an offer (Puech, n. 3, above, *Source-book* p. 336) or the element of voluntariness necessary for *gestion d'affaires*, but the duty exists only if assistance can be given without danger to the person offering it.

law that there are bound to be problems of delimiting the scope of all three defects, and especially of *erreur*, but before considering these problems we should note that the three *vices* have more in common than do the corresponding headings in the English treatment of contract. There is a fundamental unity of substance; and the legal effects of all three are the same. The unity of substance resides in the requirement, which we examine in more detail below, that the *erreur*, *dol* or *violence* must have been such as to induce the party affected by it to enter into the agreement. This and the fact that the legal effects of all three are the same has facilitated a recent tendency in the *jurisprudence* to blur the lines between the three *vices*,[6] a tendency which surprises the English lawyer, who is accustomed to seeing mistake and fraud separated by the gulf set by the distinction between a void and a voidable contract. For this reason it will be convenient here to adopt a Common law order of treatment and to deal first with remedies rather than with rights.

2 Effect of *vices du consentement*

a *Nullité rélative*

A contract vitiated by *erreur*, *violence* or *dol* is null, but the nullity is 'relative', not 'absolute'. By contrast a contract which, for example, lacks a *cause* or an *objet*, or of which the *cause* or the *objet* is illicit, is absolutely null.[7] This distinction, which is applied to all defective *actes juridiques*, is a source of some disagreement among the writers, but the disagreement is as to the theoretical basis of the distinction rather than as to the practical consequences. And these consequences relate only to the action by which the nullity is claimed (*action en nullité*). The effects of the nullity once established are the same for both types.

In practical terms indeed the distinction is rather less important than the controversy as to its theoretical basis might suggest. The most important consequence is as to who may bring the action. A relative nullity may be invoked only by the

6 See pp. 105 f, below.
7 Art 1131 Cc.

party for whose protection the law has established the nullity[8]
(the victim of the *dol*, for example). An absolute nullity,
on the other hand, may be asserted by anyone, provided that
he has an interest. This enlargement of the range of potential
plaintiffs is, however, limited by the requirement that the
interest must be directly connected with the nullity. Where,
for example, the plaintiff claims ownership of land which the
defendant has held for the period of prescription in virtue of
the *juste titre*[9] constituted by a contract of purchase from
a third party, the plaintiff may assert that the contract was
absolutely null (e g for absence of *cause*), but not that it was
relatively null (e g because induced by fraud). On the other
hand, a landowner who is inconvenienced by the activities of a
company which has purchased neighbouring land may not
assert that the contract by which that land was purchased was
absolutely null because of a defect in the incorporation of the
company. The landowner has no sufficient interest.

The other practical consequences of the distinction are (a)
that a relatively null contract may be subsequently validated by
confirmation by the person protected by the nullity, whereas
an absolutely null contract can never be confirmed; (b) that
the *action en nullité* is prescribed after five years where the
nullity is relative (the person protected being deemed to have
confirmed the contract), but only after the usual period of
thirty years[10] where the nullity is absolute.

That the nullity resulting from *vices du consentement* is
relative is clear on the face of the Code, and that absence of
cause or of *objet* produces absolute nullity is generally
accepted, but in the case of some other defects there is
uncertainty as to which type of nullity is appropriate. For the
occasions on which the practical consequences set out above
are in issue in litigation are infrequent, and the doctrinal
debate as to the theoretical basis of the distinction leaves room
for disagreement.

The classical theory, established in the nineteenth century,
bases the distinction on the nature of the act in question. The
act, on this view, may simply not exist at all (absolute nullity)

---

8 And his *ayants cause* (see p. 167, below).
9 Art 2265 Cc.
10 Or, in the view of some writers, never; Weill/Terré s. 315.

or it may exist, but defectively (relative nullity).[11] A contract which lacks a *cause*, for example, is simply incapable of existing, whereas in a contract induced by *dol* the deceived party did indeed consent, but his consent was defective. In the context of mistake this yields a distinction corresponding to that sometimes made in English law between a mistake which negatives consent, in that it prevents there ever being an agreement at all, and one which nullifies it. The former is referred to as *erreur obstacle* (the mistake being an obstacle to the meeting of minds, as opposed to a defect in a meeting which has been achieved) but it receives no express mention in the Code. It can, however, be said to be implicit in the basic requirement of consent in the same way that what is discussed under the heading of offer and acceptance has to be seen as implicit in that requirement. To put the argument in the form in which it is familiar in English law, *erreur obstacle* is not so much a mistake as a failure of the acceptance to coincide with the offer.[12]

This classical theory is nowadays, however, generally rejected as having no foundation in the Code and as not being in accord with the decisions of the courts (where there are any) as to the consequences which attach to the different types of defect. The view which is now predominant bases the distinction not on the nature of the act but on the nature of the interest protected. Thus the interest protected by attaching nullity to a contract induced by *dol* is that of the party who was the victim of the *dol*. The nullity is therefore relative (with, as we have seen, the principal consequence that only the victim can sue). On the other hand, the interest protected by declaring null a contract which has an illicit *cause* is clearly a public one and the nullity is therefore absolute. It has to be admitted,[13] however, that this theory serves better as an explanation where there is an already settled rule as to the type of nullity applicable (as in the examples given) than as a test to be applied where the rule is not settled. For the line between private and public interest is not self-evident and there is a

11 For a further distinction between nullity and non-existence see e g Weill/Terré s. 291.
12 *Bell v Lever Bros Ltd* [1932] AC 161 at 217, per Lord Atkin; Treitel *Contract* pp. 196 ff.
13 Ghestin *Contrat* s. 749.

good deal of disagreement in *doctrine* as to where in particular instances the line should be drawn. For our present purpose, however, the controversy may be left aside, since for the cases which concern us the rule is clear.

b Effects of nullity
These, as we have said, are the same whether the nullity is relative or absolute, and whatever the reason for the nullity.[14]

i *Effects as between the parties*
The contract, being null, is in principle without effect *ab initio* and each party must make restitution of what he has received.[15] Furthermore, there can be no claim for performance of the contract and no action for damages for non-performance. There may, however, be a claim in delict or quasi-delict for damage caused by the fault of either party, in the same way as there may be such a claim for damage caused by fault *in contrahendo*.[16]

The principle of retrospective nullity and consequent restitution presents practical difficulties which are familiar to students of the law of restitution, but French law so far lacks a systematic approach to the subject, either in *doctrine* or in the courts. In contracts which have involved continuous performance by both sides over a period (e g a contract of employment or of partnership) a balance has to be struck and this is left to the discretion of the judge.[17] Where, without the fault of either party, actual restitution is impossible, either in law (because the title to the object to be returned has in the meantime passed to a third party) or in fact (because the object has been destroyed or damaged), divergent answers have been given as to where the risk lies.[18]

ii *Effects as regards third parties*
Since the contract is retrospectively null, a purported transfer of property in virtue of it is also in principle without effect.

14 Including *résolution* under art 1184 Cc (pp. 236 ff, below).
15 For qualifications see pp. 127 ff, 240 ff, below.
16 Pp. 67 ff, above.
17 Pp. 238 f, below.
18 See Ghestin *Contrat* ss. 925 ff.

A distinction must, however, be drawn between movables and immovables. In the case of immovables the solution of principle applies: the transfer of property is void, no matter through how many hands it has passed,[19] and the *publicité foncière* will offer no protection. Movables, however, are subject to the rule expressed in the maxim 'en fait de meubles, la possession vaut titre'.[20] Taken literally this ought to mean that whoever possesses the thing, even in bad faith, is owner there would then, for movables,[1] be no distinction between possession and ownership. But the rule is qualified to the extent that (a) where the owner has parted with possession voluntarily under a contract (in English terms a bailment) and the 'bailee' has parted with it to a third party, the maxim applies, provided that the third party took in good faith; (b) where the owner is out of possession as a result of accidental loss or theft, he may assert his title, provided that, where the defendant is in possession in good faith, he does so within three years; and, where the defendant acquired the thing 'in a fair or market or at a public auction or from a merchant who deals in such things', he must pay to the defendant what the defendant paid for it.

3 Parallel remedies

The same facts which give rise to an *action en nullité* for *erreur*, *violence* or *dol*, will sometimes also found other remedies. In the case, for example, of the sale of a second-hand car which the buyer believed to be new, the buyer will be able to bring an *action en nullité* on the ground either of *erreur*, if it was his mistaken belief which caused him to enter into the contract, or of *dol*, if that belief was induced by the seller's bad faith; but he may, in the alternative, be able to bring two other actions. If the seller can be said to have contracted to sell a new car, the buyer may be able to bring an *action en résolution* based on the seller's non-performance; or if the fact that the car is second-hand makes it unfit for the use

19 Subject to 30 years prescription (p. 75, above).
20 Art 2279 Cc; cf p. 149, below.
 1 Except incorporeal movables, such as a business (*fonds de commerce*); see Amos and Walton pp. 113 f.

for which it was intended, the buyer may have an action on the guarantee which the law imposes on sellers.

A brief sketch of the characteristics of these other actions is necessary for an understanding of the nature of the buyer's choice in such a situation.

a *Action en résolution pour inexécution*[2]
In cases of failure to perform, the plaintiff may either seek specific performance (*exécution en nature*) or claim damages (*dommages-intérêts*), or he may claim rescission (*résolution*), with or without damages. It is this last remedy which is closest to the *action en nullité*, in that it also results in the contract's being declared retrospectively null. There is, however, this difference that in the case of the *action en nullité*, if the existence of the *vice* is established, the nullity must necessarily be decreed by the court, whereas in the *action en résolution* the court has a discretion. In exercising this discretion the courts take into account both the extent of the non-performance and the hardship to either party which may result from granting or refusing *résolution*, but they also, and especially, make a moral judgement on the conduct of the parties.

b *Recours en garantie*
Where the contract is one of sale, the Code[3] places on the seller a duty to warrant against hidden defects 'which make the thing sold unfit for the use for which it was intended or so restrict this use that the buyer, if he had known of the defects, would not have bought the thing or would have done so only for a lower price'. The *garantie* may be extended by express terms, which may, in particular, identify the intended purpose. It is to a large extent therefore an alternative, in contracts of sale, to liability for *inexécution*. The buyer who invokes the *garantie* has a choice of two remedies: the action *rédhibitoire* to obtain rescission and the *action estimatoire* (or *quanti minoris*) to obtain a reduction of the price. In these two actions, by contrast with the *action en résolution*, there is no need to show fault, but equally there is no liability in damages, save where

2 See further, pp. 236 ff, below.
3 Arts 1603, 1625-1649 Cc; cf p. 54, above.

the seller knew of the defects. On the other hand, both actions must be brought within a short time (*un bref délai*), by contrast with the prescription period of five years for the *action en nullité* and thirty for the *action en résolution*.[4]

4 *Erreur sur la substance*[5]

The Code mentions only two types of mistake: *erreur sur la substance* and *erreur sur la personne*. The courts have given to the former a very wide and flexible interpretation which contrasts markedly with the restrictive attitude of English law to mistake. Mistake is in consequence a much more common ground of relief than it is in English law. We shall consider the implications of this when we have examined all the *vices du consentement*.[6]

The *erreur* must, according to article 1110 Cc relate to 'the very substance of the thing which is the *objet* of the agreement'. The work of interpretation has centred principally on the meaning of 'substance' but also on whether it is to be taken in a subjective or an objective sense. The latter question in particular gives rise to some confusion, and since, historically speaking, the origin of *erreur sur la substance* lies in the Roman *error in substantia*,[7] clarity may be served by glancing briefly in that direction first.

a The Roman background[8]

The Roman doctrine of *error in substantia* is the subject of much controversy because the jurists themselves say next to nothing in explanation of the examples which they give. We

4 The *Cour de cassation* (first *chambre civile*) has held (Cass civ 19.7.1960, Gaz Pal 1960.2.217, *Source-book* p. 360) that a buyer cannot escape from the requirement of *un bref délai* by founding his action on the mistake arising from the defect; but in a later case (Cass com 8.5.1978; Ghestin *Contrat* s. 360) the *chambre commerciale* has held otherwise.

5 Maury in *Etudes de droit civil à la mémoire de Henri Capitant* (nd) pp. 491 ff; Ghestin *La notion d'erreur dans le droit positif actuel* (1962); Malinvaud D 1972 Chr 215 ff.

6 See pp. 105 ff, below.

7 Or, more precisely, in the interpretation given to the Roman texts in the centuries of the *ius commune*.

8 Nicholas *Roman Law* pp. 176 ff; de Zulueta *Roman Law of Sale* pp. 25 ff.

are concerned with the case where there is no *error in corpore*, i e where there is agreement as to the physical identity of the thing in question, but where there is mistake as to its 'substance'. So if bronze is bought in the belief that it is gold, or vinegar for wine, the contract is void, but not if gold-alloy is mistaken for gold, or sour wine for good. Here the word 'substance' seems to be used interchangeably with 'material', but a simply material test cannot be reconciled with the statement that the purchase of a female slave in mistake for a male is void. This example is more compatible with a metaphysical test which is implicit in the use in one text, as another alternative to 'substance', of the Greek philosophical term for 'essence'.[9]

But whatever the *rationale* of these examples, they are usually taken by modern writers as paradigm instances of 'objective' mistake.[10] The mistake is as to a quality or characteristic which is inherent in the nature of the thing and which cannot therefore vary from contract to contract. The approach would have been 'subjective' if, in the case, for example, of the purchase of a statue, it had been sufficient for the buyer to show that what determined him to buy was the mistaken belief that it was the work of a famous artist or, in the case of the purchase of a slave, the mistaken belief that the slave was an expert cook. We consider this analysis further below, but it should be noticed now that there may be degrees of 'subjectivity'. (i) It may be sufficient that the buyer's reason for buying was in fact his mistaken belief, even though the seller was unaware of this fact. (ii) It may be necessary in addition that the seller should have been aware of the buyer's reason. (iii) It may be necessary that the seller should not merely have been aware of the buyer's reason, but should have agreed that this was the reason for the contract.[11] This last verges on the 'objective', for even the Roman examples must pre-suppose an answer to the question: What were the parties buying and selling? Thus, if the sale was of a slave-cook, who was incidentally believed to be male, it would presumably not

9 *Dig* 18.1.9.2.
10 See e g Josserand's note to Cass civ 23.11.1931, DP 1932.1.129, *Sourcebook* p. 349.
11 Malinvaud D 1972 Chr 215 ff.

be open to the buyer to avoid the contract when the slave turned out to be female. There is no sign that the Romans in fact asked themselves this kind of question in this context, but they asked it in the related context of precedent destruction of the thing sold.[12] If I, having bought a piece of land, find that the olive-trees on it had been blown or burned down at the time of the sale, the sale is said to be void if I was buying the land for the sake of the trees (sc but not if I was buying it as a building-plot). The test applied is: What was the buyer buying, an olive-grove or a building-plot?

b Meaning of *substance*

Pothier,[13] while still thinking in terms of the Roman examples and of a distinction between substance and accidents, adopts a 'subjective' formulation (though in the least subjective of the three variants examined above). He says that mistake makes an agreement null 'when it relates to a quality of the thing which the parties had principally in view and which constitutes the substance of the thing'. He is applying the test, just considered, of: What were the parties buying and selling? or: What quality of the thing determined the parties to contract?

Subsequent writers, in common with the *jurisprudence*, have extended this approach far beyond the limits of the Roman examples. (We consider later which of the three variants of the subjective approach is adopted.) Although the Code speaks of 'substance', the courts and the writers commonly use terms such as 'substantial qualities',[14] 'the determining consideration'[15] or 'the quality without which the buyer would not have bought'.[16]

Some examples from the decided cases will show the elasticity of the modern test. (We ignore for the present other aspects of these cases than the interpretation of 'substance'.) We may take first the case of the Villa Jacqueline.[17] The

12 *Dig* 18.1.58.
13 *Traité des obligations* (1761; English transl. by W D Evans, 1806) ss. 17 ff, *Source-book* p. 348. On the interpretation of this in English law see David in *Etudes Capitant* (p. 80, n. 5, above) pp. 145 ff.
14 Cass soc 4.5.1956, D 1957.313 note Malaurie, *Source-book* p. 363.
15 Cass civ 17.11.1930, S 1932.1.17 note Breton, DP 1932.1.161 note Laurent, Gaz Pal 1930.2.1031.
16 Orléans 21.1.1931, DH 1931.172, *Source-book* p. 357.
17 Cass civ 23.11.1931 (n. 1, above).

plaintiff bought the villa from the defendant, intending to
parcel up the land and re-sell it in lots. The contract gave no
figure for the superficial area of the property, but the
advertisements had specified 7,800 square metres. The area
turned out to be in fact at most 5,119 square metres, an area
which was inadequate for the buyer's purpose. An obstacle to
his *action en nullité* lay in article 1619 Cc which makes express
provision for the remedy of reduction of price in cases of
deficiency of area. One might therefore have expected him to
be confined to this remedy. The court below, however, decided
that the area was 'a substantial quality of the thing sold' and
the *Cour de cassation* upheld this decision. In doing so it
declared that although deficiency of area in itself could by
virtue of article 1619 give rise only to a reduction of price, 'it is
otherwise when the deficiency of area would make the land
unfit for the purpose, known by the parties, in view of which it
was bought'. This is not an isolated case[18] and the term
'constructibility' has been coined[19] to denote the quality which
consists in land's being suitable for the intended building plots.

There are many decisions turning on the genuineness of
antiques or works of art. For example, the *Cour d'Appel* of
Orleans[20] declared null the purchase of a chest of drawers
wrongly described as Louis XV. It found that 'the antique
character of the chest of drawers was the quality which the
buyer had principally in view and without which he would not
have bought'. Similarly, in a decision which is of interest from
several points of view the *Tribunal de grande instance* of Paris[1]
allowed an *action en nullité* brought by the sellers at auction of
a picture which the sellers' experts had said was of the school of
the Carracci but which was in fact a Poussin. The court
declared that 'erreur sur la substance includes not only a
mistake as to the material of which the thing is composed, but
also a mistake which relates to the substantial qualities of
authenticity and origin'.

On the other hand, where illiterate peasants sold frescoes in
a ruined chapel which were, unknown to them, 'rare and

18 Cf e g Trib gr inst Bourges 20.1.1972, JCP 1972.II 17075 note Delpech.
19 Malinvaud D 1972 Chr 215 ff.
20 N. 16, above.
 1 13.12.1972, D 1973.410 note Ghestin et Malinvaud, JCP 1973.II.17377
   note Lindon, *Source-book* p. 354.

precious examples of primitive Catalan art' and worth forty or fifty times the contract price, a decision of nullity in favour of the sellers was quashed by the *Cour de cassation*[2] on the ground that the age and origin of the frescoes were evident on the face of the contract in general terms and the court below had therefore 'denatured' the clear terms of the contract. In other words, the sellers had contracted to sell what in fact they had sold, viz medieval frescoes of a Catalan type.

Instances from other contexts are also found. In one case, for example, a farmer bought a mare, said by the seller to be twelve years old, for work on his farm. The mare died of colic a week later and the autopsy found her to be 'beyond age', from which the court inferred that she would have been unsuitable for the purpose which the buyer had had in mind. The court therefore, upheld by the *Cour de cassation*,[3] held that the buyer's consent had been vitiated by *erreur sur la substance* (and also by the seller's *dol*).

Again, the Paris *Cour d'appel*[4] annulled a sale of a second-hand car the year of manufacture of which differed from that stated in the contract. The court found that 'the date of a second-hand car is of great importance and therefore that on the facts of the case the mistake related to what was for the buyer, and with good reason, the substance of the *objet* of the contract'.

Similarly, the purchase of a second-hand car which was found to be subject to a security interest of a third party was annulled by the *Tribunal de grande instance* of Argentan[5] on the ground that a buyer is concerned not only with the technical quality of a car but also with obtaining exclusive and peaceful enjoyment of it, and that since the buyer's consent was determined by his false idea of the extent of the rights which he was acquiring, there was *erreur sur la substance*.

These examples all concern contracts of sale, and this is true of most of the decided cases.[6] But it is plain on the face of article 1110 that *erreur sur la substance* may affect any

---

2 Cass civ 25.1.1965, D 1965.217, Gaz Pal 1965.1.251.
3 Cass civ 27.4.1953, D 1953.440, *Source-book* p. 358.
4 Paris 20.4.1964, D 1964 Somm 97, *Source-book* p. 359.
5 15.10.1970, D 1971.718 note Ghestin.
6 Cass soc 4.5.1956 (p. 82, n. 14, above and p. 86, n. 17, below) concerned a lease.

convention. A demolition contract, for example, was declared null because the contractor was mistaken (as the other party knew) as to the character of the reinforced concrete used in the structure to be demolished, with the result that the job was much more difficult.[7]

In this case there is still a physical thing involved, but this need not be so, though the interpretation of 'substance' sometimes becomes very forced.

An agreement to refer a dispute to arbitration was declared null because one party was unaware that the lawyer chosen as arbitrator had already given an option favourable to the other party's case. The *Cour de cassation*[8] held that the court below was entitled to declare that the contract was null under article 1110 because independence of mind was an essential quality of an arbitrator.

A contract of suretyship (i e a contract between surety and creditor) was declared null because the surety was unaware that the debtor was insolvent.[9] There was a mistake as to the 'principal and determining reason' for the surety's under-taking. In another similar case[10] the ground was perhaps better expressed as being a mistake as to 'the extent of the surety's undertaking'. But in either version the connection with 'substance' is very tenuous and the decisions are questionable in terms of policy.

The agreement affected may also be unilateral. A number of cases[11] concern renunciations of successions (whereby the benefits of the inheritance renounced pass to the person next entitled) and arise out of a mistake by the person making the renunciation as to the extent or nature of the rights which he is renouncing. It may be noted that it makes no difference that the mistake is one of law or, more precisely, that the mistake as to the 'substance' is caused by a mistake of law.[12]

7 Paris 14.10.1931, D 1934.2.128; cf Cass civ 23.6.1873, D 1874.1.332.
8 Cass civ 13.4.1972, D 1973.2.
9 Cass civ 1.3.1972, D 1973.733 note Malaurie.
10 Cass civ 26.1.1977, noted in the *Rapport* of the *Cour de cassation* for 1976/7, p. 44; cf Cass civ 25.10.1977, D 1978 I.R. 74. See Ghestin *Contrat* s. 414.
11 See e g Mazeaud/Mazeaud pp. 147 f.
12 Mistake of law as a ground of nullity is excluded only in two special cases: art 1356 and 2052 Cc.

These examples make plain the width of the power to intervene between the parties which the courts have derived from the apparently narrow phrase 'the very substance of the thing'.[13] This power is, moreover, largely outside the control of the *Cour de cassation*. For though the meaning of 'substance' is a question of law, we have seen that this question is answered by asking what determined the plaintiff's consent, and that question is regarded as one of fact. It has been remarked[14] that almost all decisions of the *Cour de cassation* in this area are now rejections, based on the *pouvoir souverain* of the court below. Cases in which the *Cour de cassation* intervenes on the ground that the court below has 'denatured' the contract (as it did in the case of the Catalan frescoes)[15] are rare.

There are nevertheless limits to the courts' power, which we must now consider.

c Distinction from value

It is obvious that a mistake as to 'substance' will usually entail also a mistake as to value. Indeed it will nearly always be the mistake as to value which is the real reason for the plaintiff's bringing his action. But not every mistake as to value can be allowed to be a ground of nullity without subverting the Code, which makes provision for a remedy for inadequacy of value, but only in very narrowly defined circumstances, and expressly excludes such a remedy in any other circumstances.[16]

The distinction which is drawn is between a mistaken valuation and a mistaken understanding of the facts upon which the valuation is based. If those facts can be categorised as relating to 'substantial qualities of the thing', there is *erreur sur la substance*.

The *jurisprudence*, however, shows that this is an elastic test. In one case[17] a tenant had taken a lease of a farm in the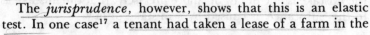

---

13 It has even been held that when a woman bought theatre tickets in ignorance of the fact that her husband had already done so, the contract was null, the 'substance' to which the contract related being the right to see the play, a right which she already had (Trib com Seine 2.4.1943, Gaz Pal 1943.2.81, Mazeaud/Mazeaud p. 149), but this is usually regarded as extreme.

14 Malinvaud D 1972 Chr 215 ff.

15 P. 84, n. 2, above.

16 Art 1674, 1118 Cc. See pp. 131 ff, below.

17 Cass soc 4.5.1956 (p. 82, n. 14, above).

belief, known to and indeed encouraged by the landlord, that the land could be rapidly put into good order. Finding that this was far from being so, he claimed and obtained a judgment of nullity for *erreur sur la substance*. The *pourvoi* before the *Cour de cassation* contended that the mistake was merely as to value, but that court held that the court below had been entitled to find a mistake as to the substantial qualities of the land.[18]

Similarly the purchase of a building, one part of which was let to tenants, was annulled because a figure had been given by the vendor for the monthly rent receivable which was in fact the quarterly figure. This mistake as to the basis of the rental figure was found to have determined the buyer's will.[19]

In another case the plaintiff had taken a villa on the Côte d'Azur for a month at a high rent. The agent had described it as comfortably equipped, but it was in fact in very bad condition in a number of respects. The *Cour de cassation*[20] held that in view of the level of the rent the court below was entitled to regard these as substantial qualities.

It is evident from these examples that mistake as to value may, where the plaintiff has the merits on his side, be confined within a very narrow area indeed.[1] For a mistaken valuation will often be based on a mistake of fact. The only clear limit is that the fact must relate to the thing in question. A mistaken reading of the current handbook of second-hand car prices, for example, would not suffice.[2]

d Distinction from motive

The difficulty here is more apparent than real. Since the substantial qualities to which the mistake must relate are those which determined the consent of the mistaken party, there will commonly be no distinction between mistake as to substance and mistake as to motive.[3]

18 The trial court spoke of 'la valeur culturale'. It is clear that there was *dol par réticence* (pp. 98 ff, below), but the decision was based on *erreur*.

19 Trib gr inst Fontainebleau 9.12.1970, D 1972.89 note Ghestin.

20 Cass civ 29.11.1968, Gaz Pal 1969.1.63.

1 But contrast the case of the Catalan frescoes (p. 84, n. 2, above).

2 What amounts to mistake as to value may also sometimes be expressed in terms of absence of *cause*; see pp. 114 f, below.

3 But there may be more than one motive.

If, for example,[4] I buy a napkin which I believe to have belonged to Louis XVI and my motive for buying it is my desire to acquire a relic of that king, the substantial quality of the napkin is the quality of being such a relic and (subject to what is said below as to the knowledge of the seller) I can claim annulment if my belief is unfounded. Similarly, in the 'constructibility' cases[5] the buyer's motive for buying the land is the desire to build on it (or sell it for building) and the possibility of fulfilling that desire (i e the suitability of the land for building) is the 'determining consideration' for the purposes of *erreur sur la substance*. But what if the buyer's motive for buying a house is the desire to live in it with his prospective wife and she dies before the marriage can take place? Here the possibility of fulfilling the buyer's desire does not depend on any quality of the house. Or, to put the matter in another way, in the 'constructibility' case the agreement was made under the influence of a mistaken belief as to a present fact, whereas in the marriage case the mistaken belief was as to a future event, and that can never be a 'substantial quality of the thing'.

e State of mind of the other party

We saw[6] that there are three possible variants of the 'subjective' approach. It may be sufficient that the determining consideration for the mistaken party was in fact his mistaken belief; or it may be necessary in addition that the other party should have been aware that this was so, whether or not he shared the mistake; or it may be necessary that both parties should have agreed that this was the determining consideration.

Classical *doctrine*, in accordance with its subjective approach to consensus, adopted the first variant, but this has clearly been rejected by the *jurisprudence* and by contemporary *doctrine*. It would indeed be unacceptably

---

4 Cf *Nicholson and Venn v Smith-Marriott* (1947) 177 LT 189, in which Hallett J's dictum that the contract might have been held void would be sound for French law.

5 P. 83, above.

6 P. 81, above. On what follows see especially Maury in *Etudes de droit civil à la mémoire de Henri Capitant* pp. 491 ff, with references.

disruptive of the stability of contracts, even in a system which finds in the law of delict a corrective of the subjective approach.[7] Some writers, on the other hand, argue for the third variant. The mistake, it is said, must relate to a *qualité convenue*:[8] the parties must have agreed that this quality was the determining consideration. There is, however, a logical difficulty in requiring that the same consideration should be determining for both parties. The buyer's decision to buy may have been determined by the belief that the picture was a Rubens and the seller may know this, but the same belief can hardly be determining for the seller. He would presumably be all the more willing to sell if the picture turned out to be a copy. The requirement of a *qualité convenue* would relate rather to the existence of the quality (e g that the painting was by Rubens) than to the fact that this was the determining consideration. And it would be a requirement that, as a Common lawyer might say, the existence of this quality should be a term of the contract. In other words, where there was *erreur sur la substance* there would also be *inexécution*. This will indeed sometimes be the case, but to require that it should always be so is to risk blurring the distinction between what is agreed and what is taken for granted, a distinction which is sharper in French law, which resorts relatively little to the implied term, than it is in English law.

In any event most modern writers adopt the second variant and this is the usual approach of the *jurisprudence*. The fact that the mistaken belief was the determining factor for the mistaken party must have been known to or taken for granted by the other party. Thus, in the *Villa Jacqueline* case[9] the *Cour de cassation*, in the passage quoted above,[10] makes a point of the fact that the buyer's purpose was 'known by the parties', and Josserand in his note on the case insists that 'the *jurisprudence* does not require that the seller should himself have fallen into the error of which the buyer is the victim; it is enough that he had knowledge of the conditions in which the

7 See pp. 104 f, below.
8 The most recent exponent of this view is Ghestin. See his notes to Cass com 20.10.1970, JCP 1971.II.16916 and Cass com 4.7.1973, D 1974.538.
9 P. 82, n. 17, above.
10 P. 82.

buyer thought that he was negotiating, of the belief by which he has been misled'.[11]

It should be noted that there is nothing to correspond to the English principle that if mistake as to quality ever affects assent, it does so only if it is the mistake of both parties.[12] This principle would make no sense in French law. For the 'passive acquiescence of the seller in the self-deception of the buyer'[13] which English law in the ordinary case regards with indifference, will in French law usually amount to *dol*.[14] Many decisions in this area are indeed based on both *erreur* and *dol*, and in others, though *dol* is not invoked, the facts are sufficient to establish it. It has been remarked that even in English law the principle makes little sense, since it has the paradoxical result that if I share the buyer's mistake, I may find that the contract is void, whereas if I know of the buyer's mistake and yet do nothing to disabuse him of it, the contract will stand.[15]

f Relevance of conduct or knowledge of the mistaken party

The subjective character of the French doctrine is therefore limited by the need for the other party to have been aware of what determined the mistaken party's consent. It is also limited by the requirement, as to which there is no question, that the mistake must not have been 'inexcusable'.[16] What is excusable will depend on the knowledge or the expertise of the mistaken party. These same factors may, however, show that the mistake did not exist at all. This is exemplified in a case[17] in which the plaintiff, who made ladies' clothes, bought from the defendant some velvet furnishing material, intending to use it, as the defendant knew, for making trousers. It turned out to be unsuitable for this purpose and the plaintiff refused to pay,

---

11 Cf, for the attitude of the courts, note by Delpech (a leading *magistrat*) to Trib gr inst Bourges 20.1.1972 (p. 83, n. 18, above).

12 Expressed in the much-quoted dictum to this effect by Lord Aitkin in *Bell v Lever Bros Ltd* [1932] AC 161 at 218; Treitel *Contract* p. 201.

13 *Smith v Hughes* (1871) LR 6 QB 597 at 606, per Cockburn CJ.

14 See pp. 98 ff, below.

15 *Bell v Lever Bros Ltd* [1932] AC 161 at 235, per Lord Thankerton; *Source-book* pp. 353 f.

16 Ghestin *Contrat* s. 398.

17 Cass com 4.7.1973 (p. 89, n. 8, above); cf Cass com 20.10.1970 (ibid).

contending that the contract was null on the ground that the *qualités substantielles* in view of which he had bought the cloth were, as the defendant knew, its suitability for trousers. The *Cour de cassation* held that the *juges du fond* were entitled to find that the plaintiff was not in error because he was in the business of making clothes and had bought the cloth with his eyes open, knowing it to be furnishing material.

g Relevance of conduct or knowledge of the other party

These also may be taken into account as evidence that, for example, the mistake was a determining one or was not 'inexcusable'.

For example, in the case of the Louis XV chest of drawers,[18] the seller carefully avoided any express exclusion of a guarantee that it was an antique and this was taken as evidence that he knew that what determined the buyer's consent was the belief that he was buying an antique.

The case of the Poussin[19] provides another example. One of the reasons why this case was much noticed was that the buyer/ defendant was the *Musées Nationaux* (and the painting had been put on exhibition at the Louvre as a Poussin). One of the *attendus* in the court's judgment notes somewhat cryptically that 'the *jurisprudence*, in annulling an act vitiated by *erreur sur la substance*, identifies as a determining element of this situation the artistic or technical competence of the party who has benefited from the mistake'. The relevance of this competence is presumably that it helps to establish the determining character of the mistake and to show that it was, in the circumstances, excusable.

h Mistake as to the mistaken party's own *prestation*

The case of the Poussin is noteworthy also as a rare instance of a claim arising out of the mistaken party's own 'prestation'. It was the converse of the usual case in which the buyer seeks to escape from the purchase of a picture which has turned out to be not what he thought it was. The court expressly adverts to

18 Orléans 21.1.1931 (p. 82, n. 16, above).
19 Trib gr inst Paris 13.12.1972 (p. 83, n. 1, above).

the fact that article 1110 makes no distinction in this matter. The reason, one may assume, why cases of this kind are rare is that the seller will not often discover the truth.

5 *Erreur sur la personne*

Article 1110 Cc declares that mistake as to the person with whom one intends to contract is not a cause of nullity 'unless the consideration of this person is the principal cause of the agreement'. In most contracts mistake as to the person with whom one is dealing is irrelevant because one is willing to contract with anyone. One is not contracting, in the phrase which is traditional in French expositions of this subject, *intuitu personae*. That contracts are usually in this sense not personal is as true in English law as it is in French law, save that French law recognises the category of contracts *à titre gratuit* and such contracts will usually be made *intuitu personae*. Beyond this the two systems diverge markedly. As in the area of *erreur sur la substance*, French law adopts a much broader and more flexible and 'subjective' approach.

In English law mistake as to person falls into the category of mistakes which negative consent: it embraces only the case in which A, intending to contract with B, in fact deals with C. In such a case there is simply no agreement. But the interpretation which French *doctrine* and *jurisprudence* has given to article 1110 goes much further. It is sufficient that A, though he was under no mistake as to the identity of the person with whom he was dealing, would not have entered into the contract if he had known of some attribute of that person's of which he was then ignorant. In English law the reason why A dealt with C must be that he thought he was dealing with B, whereas in French law it is sufficient that A dealt with C because he thought that C had some attribute or quality which he in fact lacked or lacked some attribute or quality which he in fact had. In crude terms, it is enough that A would not have contracted with C if he had known what kind of a person C was. Thus, if A gives a lease of a house to C in ignorance of the fact that C has previously been convicted of keeping a disorderly house, and if A would not knowingly have given the lease to such a person, he can claim nullity of the lease.[20] These are, of course, broadly the facts of the now discredited English case of *Sowler v Potter*,[1] in which Tucker J was persuaded to apply what was in effect the French rule.

Erreur sur la personne is thus closely parallel to *erreur sur la substance*. In both the mistaken party must have been mistaken as to a quality of the thing/person, and that quality must have determined his consent. In both the matter is one within the *pouvoir souverain du juge du fond* and in both the same considerations as to the state of mind of the other party and the conduct or knowledge of each party apply. There is, however, this difference, that since the other party must be aware of the fact that the quality in question is the determining consideration for the mistaken party, and since in the case of *erreur sur la personne* the other party will rarely be unaware of the absence of that quality, the likelihood of an overlap with *dol* is obviously much greater.

We have seen that mistake as to value is excluded from the ambit of *erreur sur la substance*. Similarly a mistake as to the solvency of the other party is not a ground for claiming nullity. The reasons of policy are similar and there is a similar difficulty in drawing a distinction between mistake as to solvency and mistake as to other qualities from which insolvency results.

In the case[2] of the sale of land to a man who, unknown to the seller, had been condemned to confiscation of his assets, both existing and prospective, and was thus not only insolvent, but also incapable of conducting his affairs without the intervention of the official sequestrator, the *Cour de cassation* held that the court below was entitled, in exercise of its *pouvoir*

20 Cf Trib civ Nantes 10.7.1894, D 1894.2.176; for other cases see Ghestin *Contrat* s. 412.
1 [1940] 1 KB 271. Tucker J purported to follow Pothier, but while Pothier's formula ('whenever the consideration of the person with whom I am willing to contract enters as an element into the contract . . .') is wider than that of art 1110 Cc, the examples which he gives (and which were not before Tucker J, as to which see Smith and Thomas (1957) 20 Mod L Rev 38 ff) are compatible with the narrow English rule; see Treitel *Contract* pp. 216 f.
2 Cass civ 20.3.1963, D 1963.403, JCP 1963.II.13228 note Esmein, *Sourcebook* p. 368.

souverain, to find that the vendor had intended to deal only with a buyer who was 'in free control of his rights and legally capable of making a payment of the price which would be valid against the world' and that the seller was therefore the victim of an error which vitiated his consent (and not, as the *pourvoi* had contended, merely an error in assessing the buyer's solvency).

6 *Erreur obstacle*

We have seen[3] that *erreur obstacle* is the term applied by *doctrine* to those mistakes which negative consent and that, though there is no express mention of it in the Code, it can be said to be implicit in the fundamental requirement, in article 1108, of consent. According to the classical theory the consequence of *erreur obstacle* should be absolute nullity. The *jurisprudence*, however, has shown little inclination to accept *erreur obstacle* as an independent category. In the relatively rare cases which have arisen in practice it has preferred to see no more than an *erreur sur la substance*. This has not been possible without some straining even of that elastic category, but it is difficult to disagree with the conclusion that the nullity should be relative.

There seems to have been no instance of *error in corpore*, but there have been several cases of *error in negotio* (i e mistake as to the nature of the transaction into which the party is entering). A controversial decision[4] involved three peasants who signed a guarantee of a loan made to a widow. They were described as illiterate and the document was not read to them before they signed. When the widow defaulted and they were called upon to pay, they pleaded that they had thought that the document was no more than a moral guarantee. The *Cour de cassation* held that the court below had been entitled to find that the agreement which they had signed had an *objet* other than that of the contract into which they thought that they were entering, and that in making this finding the court had necessarily concluded that their mistake related not to 'the

3 P. 76, above. For *erreur sur la cause* see pp. 119 f, below.
4 Cass civ 25.5.1964, D 1964.626, *Source-book* p. 361; cf RT (1965) 109; also Cass civ 25.5.1968, JCP 1968.II.15611.

consequences of the undertaking, but to its very substance' and that this mistake had determined their consent.

In this case there was a mistake as to whether there was a legal transaction at all. In a number of other cases[5] the mistaken party knew that he was entering into a legal transaction (he was borrowing money), but thought that the loan was to be immediate whereas in fact it was deferred. In short, the mistake was as to the terms of the contract. Here too the mistake was found to relate to the 'substance' of the agreement or to 'an essential element' of it.

There were also cases arising out of the change from old francs to new. For example, a laundry agreed to place an advertisement in the municipal news-sheet at a cost of 1,000 francs, assuming that the unit was the old franc. The publisher claimed 1,000 new francs. The trial court found the contract to be 'vitiated by a fundamental mistake' and the *Cour de cassation*[6] held that the trial court had been entitled to find that the laundry was mistaken as to the substance of its *prestation*, that substance being the monetary unit used to measure the price.

It can be objected that money can hardly have 'substance' or 'substantial qualities', but the English reader will have other difficulties also. He will notice that in none of the cases discussed in this section is there any attempt to give an objective meaning to the contract, i e to ask what the reasonable man would have taken the parties to have intended. This is not, however, surprising. We have repeatedly found that the French approach to consensus is, from the English standpoint, markedly subjective. But these cases go further. They do not even apply the usual French corrective of this subjectivity by requiring that the mistaken party's assumption (as to the type of franc in question, or the type of loan) should have been known to or taken for granted by the other party.[7] This, as well as the need to stretch the meaning of 'substance', is the objection to expressing *erreur obstacle* as *erreur sur la*

5 Rennes 26.10.1950, Gaz Pal 1951.1.27; Lyon 5.7.1951, D 1951.614; Lyon 13.3.1952, S 1953.2.21; Lyon 15.7.1952, D 1952.753.
6 Cass civ 14.1.1969, D 1970.458 note Pedamon; for other cases see Loussouarn RT (1971) 625.
7 The other corrective (p. 104, below) would be available.

substance. An acknowledgment of this objection may underlie a recent decision of the *Cour de cassation*.

The case concerned the sale of 60,000 bottle-openers. The buyer thought that the price was 55 francs per 1,000, but the seller thought it was 550 francs. The court below had given judgment for the seller on the ground in particular that mistake as to price is not a ground of nullity. The *Cour de cassation*[8] quashed this decision because the court had not dealt with the buyer's argument that there had been a 'fundamental misunderstanding' (*malentendu fondamental*). This is the language of *erreur obstacle*, not of *erreur sur la substance*, but one must not read too much into its use by the *Cour*. For the legal basis of the *cassation* is the provision of the *loi* of 20 April 1810 on the administration of justice[9] which declares null any judgment which does not give reasons (*motifs*) and the language used is taken from the buyer's *conclusions* before the court below, with which the court had not dealt. At least formally therefore the *Cour de cassation* is expressing no opinion as to whether the contract should or should not have been declared null for *malentendu fondamental*.

7 *Dol*

a Essential elements
Article 1116 Cc provides that:

> *Dol* is a cause of nullity of the agreement when the artifices (*manoeuvres*) practised by one party are such that it is evident that without those artifices the other party would not have contracted.

Dol and *erreur* are very closely akin. At least on the traditional view,[10] *dol* has a place in the treatment of *vices du consentement* only in so far as it produces a mistake. It would indeed be clearer to say that there are two categories of mistake: those mistakes which are and those which are not produced by *dol*. Since in both categories the mistake must

---

8 Cass civ 28.11.1973, D 1975.21 note Rodière, *Source-book* p. 362; RT (1975) 702.
9 Art 7; *Source-book* p. 276.
10 For a different view see p. 106, below.

have induced the mistaken party to contract, the difference lies in the subject matter of the mistake. A mistake induced by *dol* need not relate to a 'substantial quality' of the thing or person. Hence a deception as to value or solvency or one which affects the other party's motive may constitute *dol*, but will not be a ground of nullity for *erreur*. The reason of policy for the wider range within which mistake induced by *dol* is allowed to vitiate consent lies, of course, not in the *vice* itself, but in the wish to deny to the deceiver the benefit of his deceit. It is for this reason that the *dol* must be that of a party. If D, fraudulently representing that he is solvent, persuades S to be a surety for the debt which D owes to C the *dol* of D cannot be adduced by S as a ground for declaring null his contract of suretyship with C[11] (But, as we have seen, the courts have, by a rather forced interpretation, granted nullity under the heading of *erreur sur la substance*.)

Nevertheless, the range of *erreur sur la substance* is, as we have seen,[12] so wide that in most cases of *dol* there will also be *erreur*.

The *Cour de cassation* has a rather larger role to play in the interpretation of *dol* than in that of *erreur*. For it has held[13] that though the primary facts are within the *pouvoir souverain du juge du fond*, the qualification of those facts as *dol* is a matter of law.

The principal difficulty has lain in the meaning of the term 'manoeuvres'. That they must be 'illicit' is universally accepted.[14] The English lawyer needs to bear in mind that an innocent (i e non-fraudulent, non-negligent) misrepresentation has no legal consequences in French law (except in so far as it may produce *erreur*). But he needs also to notice that *dol* is not confined to representations and there is therefore in French law none of the difficulty with which we are familiar of distinguishing representations of opinion or intention from representations of fact, or representations as to the future from those as to the present. 'Manoeuvres' is an elastic word which

11 Cass civ 28.6.1978, D 1979 I.R. 149.
12 P. 86, above.
13 Cass civ 30.5.1927, S 1928.1.105 note Breton, *Source-book* p. 371.
14 Some lapses from the truth are habitually tolerated (as with the English 'puff') under the heading of *dolus bonus*; see Ghestin *Contrat* s. 429, Mazeaud/Mazeaud s. 191.

looks more to the state of mind of the actor than to the precise nature of the act itself.[15] The difference between the two systems is less great, however, in this respect than it might seem, because of the elasticity of the English idea of representation by conduct.[16] The greatest difference and the principal area of uncertainty in French law lies in the extent to which the requirement of 'manoeuvres' can be satisfied by silence. This is the problem of *dol par réticence*.

b *Dol par réticence*[7]

The starting-point is the same in French as it is in English law. Since in most contracts the interests of the parties are opposed, each must look after his own interests.[18] Silence is not blameworthy unless there is a duty to speak. In French law, however, the extent of the duty, particularly in the light of recent developments in *jurisprudence* and in legislation, is wider than in English law. One may leave aside duties for which there is a parallel in English law, such as those expressly laid down by statute (in contracts of insurance, for example) or arising from relationships in which the interests of the parties are not, or should not be, opposed (partnership or agency, for example). But the wider context is more favourable in French law to the importation of ideas of good faith or fair dealing (*loyauté*). In a contract of sale, for example, since the seller is liable for defects which make the thing unfit for its intended use, even if he is not aware of them, the French lawyer, who is accustomed, as the English lawyer is not, to seeing particular statutory provisions, especially those in the Code, as expressions of broad underlying principles, can infer a duty to disclose. And since, as we have seen, many cases which could be seen as instances of *dol par réticence* can as easily be decided on the ground of *erreur sur la substance*, there is a greater pre-disposition to seeing silence (as to a fact which determined the other party's consent) as reprehensible. To these factors has been added in recent years a flow of legislation (which is, of course, paralleled in English law) directed to

15 See Breton (n. 13, above).
16 *Chitty on Contract* (24th edn) s. 359.
17 Ghestin D 1971 Chr 247.
18 See Breton, above, quoting Ripert.

correcting disparities, whether of information or of bargaining power, between the parties.[19]

Where exactly the law now stands on *dol par réticence* it is difficult to say. The starting-point referred to above remains. It is exemplified in a decision of the *Cour de cassation* in 1927 which is offen cited.[20] A divorced wife had assigned to her former husband for a sum in francs all her rights in the matrimonial property situated in Indo-China. Her husband immediately re-sold for a sum in Indo-Chinese currency which, owing to the state of the exchange-rate, enabled him to make a fourfold profit. The Court below, holding that his conceal-ment of his intention to re-sell immediately amounted to *dol*, annulled the contract, but this decision was quashed on the ground that the mere fact of not telling his wife of his intention and of his expected profit 'was not sufficient, without some other circumstance, to establish a *manoeuvre illicite*'.

Everything in this statement turns on the meaning of 'some other circumstance' and until quite recently both *jurisprudence* and *doctrine* seemed to adopt a restrictive attitude, requiring some specific duty. But even in 1947 the *Chambre sociale* of the *Cour de cassation*[1] could decide that:

> though in principle mere *réticences* do not constitute *dol*, it is otherwise when, as in this case, the seller, after vainly trying to sell to a third party, nevertheless sold [to the plaintiff] the same horse, of the unsuitability of which for agricultural work he could not be ignorant.

By 1971, however, the emphasis has shifted and there appears[2] an *attendu* which seems now to have been adopted as a recurrent formula:

> *Dol* can consist of the silence of one party concealing from the other a fact which, if he had known it, would have prevented him from contracting.

This was repeated in a case in which the vendor of a house in the country had not revealed to the purchaser the existence of a plan to set up a piggery nearby.[3]

19 See pp. 135 ff, below.
20 Cass civ 30.5.1927 (p. 97, n. 13, above).
 1 Cass soc 30.5.1947, S 1949.1.24.
 2 Cass civ 15.1.1971, D 1971 Somm 148; cf Loussouarn RT (1971) 839.
 3 Cass civ 2.10.1974, D 1974 I.R. 252.

Among other recent cases in which a finding of *dol* has been upheld have been the following:

The seller of land, who knew that the buyer intended to build a hotel on it, did not reveal that the only water supply was from a spring which was on land retained by the seller and which was in any event quite inadequate.[4]

The seller of a site for commercial purposes did not reveal that a level-crossing by which customers approached the site was to be suppressed.[5]

The dealer who sold a second-hand car did not reveal that the odometer had been altered.[6]

It is not easy to see what principle can accommodate decisions such as these, still less the formula quoted above, without rejecting the much-cited decision of 1927, and, more fundamentally, without abandoning the axiomatic starting-point set out above. What 'other circumstance' accounts for decisions such as these? *Doctrine* offers various answers:[7] that the fact which is not revealed is within the knowledge of the 'reticent' party alone, or at least is something which the other party could not find out for himself, that the 'reticent' party has an expertise in the matter on which the other relies. But it is obvious that the recent *jurisprudence* has outstripped limits such as these. One is left with a very elastic principle that *réticence* will constitute *dol* if it amounts to a failure of the good faith or fair dealing (*loyauté*) which the other party is entitled to expect. It is obvious that French law is in this respect far more demanding than English law. *Dol par réticence* merges in fact into a general duty to inform,[8] which itself is part of a broad principle of fair dealing.

8 *Violence*

a The classical *vice*

Violence is not defined in the Code, but it can be said to be a constraint, physical or moral, placed on the will of a person,

4 Cass civ 7.5.1974, Gaz Pal 1974.2.184.
5 Cass com 21.3.1977, JCP 1977.IV.135.
6 Cass civ 31.1.1979, D 1979 I.R. 288.
7 Ripert/Boulanger s. 183; Marty/Raynaud s. 134; Mazeaud/Mazeaud s. 193 and pp. 166 ff; Flour and Aubert *Droit civil - Les obligations* vol 1, s. 211.
8 Cf Ghestin *Contrat* p. 350.

which induces him to consent. Just as in the case of *dol* the *vice du consentement* consists in the mistake which results from the *dol*, so also here the *vice* is not the *violence* itself, but the fear which the *violence* creates in the mind of the person constrained.[9]

(i) As with the other *vices*, the *violence* must have determined the consent of the person constrained. The Code is self-contradictory in the two *alinéas* of article 1112 as to whether the test is objective (was the *violence* such as to constrain a reasonable person?) or subjective (did it in fact constrain this person?), but *doctrine* and *jurisprudence* are at one in adopting (as for the other two *vices*) the objective test.[10] Article 1112 is an unfortunate conflation of the objective Roman rule and the subjective approach preferred by Domat and Pothier.[11]

(ii) The constraint must be illegitimate. This appears *e contrario* from article 1114 which excludes 'reverential fear, without more, directed to a father, mother, or other ascendant'. In particular, pressure is prima facie legitimate when it is applied in exercise of a right. For example, an employer cannot escape from an agreement to pay higher wages because it was made under the threat of a strike. But the commonest instance of a legitimate threat is that of legal action. For example, an agreement by a debtor to create a mortgage is not vitiated by its having been made under the threat of an action to enforce the debt. There are, however, two limits to this type of legitimate threat, both of which can be seen as aspects of the doctrine of abuse of rights.[12] There must be a direct connexion (as there is in the example of the mortgage) between the right which gives rise to the threat and the agreement which is exacted. For example, a husband has a right to prosecute his wife for adultery, but to use the threat of such prosecution to extract from her an acknowledgment of debt is not legitimate.[13] Or a creditor may use the threat of

9 The draft of a revision of the Civil Code of Quebec, *Obligations*, art 34, expresses this: 'Fear of serious harm vitiates consent when induced by violence on the part of either contracting party.'
10 Cass req 27.1.1919, S 1920.1.198, *Source-book* p. 380; Cass req 17.11.1925, S 1926.1.121 note Breton, *Source-book* p. 381.
11 Mazeaud/Mazeaud s. 204.
12 Cf p. 66, above.
13 Cass req 6.4.1903, S 1904.1.505 note Waquet, D 1903.1.301.

action to obtain a benefit from his debtor, but not to obtain such a benefit from the debtor's relatives.[14] Or again a local authority is not entitled to use a refusal of planning permission as a lever to obtain a free gift of other land owned by the applicant.[15] The second limit is that there must be a reasonable proportion between the right asserted and the advantage obtained. This is illustrated by a case which came before the Paris *Cour d'appel*.[16] A woman was caught shoplifting in a branch of Monoprix and, in order to induce the firm not to take proceedings, agreed to pay 5,000 francs as compensation. This was held to be a compromise (*transaction*)[17] and therefore prima facie valid, but since 5,000 francs was appreciably greater than the amount of the firm's loss (and the woman was in a disturbed psychological condition), there was held to be an abuse of right.

(iii) The *violence* may be directed against either the person or property of the party whose consent is exacted or even against that of a third party. The Code[18] speaks in this connexion only of certain close relatives (husband, wife, ascendants, descendants) but since, on the subjective test, the question should be simply whether the threat to the third party, whatever his relationship, in fact did constrain the contracting party, this provision is interpreted either as establishing merely a presumption that threats to these particular third parties did constrain the contracting party, or simply as giving examples.

(iv) The Code expressly provides that the *violence* may emanate from a third party. Anyone therefore who benefits, even innocently, from someone else's *violence* may be deprived of what he has received. As we have seen, this is not so in the case of *dol*. The rule originates in Roman law, which was concerned to repress a wrong rather than to grant relief for defective consent (and *violence* is a particularly grave wrong in unsettled times), but in the modern context also it can be justified. For, as with *violence* directed *against* a third party, the question should be simply whether consent was in fact

14 Mazeaud/Mazeaud, s. 204; note by Holleaux to Cass civ 3.11.1959 (p. 103, n. 1, below); *Source-book* pp. 385, 387.
15 Cass civ 16.10.1962, cited by Ghestin *Contrat* p. 370, n. 37.
16 Paris 31.5.1966, Gaz Pal 1966.2.194; cf RT (1967) 147.
17 Art 2045, 2053 al 2 Cc.
18 Art 1113 Cc.

vitiated, regardless of whether the other party was to blame. The difference from *dol* can be justified on the ground that a third party's *dol* will be a ground of nullity if it creates *erreur sur la substance* or, conceivably, *sur la personne*, and that, as we have seen, the reason of policy for the wider range of mistake in the case of *dol* by a party can be said to be the wish to deny him the benefits of his wrong.

b Abuse of a state of need or dependence

Since the *violence* may be that of a third party it can be argued that it may also arise from the external circumstances in which the plaintiff finds himself, provided that the constraint resulting from those circumstances satisfies in other respects the requirements of the *vice*. On the other hand, in article 1109 the Code speaks of there being no valid consent 'if it has been *extorted* by *violence*', echoing in this the approach of Roman law. *Doctrine* is therefore divided. The jurisprudence is likewise not clear. In an early *arrêt de principe*[19] the *Cour de cassation* took the broad view and declared that when the consent of the person obliged 'is not free, but is given under the influence of fear inspired by a real, considerable and present evil to which his person or fortune is exposed, the contract is tainted by a *vice* which makes it annullable'. The case concerned a ship which was in imminent danger of being lost unless it was pulled off the sandbank on which it had grounded. The captain of the only available tug insisted on a fee which, the trial court subsequently held, was more than four times the reasonable figure. The captain of the stranded ship protested, but agreed to pay, When later sued, however, on this agreement, he pleaded that his consent was not freely given.

The particular matter of salvage out of which this case arose was later dealt with by statute,[20] but in other situations the *jurisprudence* has not been clear. We may leave aside situations in which there is a special relationship of trust or dependence such as might in English law raise a presumption of undue influence, as where an elderly widow was pressured by her business agent,[1] or a bed-ridden farmer yielded to the

19 Cass req 27.4.1887, S 1887.1.372, D 1888.1.263, *Source-book* p. 378.
20 *Loi* of 7.7.1967, art 7 (replacing a *loi* of 1916).
1 Cass civ 3.11.1959, D 1960.187 note Holleaux, *Source-book* p. 385.

fear that his share-cropping tenants would not continue to look after him.[2] Cases such as these could fall within what we have called the classical *vice*, but in other contexts there has been no clear line. In recent years, however, there has been a number of decisions which can be seen as applying the principle that a contract may be null for *violence* if one party's freedom of choice is limited by the state of necessity or of economic dependence in which he finds himself. Such decisions are seen by some as applying the same policy as is embodied in recent legislation restricting or invalidating, for example, exemption clauses and penalty clauses[3] or the excesses of door-step contracts and the unsolicited delivery of goods.[4] This is obviously an area in which it is difficult to achieve a just balance and even more difficult to formulate a general criterion,[5] since in every contract the parties must be influenced by the circumstances in which they find themselves. But a disadvantageous contract of employment, for example, entered into by the employee under a pressing need of money occasioned by the illness of one of his children has been declared null,[6] and the *Cour d'appel* of Paris[7] has held that alterations to the contract under which a distributorship of cars was granted were not freely accepted on the ground that the two parties were not on an equal footing because of the 'economic subjection' of the distributor.[8] It is too early, however, to say that any clear *jurisprudence* has emerged.

9 Liability in damages

Since a *vice du consentement* makes the contract null, there is no obstacle to an action for damages founded in delict,[9] and,

---

2 Cass req 27.1.1919, S 1920.1.198, *Source-book* p. 380.
3 See pp. 226 ff, below.
4 See pp. 135 ff, below.
5 Cf the formulation propounded by Lord Denning MR in *Lloyds Bank Ltd v Bundy* [1975] QB 326; Treitel *Contract* pp. 313 f.
6 Cass soc 5.7.1965; see Starck s. 1381.
7 Paris 27.9.1977, D 1978.690 note Souleau, Gaz Pal 1978.1.110 note Guyenot, RT (1978) 595.
8 On the courts' approach to sales of property entered into by Jews during the German occupation of 1940–1944 see Weill/Terré p. 215; Ghestin *Contrat* p. 367.
9 Cf p. 30, n. 6, above.

as we have seen in connexion with pre-contractual fault, the French remedy in delict is very flexible. Wherever the fault of the defendant, intentional or negligent, has caused the plaintiff damage which is sufficiently direct in character, there is in principle liability. And this liability is often invoked. In the case, for example, of the chest of drawers culpably, if not knowingly, misdescribed as Louis XV,[10] the vendor was condemned in damages, as was the lessor of the villa on the Côte d'Azur.[11] In the case of the second-hand car burdened with a security interest, the vendor, though he was unaware of the encumbrance, was held, because he was a dealer, to have owed a duty to the plaintiff to find out.[12] In the case of *dol* or *violence* the existence of fault and therefore the availability of an action in damages is self-evident.

10 Conclusion

a The distinctions between the *vices*
We remarked above on a tendency to blur the distinctions between the three *vices*. As between *erreur* and *dol*, it has long been settled[13] that a court may give judgment on the ground of *erreur* even though the case has been pleaded in *dol*. And this is not surprising since, as we have seen, *dol* can be said to constitute a *vice* only in that it produces *erreur*. And many cases decided on the ground of *erreur* could, it would seem, have been equally well founded on *dol*, if *dol* is allowed to extend to *dol par réticence*. Obviously the converse is not necessarily true (i e that what is decided in terms of *dol* could have been decided in terms of *erreur*), since the scope of *dol* is wider. And *violence* is independent of the other two in that it lacks the common ground of mistake.

In a recent case,[14] however, the *Cour de cassation* seems to have held that the courts are entitled to base their decisions on the ground of defective consent without specifying the particular *vice* involved. A land-owner, in order to obtain a

10 P. 83, above.
11 P. 87, above.
12 P. 84, above.
13 Cass civ 5.11.1900, D 1901.1.71.
14 Cass civ 9.11.1971, D 1972 Somm 37.

building-permit from the local authority, had signed a renunciation of any claim he might have to compensation in the event of expropriation. He later sought to have this agreement declared null. The only arguable ground, one would think, was *violence* in its extended form, but the plaintiff in fact based his claim on *erreur*. The court, however, gave judgment for him on the undifferentiated ground of defective consent, and the *Cour de cassation* held that it was entitled to do this.

A much more sweeping disregard of the distinctions was shown by the *Cour d'appel* of Colmar in a learnedly argued decision in a case concerning a family company.[15] An old woman had, after much pressure and late at night in highly suspect circumstances, signed over to her daughter and son-in-law sufficient shares to give them a controlling interest (to the disadvantage of her son). This was declared void on the ground, not of *violence*, but of *dol*. The court held that *dol* did not require any element of deceit. The victim of *dol* had not necessarily been deceived; 'the idea of *dol* overlaps with those of *erreur* and *violence*'. Any dishonest act tending to 'surprise' a person with a view to making him sign an undertaking into which he would not otherwise have entered could, the court held, be qualified as *manoeuvres dolosives*.

b Relative importance of *erreur*

There is no question but that of the three *vices* the one most frequently invoked is *erreur*. Nor is this surprising. For the circumstances of *violence* (unless it is to expand into a remedy for abuse of economic power) will only rarely occur, and *erreur* is more easily proved than *dol*. What does surprises the English lawyer is the sheer number of cases in which *erreur* is invoked, by comparison with the rarity of such cases in English law. We have seen[16] that there may be alternative remedies in the *action en résolution* or the *recours en garantie*. Why does the French litigant have recourse to the *action en nullité* rather than to the alternatives? To this there are a number of possible

15 Colmar 30.1.1970, D 1970.297 note Alfandari, Gaz Pal 1970.1.174, *Source-book* p. 376.
16 **Pp.** 78 ff, above.

answers. (i) The *action en nullité* provides an escape from the discretionary elements in the *action en résolution*. Where non-performance and mistake overlap (e g in the case of the mare,[17] whose age could be seen as the subject matter either of a mistake - as in the actual decision - or of a term in the contract) the non-performance of which the plaintiff can complain is necessarily partial (he has received a mare, but an over-age one) and the judge will therefore have a discretion as to whether or not to resolve the contract. If *erreur* is established, however, the contract is necessarily null. (ii) French law is much less ready to imply terms than is English law. As was pointed out above in connexion with the thesis that the *erreur* must be as to a *qualité convenue*, the French are more likely than we are to distinguish between what is agreed and what is taken for granted. In most of the cases cited above it is in fact unlikely that a French court would have found the subject matter of the mistake to have been a term in the contract. (iii) In the rare cases where the mistake relates to the mistaken party's own *prestation* there can obviously be no other remedy. (iv) As far as the *recours en garantie* is concerned, there will be an overlap only if the absence of the quality which was mistakenly thought to exist can be said to constitute a *vice caché*, and this would not have been so in many of the cases which we have examined. Moreover, the *action rédhibitoire* must be brought within a *bref délai*, by contrast with the prescription period of five years for the *action en nullité*.[18]

If one asks for the reason for the much greater frequency of recourse to *erreur* in French law than to mistake in English law, the answer no doubt lies principally in the much greater width and flexibility of the meaning given to *erreur* - a width and flexibility which can be criticised as subverting the security of transactions. One must, however, bear in mind that French law has no independent remedy for misrepresentation not amounting to *dol*. Moreover, as has been said above, French law resorts less easily than English law to implied terms. The gap thus created is to some extent filled by *erreur*.

17 P. 84, above.
18 But see p. 80, n. 4, above.

C *Objet*

Article 1108 Cc lays down four requirements for the validity of a contract: consent, capacity, an *objet* and a *cause*. We have now examined the first of these requirements. The second may here be passed over, since such differences as there are from English law throw no special light on the French idea of contract. The requirement of *cause*, as we shall see, is in some respects comparable to that of consideration, but there is no concept in the Common law which corresponds to *objet*. To the Common lawyer indeed it seems to embrace a number of disparate ideas which in his system are subsumed under other headings.

1 Terminology

The language of the Code, and also of the courts and the writers, is shifting and imprecise. Article 1108 speaks of the *objet* of a contract[19] as being the content of what a party undertakes (*la matière de l'engagement*). But here already there is an ellipse. What is defined is not the *objet* of the contract, but the *objet* of the obligation which the contract creates, i e the *prestation* which the party obliged is bound to perform. For example, in a contract of sale the seller is obliged, among other things, to convey the thing sold to the buyer and this conveyance is the *objet* of his obligation. There is a further ellipse in the articles (1126–1130) which set out some details of the requirement of *objet*. Thus, article 1126 lays down that every contract must have as its *objet* a thing (*une chose*) which a party obliges himself to convey or to do or not to do (*donner, faire, ne pas faire*). Here the *chose* is the *objet* not of the contract or even of the obligation, but of the *prestation*. (As we have seen, every *prestation* must consist of either *donner, faire* or *ne pas faire*.) If both the ellipses are removed we have to say (to take again the example of a sale) that the *objet* of the contract is found in the obligations which it creates, that the *objet* of the seller's obligation is, among other things, the *prestation* consisting in the conveyance of the

19 Or, to be precise, of a *convention*; see p. 36, above.

thing, and that the *objet* of that *prestation* is the thing (*chose*) itself. Where, as in a contract of sale, the obligation consists of *donner*, the *chose* is a physical thing, but where the obligation consists of *faire* or *ne pas faire*, the *chose* is an act or abstention.

The term *objet* may therefore be used in three different senses, as applied either to a contract or to an obligation or to a *prestation*. Most of the practical consequences which attach to the requirement relate to one or other of the latter two senses, particularly the last, and the shift between them presents no difficulty.

2 Particular applications of the requirement of an *objet*

From the general requirement that there should be an *objet* are derived three consequences in particular.

a The *objet* must be determined or determinable

There is nothing surprising in a requirement that the content of a contract should be sufficiently certain. Different systems of law will differ as to what is sufficient (in the contract of sale, for example, French law,[20] in common with all Civil law systems, requires that the price be determined or determinable, whereas the Common law is content with a reasonable price), but the general requirement must be universal. What surprises an English lawyer, who sees the requirement as no more than an aspect of the primary requirement of agreement,[1] is that is should be given separate treatment under the heading of *objet*. The explanation is probably to be found in the imperfect generalisation at the time of the Code from specific contracts (*contrats nommés*) on the Roman pattern, each having certain identifying elements (in sale, for example, a thing and a price), to a general principle of contract. The process of generalisation can be seen in Pothier[2] and echoes of it are to be found in those

20 Arts 1591, 1592 Cc.
1 E g Treitel *Contract* pp. 40 ff.
2 *Traité des obligations* (p. 82, n. 13, above) ss. 53, 129-40, 649, 650.

articles of the Code which identify the *objet* with a *chose*.[3] In short, because Roman law thought in terms of specific contracts which required agreement as to certain necessary elements, French law still thinks of contract in general in similar terms. English law, on the other hand, thinks in terms simply of agreement, the content of the agreement being a matter for the parties, provided that it is sufficiently certain (and, of course, lawful).

b The *objet* must be possible[4]

An impossible *object* has no content and therefore a promise of an impossibility is null (*impossibilium nulla obligatio*).[5] It follows from this that if the *objet* of the *prestation* is a specific thing[6] and that thing has ceased to exist when the contract is made, there is no *objet*. Here, however, the difference from English law is not merely one of formulation. For French law sees a contract as a promise of a performance, whereas English law sees it as a guarantee of a result.[7] Hence there is in English law nothing inconceivable in a promise of the impossible or a promise to deliver a thing which does not exist.[8] It is a matter of construction in each case whether the promise was an unconditional guarantee or was conditional upon (or took for granted) the possibility of performance. Hence in French law the contract in *McRae v Commonwealth Disposals Commission*[9] (for the sale of a non-existent ship) would necessarily have been void for lack of an *objet*, whereas the Australian High Court was able to construe it as a contract which embodied a promise that the ship existed. It should be remembered, however, that this does not mean that in French law the seller would have been without a remedy at all. The limits imposed on the contractual action by the requirement of an *objet* make the existence of a remedy for pre-contractual fault the more important.[10]

3 Arts 1108, 1126–1130.
4 See Nicholas (1974) 48 Tulane L Rev 966 ff.
5 Cf p. 193, below.
6 But a contract may relate to a future thing: art 1130 al 1 Cc.
7 Cf pp. 53 f, above and pp. 193 ff, below.
8 Atiyah *Sale of Goods* (5th edn) ch 7.
9 (1950) 84 CLR 377.
10 Pp. 67 ff, above.

c The *objet* must be licit

A contract to commit a crime or a civil wrong is null, as is also, for example, an agreement to sell an infected animal, the sale of which is forbidden, or an agreement by an unlicensed vendor to sell tobacco, which is the subject of a state monopoly, or an agreement to sell something for more than the price allowed by law. In all these instances the *objet* of the obligation is illicit and the contract is therefore null. There is, it is true, no explicit authority for this proposition in the Code, but it is treated by *doctrine* either as an aspect of the requirement that the *objet* must be possible or as being implicit in the provision that things which are *hors du commerce* (i e which cannot be dealt with in a private legal transaction)[11] cannot constitute the *objet* of an agreement. The matter is not, however, of great practical importance because the illicitness of contracts is usually dealt with under the heading of cause rather than that of *objet*. For this there are two reasons. The first is that, as we shall see, cause (in its primary sense) is simply the correlative of *objet* and therefore wherever, as in the instances given above, the *objet* of one party's obligation is illicit, the cause of the other party's obligation must also be illicit. This would not, however, lead to the choice of one concept rather than the other were it not that (and this is the second reason) there are situations in which policy requires that the contract be declared null for illicitness, but in which this conclusion cannot be attached to any illicitness in the *objet*. If, for example,[12] the owner of a café agrees with a candidate in a local election to supply free drinks to electors at the candidate's expense, the *objet* of the café owner's obligation (to supply drinks) is licit and so also is that of the candidate's obligation (to pay for them), but the purpose of the transaction (to buy votes) is illicit. Here, as we shall see, the concept of cause is invoked. Further discussion of the problems posed by illicit contracts is therefore postponed until the meaning of cause has been unravelled.

---

11 The word *commerce* here does not bear its usual meaning: it translates the Latin *commercium*. For examples of *choses hors du commerce* see e g Weill/Terré s. 232.

12 Trib Tarbes 14.3.1899, S 1900.2.219.

D Cause[13]

1 Introductory

Article 1108 Cc lays down as the fourth requirement of a valid contract that there must be 'a licit cause in the obligation'. More precisely, a contractual obligation is valid only if it has a cause and if that cause is licit.

This requirement of cause is one of the distingishing marks of the French family of legal systems; it is not found in German law or in other systems not derived from the French. Although the term originates in Roman texts, the doctrine was first formulated by the canonists. Wishing to go beyond the Roman principle that only certain types of contract were binding and to establish the moral principle that agreements should be observed (*pacta sunt servanda*), but recognising that there must be some limit to this principle, they found this limit in the cause of the promise, which they interpreted as its motivating reason or purpose. And this, in the very broad sense of 'final cause' or, from another point of view, 'the end pursued' is still the accepted meaning of the term in modern French law. To use a much-repeated aphorism, whereas *objet* provides an answer to the question *quid debetur?* (what is owing?), cause answers the question why it is owing (*cur debetur?*).

The difficulty has lain, as the vast literature on the subject attests, in giving precision to this broad concept in such a way as to account for the practical consequences which both *jurisprudence* and *doctrine*, without much difference of opinion, attach to it. This has led some, following Planiol,[14] to argue that the theory of cause is both unworkable, in that it does not satisfactorily account for those consequences, and unnecessary, in that the consequences can be equally well accounted for in other ways. These 'anti-causalist' arguments (which are considered in the appropriate places in what follows) have not carried the day, but there has in recent years been a general retreat from the attempt to find a single

13 Marty/Raynaud ss. 170 ff; Maury 'Cause' *Encyclopédie Dalloz* (*Civil*) (1951) vol 1, pp. 514 ff.

14 *Traité élémentaire de droit civil* vol 2, s. 1037; cf Ripert/Boulanger, s. 287.

meaning which will be appropriate both for situations in which there is no cause and for those in which the cause is illicit. Many writers now acknowledge, in one way or another,[15] that in order to accommodate the actual practice of the courts 'the end pursued' in these two situations must be differently defined. In what follows we start from this position and leave aside the elaborate arguments which lead up to it.

2 Absence of cause

The 'end pursued' by a party who enters into an obligation (e g the buyer in a contract of sale) may be variously defined, but there is a broad distinction between a subjective (or concrete) meaning which will differ from person to person (e g, where what is bought is a house, the buyer's purpose in this sense may be to get somewhere for his family to live, or to acquire an investment), and an objective or abstract meaning which will be the same for everyone entering into that type of contract. It is with the latter meaning that we are now concerned and the types of contract to be distinguished are, first, the onerous as opposed to the gratuitous and then, within the category of onerous contracts, the synallagmatic as opposed to the unilateral. And within each of these sub-categories there are other distinctions.

a Onerous contracts

i *Synallagmatic contracts*
In these, which in practical terms, as we have seen, are the most important contracts, the cause of each party's obligation is to be found, according to the classical theory, in the obligation of the other. Each obligation is the counterpart of the other. In a contract of sale, for example, the buyer incurs his obligation in order to obtain the obligation of the seller, and vice-versa. Here to the Common lawyer it is obvious that, though the concepts used are different, cause coincides with consideration. And each meets a similar difficulty. In English

---

15 Most explicitly, Carbonnier s. 26; see also Ghestin *Contrat* s. 692 and the citations in Marty/Raynaud s. 183.

law we say that where a contract is wholly executory, each promise is consideration for the other, but to this it is objected that the reasoning is circular. For a promise will only constitute a detriment to the promisor or a benefit to the promisee if it is legally binding, and that depends on there being consideration. The anti-causalists make a parallel objection to the proposition that each obligation is the cause of the other. It is therefore now normally said that the cause of one party's obligation is the consideration (in a non-technical sense), or the expectation, that the other party will be obliged.[16]

Cause in synallagmatic contracts may be practically relevant either because it was non-existent from the beginning or because it subsequently failed.

(a) *No cause from the beginning*   Here the anti-causalist objection is easily seen. If one party's obligation has no cause, it is because the other's obligation has no *objet*. For example, if the thing sold has perished at the time of the agreement, the seller's obligation has no *objet* and the buyer's has no cause. Cause is therefore a superfluous concept. Thus, when, in 1871, M agreed with R (as was legally permissible) to do R's military service for him, R was, unknown to either of them, no longer liable for such service. The *Cour de cassation*[17] held that M's obligation had no *objet* and R's had no cause and that the contract was therefore void.

To the anti-causalist objection there are two answers. The first concedes that decisions which are founded on absence of cause could also be, and indeed often are,[18] justified by absence of *objet*, but points out that there are situations in which the courts find it easier to rely on the absence of cause because the *objet*, though trivial or illusory, cannot strictly be said to be non-existent. There are, for example, a number of cases concerning claims by genealogists for services rendered in drawing the attention of beneficiaries to their rights of succession on intestacy.[19] (The range of persons entitled on intestacy is much wider in French law than in English; and intestacy is

16 Mazeaud/Mazeaud s. 265.
17 Cass req 30.7.1873, S 1873.1.448, D 1873.1.330, *Source-book* p. 404.
18 As in the case just cited.
19 E g Cass civ 18.4.1953, D 1953.403, JCP 1953.II.7761; Cass civ 9.11.1960, JCP 1960.II.11884. See further, Ghestin *Contrat* s. 663.

more common because a testator's freedom is restricted in favour of certain relatives.) The courts have held that there is no contract where there is no serious likelihood that the beneficiary would in the ordinary course of events have failed to discover his entitlement. In such cases there is in a sense an *objet*, in that the genealogist has supplied information, but the information is superfluous.

A similar situation may arise where the contract is not, as in the examples so far considered, commutative, but aleatory. It is of the essence of such a contract that the content of one party's obligation is variable and may in the event even be non-existent. The cause of the other party's obligation is therefore said to be the *aléa* or chance. A number of cases concern *rentes viagères* or *baux à nourriture*.[20] When an old man parts with his land in return for a promise that he will be looked after, or paid an annuity, for the rest of his life, and he dies unexpectedly the next day, the contract is unaffected because the *aléa* was genuine.[1] But if he is already mortally ill when he makes the agreement and the promisor knows this, there is no substantial *aléa* and therefore no cause.[2] The same will be true when the income from the property transferred is greater than the amount of the annuity payable. The promisor takes no risk; there is no *aléa*.[3]

In situations such as these, where the *objet* is insubstantial rather than plainly non-existent, the courts may prefer to rely on cause. But there is a second and more direct answer to the anti-causalist argument that cause is superfluous in synallagmatic contracts. Cause, it is said, expresses the idea of the interdependence of the obligations of the parties. Where the thing sold has perished at the time when the contract is made, the absence of *objet* will explain why the seller's obligation is null, but it cannot explain why the buyer is not obliged to pay the price. Only cause it is argued, can do that.[4]

(b) *Subsequent failure of cause* Since article 1108 relates cause only to the formation of contract, one might think that it would have no bearing on the subsequent relations of the

20 See p. 44, above.
1 Cass req 15.6.1933, DH 1933.377, Gaz Pal 1933.2.482.
2 Art 1975 Cc; Ghestin *Contrat* s. 675.
3 Cass req 29.12.1930, DH 1931.53; Ghestin *Contrat* s. 676.
4 See further, p. 121, below.

parties. The principle of interdependence, however, whatever its theoretical foundation, continues to apply and is expressed in the so called *exceptio non adimpleti contractus*[5] or *exception d'inexécution* (defence of non-performance) which enables a party to refuse performance if the other party has failed to perform or is not ready to do so. The *exceptio*, however, will be of no use to the aggrieved party if he has already peformed. He will then wish to obtain restitution of that peformance. That he can do so there is no doubt. What is disputed is whether his remedy should be an action asserting that the contract is null for failure of cause (*action en nullité*) or an action claiming resolution of the contract on the ground of the other party's non-performance (*action en résolution*). In the former case there is a clear parallel with the English doctrine of total failure of consideration (though there is no requirement that the failure of cause should be total). And within both concepts there is a shift of meaning.[6] In the formation of the contract consideration is commonly a promise, but in the context of total failure it is the performance of the promise. And so it is also with cause. The cause for the aggrieved party's promise was the promise of the other party; what has failed is not the promise, but its performance. This shift in the meaning of cause is criticised,[7] but there are difficulties also in the approach via the *action en résolution*.[8] The *Cour de cassation* long ago adopted an irrational amalgam of both approaches by upholding a grant of resolution but founding it on failure of cause. This is considered below.[9]

ii *Unilateral contracts*

Here cause has to bear a different meaning, or indeed two different meanings, according as the contract is real or consensual.

(a) *Real contracts*[10]   On the classical theory the cause of, for

5 See further, pp. 207 ff, below.
6 Cf Treitel *Contract* p. 773.
7 Ripert/Boulanger s. 522; Mazeaud/Mazeaud p. 223; Marty/Raynaud s. 190.
8 In that it is normally seen as a remedy for imputable non-performance, i e for breach (see p. 237, below).
9 Pp. 199 ff.
10 The conservative view (p. 40, above) is here adopted.

example, the borrower's obligation to repay money lent to him lies in the preceding delivery to him of the money.[11] But this is unsatisfactory because the delivery is itself a condition of the formation of the contract. If there has been no delivery there is indeed no contract, but this is not because of absence of cause, but because the essential condition for the formation of the contract has not been satisfied.

(b) *Consensual contracts* Here we are concerned with a promise which is given neither with the intention of conferring a gratuitous benefit on the promisee nor in consideration of an obligation to be incurred by him. It will commonly be a promise to pay an existing debt. The reason for making the promise may be to liquidate an otherwise unliquidated debt (e g one arising out of a civil wrong committed by the promisor) or to give legal effect to an obligation of conscience or a natural obligation (e g to pay a pension to an old retainer[12] or to support a natural child of the promisor). This existing debt will be the cause of the promisor's obligation and therefore if the debt did not exist (e g because the promisor is not in fact the father of the child) the obligation will be null. But not all unilateral consensual contracts are promises to pay existing debts. We have already considered[13] the *promesse unilatérale de vente* or granting of an option. Here the cause must presumably be found not in the past but in the future, in the prospect of the option's maturing into a contract.[14]

What emerges from this consideration of unilateral consensual contracts is that the cause is not, as in the synallagmatic or the real contracts, entirely objective or abstract, but varies according to the circumstances of each particular contract. This is the subjective or concrete cause referred to at the beginning of this chapter. It is probably because of this shift in meaning that the courts have tended to rely not simply on absence of cause, but on mistake as to cause (*erreur sur la cause*).[15] This approach is considered below.

11 Cass civ 18.5.1898, D 1900.1.481.
12 Cass civ 3.2.1846, D 1846.1.159.
13 P. 63, above.
14 Carbonnier s. 27.
15 Cf Ghestin *Contrat* s. 682.

b Gratuitous contracts

Here it is difficult to give any effective meaning to the requirement of cause. According to the classical theory the cause of a
gratuitous promise lies in the promisor's *intention libérale*, i e
his intention to confer a gratuitous benefit on the promisee.
But absence of cause in this sense is inconceivable. A promisor
who neither expected anything in return for his promise nor
intended thereby to confer a gratuitous benefit would be
insane. In other words, here as in the case of the real contracts,
cause in the classical sense merely repeats one of the elements
in the definition of the transaction in question; it has no
independent function. The truth is that in gratuitous transactions the main practical importance of cause lies in situations
in which it is held to be illicit, but there, as we shall see, it bears
the different and subjective sense of the motive which in each
case determined the promisor to make his promise.

There are however, some instances in the *jurisprudence* of
this subjective sense even in the area of absence of cause. Those
which concern indisputably gratuitous acts have arisen not out
of contracts but out of wills (e g where the testator made his
will on the clear assumption that he had no children, but his
wife was in fact pregnant when he died).[16] Others which are
sometimes cited in this connexion can alternatively be seen as
instances of unilateral consensual contracts *à titre onéreux*. For
example, the grant of a supplementary pension by a company
to its retiring chairman was annulled for absence of cause (and
on the subsidiary ground of *dol*) when it was discovered that he
had already agreed to enter the service of a competitor.[17] The
cause was the company's debt of gratitude for past services, but
this, it was held, presupposed that he remained loyal to the
company.

It is obviously not easy to distinguish between a 'gratuitous'
promise motivated by a sense of gratitude and an 'onerous'
promise made in recognition of an obligation of conscience or
a natural obligation, but however any individual case is
categorised, we are plainly dealing with a subjective cause or
motive, and, as has been said above, it is in cases of this kind
that the approach via mistake is most commonly found.

16 Douai 30.1.1843, S 1843.2.69.
17 Cass com 8.4.1976, cited by Ghestin *Contrat* p. 577.

c 'Erreur sur la cause'

Article 1131 Cc confusingly says that an obligation is without effect not only if it has no cause or has an illicit cause, but also if it has a 'false cause'. This does not refer, as might be imagined, to the case in which the apparent cause is not the real cause (when the validity of the obligation is usually unaffected). 'False cause' is not a third category, but merely absence of cause looked at from a subjective point of view. In a contract of sale, for example, where, unknown to the parties, the thing sold did not exist when the contract was made, the buyer's obligation objectively has no cause, but subjectively, from the buyer's point of view, it has a cause, though one as to whose existence the buyer is mistaken. 'False cause' is therefore a superfluous term, but it, or more commonly the concept of mistake as to the cause, is sometimes invoked when cause has to be given a subjective meaning. This, as we have seen, occurs in some unilateral onerous promises and occasionally in gratuitous transactions.

The general rule, which is always applied in synallagmatic contracts, is that a mistake affecting a party's motive is irrelevant, though the line between mistake as to motive and mistake as to 'substance' may not always be easy to draw.[18] But where, for example, a man undertakes to maintain a child in the mistaken belief that he is the natural father, or to compensate for damage caused by a fire in the mistaken belief that he is responsible for it, or where a testator gives his property to charity in the mistaken belief that he has no heirs, the courts, in declaring the transaction void, commonly speak of 'mistake as to the cause' or 'mistake as to the legal validity of the cause' or 'mistake as to the determining reason (*motif déterminant*)'.[19] In view of the subjective character of *erreur sur la substance* and *sur la personne* and the expansionist use which the courts have made of *erreur sur la substance*, this resort to mistake is not surprising, but it presents difficulties. For *erreur sur la cause* is not excluded, as are the other two types of *erreur*, by its being 'inexcusable', nor is there any need for the other party to be aware of the determining character of

18 Cf pp. 87 f and Cass civ 3.8.1942, DA 1943.13.
19 Cass req 7.7.1931, DH 1931.445; Cass req 1.7.1924, D 1926.1.27; Paris 3.2.1944, DA 1944.71.

the mistaken party's motive. More importantly, views differ as to whether the nullity which results from *erreur sur la cause* is relative, as in the other two types of mistake, or absolute as in the normal case of absence of illicitness of cause. This question is in turn related to the question whether *erreur sur la cause* is to be seen as a *vice du consentement* or as *erreur obstacle*. The preponderance of *doctrine*[20] favours relative nullity and certainly if the criterion for distinguishing the two types of nullity is the existence or not of a public interest, one would expect the line to be drawn between absence of cause and *erreur sur la cause* on the one hand and illicit cause on the other.

d Utility of the concept of cause

That cause is, and is likely to remain, a central feature of French law is clear. It is embedded in the Code and has general, even if sometimes qualified, support in current *doctrine*.[1] But external observers are less convincd that it serves a useful purpose.[2] Within the French family of legal systems the draft of a new Civil Code for Quebec[3] omits the concept on the grounds that it has in practice been very little invoked and that the purposes which it is supposed to serve are adequately provided for by other institutions and rules. We may therefore, before going on to consider *cause illicite*, review the anti-causalist case in the context of absence of cause.

As we have seen, the argument against cause is twofold. It is said to be unworkable in that it does not satisfactorily account for the practical consequences attributed to it, and unnecessary in that those consequences can equally well be accounted

20 Planiol and Ripert *Traité de droit civil* vol VI, s. 176; Maıty/Raynaud ss. 126, 195; Starck s. 139; Weill/Terré s. 164; *contra* Colin et Capitant *Traité de droit civil* II s. 55.

1 Ghestin *Contrat* s. 722.

2 Zweigert/Kötz vol 2, p. 67; J P Dawson *Gifts and Promises* pp. 113 ff; F H Lawson *A Common Lawyer Looks at the Civil Law* pp. 159 f; *contra* Markesinis (1978) 37 Camb LJ 53,54, but he is concerned to show that French law, through the medium of cause, reaches the same conclusions as English law attains by a variety of conceptual routes, rather than to consider the question discussed here, of whether cause itself is a single concept.

3 *Report on Obligations* p. 13.

for in other ways. We have found that the first argument is made out, in the sense that the consequences can only be accommodated by allowing in some cases a shift from the objective to the subjective meaning, i e by employing two concepts. And we have seen that the second argument also can largely be sustained. In synallagmatic contracts *objet* will do the work of cause except that it cannot account for the interdependence of obligations. (The fact that cause will more easily accommodate the cases in which the *objet* is derisory is hardly in itself a sufficient reason for retaining the concept.) In real and gratuitous contracts cause is plainly superfluous in that in each case it simply duplicates one of the conditions for the formation of the contract; and in unilateral consensual contracts the practical consequences could be, and, as we have seen, sometimes are, accommodated within the doctrine of mistake.

If therefore there were no doctrine of nullity for absence of cause, the important practical consequence which would remain unaccounted for would be the interdependence of obligations in synallagmatic contracts. In the German Civil Code, which, as has been said above, has no concept of cause, the principle of interdependence is simply embodied in express provisions, a solution which is intellectually perhaps less elegant but practically more convenient than the shifts and complexities of the theory of cause. But there is another and much more far-reaching difference between French and German law. For German law adopts the principle of the abstract conveyance. A conveyance or assignment made in pursuance of a void contract is nonetheless valid, whereas in French law, in which, in general, conveyances are causal, no title will pass. The consequence of this difference is that whereas in French law the conveyor's remedy is to have the contract declared void and to reclaim his property, in German law he must accept that the conveyance is effective but may claim restitution on the ground that the resulting enrichment is unjustified. This difference accounts for the much greater importance and sophistication of the German doctrine of unjustified enrichment.[4] While the French concept of cause as

4 Zweigert/Kötz vol 2, pp. 112 f, 212 and vol 1, pp. 177 ff; Weill/Terré s. 272.

an element in the validity of a contract is not the same as the German concept of ground (*Grund*) as justification for an enrichment, it can broadly be said that in German law the question of cause is transfered from the formation of contract to the restitution of enrichment. In this respect, of course, English law is in princple, like French law, a system of causal conveyances.

3 Illicitness of cause

a Meaning of cause

We have seen that, on the classical theory, in synallagmatic contracts cause and *objet* are correlative. Thus, if X agrees to commit a crime in return for Y's promise to pay him a sum of money, the *objet* of X's obligation is illicit and therefore the cause of Y's obligation is likewise illicit, though its *objet* (the payment of money) is not. The contract is therefore null. In cases such as this the classical theory is adequate (though it makes cause duplicate the function of *objet*), but if the *objet* of each obligation is licit, even though the remoter purpose of one or both parties is illicit, the classical theory has nothing to say. For example, if X takes a lease of Y's house, intending to use it as a brothel, the *objet*, and therefore, on the classical theory, the cause, of neither obligation is illicit. Again, in real contracts or gratuitous contracts there can never, on the classical theory, be an illicit cause, since neither the handing over of a thing nor an *intention libérale* can, in themselves, be illicit. Hence the return of money lent to launch a brothel or of equipment lent to enable a crime to be committed would be enforceable and a gift made to secure an adulterous relationship would be valid. These obviously unsatisfactory results have led to the adoption for all types of contract of a definition of cause (when its licitness is in question) as the determining reason or purpose (*motif déterminant, cause impulsive et déterminante*) which led the parties, or one of them, to enter into the contract. Thus a lease of a house for use as a brothel or a loan for such a purpose or a gift to achieve an immoral end all have an illicit purpose and therefore an illicit cause. In this sense, it will be seen, cause has no connexion with *objet* (though the courts sometimes confusingly use the latter term, as the English word 'object' can be used, to denote the parties' purpose).[5] It is indeed no longer the cause of an obligation, but the cause of the contract. This subjective or concrete meaning of cause as the determining reason or purpose is, it will be seen, the same as that adopted, in the instances discussed above, in the context of *erreur sur la cause*.

b Meaning of illicit and the concept of *ordre public*

Article 1133 Cc provides three headings. It declares the cause to be illicit 'when it is prohibited by *la loi*, or when it is contrary to *bonnes moeurs* or to *ordre public*'. The first heading is self-explanatory. The second is of course the French translation of *contra bonos mores*, a term which has sometimes been invoked in this context in English law also. It imports the idea of immorality, but has not achieved, in either *doctrine* or *jurisprudence*, any precise meaning. It is commonly subsumed under the third and broader heading of *ordre public*.[6]

The term 'ordre public' is confusing to the English lawyer because it embraces two ideas between which he does not normally see a connexion. Thus it occurs not only in article 1133, but also in article 6, which provides that 'One cannot by agreements between individuals derogate from *lois* which involve *ordre public* or *bonnes moeurs*'. This looks to the provision in article 1134 that 'Agreements legally formed have the character of *loi* for those who have made them' and indicates the extent to which the law thus made by the parties must give way to the general law. The *lois* from which private agreements cannot derogate are the *lois impératives* which have been mentioned above,[7] and they are *impératives* because they concern the public interest. The parallel here in English law is with provisions such as those in the Unfair Contract Terms Act 1977 or the Supply of Goods (Implied Terms) Act 1973 which declare certain types of term ineffective or impose certain terms regardless of the intention of the parties. From

---

5 E g Cass civ 4.12.1929 note Esmein, S 1931.1.49, DH 1930.50, *Source-book* p. 253; Cass civ 23.6.1879, S 1879.1.473, *Source-book* p. 415.
6 Julliot de la Morandière in *Etudes Capitant* (p. 80, n. 5, above), pp. 381 ff; *Source-book* pp. 241 ff.
7 Pp. 32 ff.

the French point of view such provisions have this overriding effect because they are an expression of *ordre public*, and likewise contracts which have an illicit cause are null because their purpose is contrary to *ordre public*.[8] In the latter context we find no difficulty in translating the term into English as 'public policy', but we see no such broad principle in the former. This is perhaps because we still see statutes as isolated irruptions into the ordered framework of the Common law, each perhaps giving effect to a policy, but embodying as a whole no general ideas.

There is a difference in formulation between article 6 and article 1133, in that article 6 speaks only of *lois* which concern *ordre public*, which might suggest that *ordre public* is to be found only in the enacted law, whereas article 1133 distinguishes between a cause which is forbidden by *la loi* and one which is contrary to *ordre public*. But no point is made of this difference and it has indeed long been accepted that, even in the absence of any express provision, the judge may, and indeed must, decide whether *ordre public* is involved (and, of course, whether a given contract or term is inconsistent with it). And the *Cour de cassation* has laid down in an *arrêt de principe*[9] that 'the cause is illicit when it is contrary to *ordre public*, without there being any need for it to be forbidden by *loi*'. The distinction between enacted and unenacted *ordre public* is sometimes expressed in the terms *ordre public textuel* and *ordre public virtuel*,[10] but it is obvious that since even *ordre public textuel* has to be interpreted, and since *ordre public*, like public policy in English law, is not fixed but changes as social and economic conditions and ideas change, the part played by the courts in its formulation must in any event be central.

Modern writers[11] distinguish between a traditional *ordre public* with a political and moral content and a more recent *ordre public économique et social*. The division is not sharp,

8 *Contra*, Malaurie 'Ordre public' *Encyclopédie Dalloz (Civil)* (1st edn) vol III, p. 668.
9 Cass civ 4.12.1929, n. 5, above.
10 Carbonnier s. 32; Ghestin *Contrat* s. 100. Nevertheless the courts rarely rely only on *ordre public virtuel*: Hauser 'Ordre public' *Encyclopédie Dalloz (Civil)* (2nd edn) vol V, s. 13.
11 Carbonnier s. 32; Ghestin *Contrat* ss. 106 ff.

but it is convenient for exposition and it corresponds very roughly to the difference between article 6 and article 1133. *Ordre public économique et social* is more likely to be relevant to the question of excluding an objectionable term from a contract or including one which is required by, for example, the policy of protecting the weaker party to a bargain, whereas *ordre public politique et moral* is more likely to be relevant to the determining purpose of the contract and therefore to the illicitness of its cause.

Ordre public politique et moral embraces in particular the protection of the functioning of the state and the public services, the preservation of the integrity of the family and the maintenance of *bonnes moeurs*. As illustrations to be found in the *jurisprudence* of the first of these categories one may cite (leaving aside *ordre public textuel*) an agreement to supply free drinks with the aim of influencing the voters in an election,[12] or an agreement the purpose of which was to secure favours from the administration,[13] or an agreement for the hire of equipment to carry out work for the German occupation forces.[14] The protection of the integrity of the family has led to an extensive case law on the validity of a gift to a mistress,[15] the effect of which is to declare such a gift void if 'its cause is either the formation or the continuation or the renewal of immoral relations',[16] but not if it is made, on the termination of those relations, in order to 'guarantee the future of a woman who has given to her lover the best part of her youth'.[17]

The notion of *bonnes moeurs* is a fluid one, not least because of the diversity of moral attitudes which is found in modern France as in modern England.[18] Mention has already

12 Trib Tarbes 14.3.1899, S 1900.2.219.
13 Cass req 5.2.1902, DP 1902.1.158.
14 Paris 12.5.1949, Gaz Pal 1949.2. 48, Mazeaud/Mazeaud p. 674.
15 Or by her: Cass req 17.4.1923, D 1923.1.172, Mazeaud/Mazeaud p. 228.
16 Cass civ 14.10.1940, DH 1940.174, Gaz Pal 1940.2.165, Mazeaud/ Mazeaud p. 227.
17 Cass civ 6.10.1959, D 1960.515 note Malaurie, *Source-book* p. 405 (but the question in issue was one of absence of cause, not of *cause illicite*; see the note).
18 Thus the increasing acceptance of stable relationships outside marriage has led the *Cour de cassation* to allow a partner in such a relationship to sue in delict for the death of the other; Cass ch mixte 27.2.1970, D 1970.201 note Combaldieu, JCP 1970.II.16305 concl Lindon, note Parlange.

been made of some of the many cases relating to brothels,[19] and gambling houses have been treated similarly, but in other matters the attitude of the courts is, not surprisingly, uncertain.[20]

Ordre publique économique et social embraces, as has been said, the large amount of recent 'imperative' legislation on consumer contracts, rent restrictions, insurance etc, and, of course, many provisions of labour law. The principles which have been evolved by the courts to govern contracts in restraint of trade between employer and employee and which closely parallel the corresponding principles of English law, are seen as expressions of an *ordre public* which protects 'liberty of commerce, industry and labour'.[1]

c State of mind of the parties

We have seen that except in the simplest case, where the *objet* itself is illicit, 'cause' in the present context bears the meaning of 'determining purpose'. But this leaves open the question whether it is sufficient that this purpose motivated one party, or whether it must be known to or even shared by the other.

If either of the latter alternatives is adopted, the result will be that the guilty party will be able to enforce the contract against the innocent party. And yet this was the result of a case before the *Cour de cassation*[2] which gave rise to an *arrêt de principe* in the matter. A landlord had agreed to let premises not knowing that the tenant intended to use them as a brothel. The tenant was allowed to enforce the contract and the landlord's *pourvoi* on the ground that the contract was null was rejected, the court adopting the extreme position that the cause would be illicit only if the parties had agreed on the exploitation of the premises as a brothel. Even apart, however, from the undesirability of this practical result, the principle can be questioned. Since the reason of policy for importing

19 Which have been formally illegal only since the *loi* of 13.4.1946.
20 See Ghestin *Contrat* s. 112, with examples.
 1 Cass civ 20.3.1928, DP 1930.1.145 note Pic; Cass civ 20.8.1938, DH 1938.513; Cass req 22.1.1941, DA 1941.163; Amiens 23.1.1940, DH 1940.55.
 2 Cass civ 4.12.1956, JCP 1957.II.10008 note Mazeaud, Gaz Pal 1957.1.183. See generally Weill/Terré s. 283, Ghestin *Contrat* ss. 704 f.

nullity for *cause illicite* is the need to discourage the pursuit of illicit aims, it should be irrelevant whether the pursuit is by one or both parties. To this it is objected that since, for the same reason, the nullity is absolute, the nullity can in principle be invoked by either party and therefore (in the converse situation to that in the case discussed above) the guilty party would be able to assert the nullity of the contract against the innocent party. This consequence is, however, mitigated by another principle, which is discussed in the next section.

In gratuitous contracts the question will in practice rarely arise, since the beneficiary will normally know what his benefactor's purpose is, but the predominant opinion, even among those who take the opposite view in the case of onerous contracts, is that the beneficiary need not have been aware of the illicit purpose. In favour of this opinion it is argued that, though the beneficiary's participation in the act is necessary to the extent that he must give his agreement, the dominant intention is that of the benefactor and, moreover, that what the beneficiary loses is a benefit for which he has given nothing in return.

d Effects of *cause illicite*

Article 1131 Cc declares that where there is no cause or the cause is illicit, 'the obligation can have no effect' and we have seen that classical theory accordingly treats the contract as in both cases absolutely null.[3] The modern doctrinal approach, which bases the distinction between absolute and relative nullity not on the nature of the act but on the nature of the interest protected,[4] has difficulty in accepting that absolute nullity is appropriate in the case of mere absence of cause (or *objet*), since the public interest involved is tenuous,[5] but there can be no such hesitation where the cause or the *objet* is illicit. Both doctrine and *jurisprudence* are clear that here the nullity is absolute. Any person interested may therefore invoke it and the courts will take notice of it in the course of litigation, even if the parties do not put it in issue.

3 See, for a case of absence of cause, Cass civ 17.12.1959, D 1960.294.
4 See p. 76, above.
5 See Ghestin *Contrat* s. 776.

From this it follows that the courts will not specifically enforce an illicit contract or give damages for its non-performance,[6] but it also follows, as has been said above, that even a guilty party may, either by way of defence or by *action en nullité*, have the contract declared null. It might be thought that from this latter consequence it would further follow that a claim for restitution of any benefit conferred in pursuance of the null contract (*action en répétition*) would also be allowed, but no such simple proposition can account satisfactorily for the practice of the courts.

Two maxims are invoked in this connexion by *doctrine* and, on occasion, by the courts: *Nemo auditur propriam turpitudinem allegans* (no-one can be heard to plead his own turpitude) and *In pari causo turpitudinis cessat repetitio* (where the turpitude of both parties is equal, there is no restitution).[7] The former is the more commonly cited of the two, but it is in fact the less precise. For, as we have said, a party is allowed to invoke his own wrongdoing to the extent that he can obtain a declaration that the contract is null. What he cannot do, as the second maxim indicates, is to obtain restitution of his own performance. But even this proposition has to be considerably qualified. The maxim *In pari* . . . itself expresses one qualification: the party claiming restitution may succeed if his turpitude is less reprehensible than that of the other party.[8] Again, restitution is always available in the case of gratuitous contracts. (The reason for this is considered below.) Beyond these two qualifications it is usually said that restitution is excluded only where the cause is immoral, as opposed to simply illicit. The preponderance of decided cases can be seen as applying this distinction,[9] but there are many decisions which depart from it in both directions[10] and the distinction itself is not easy to make. The immorality in question is most commonly sexual, and examples have been given above, but

6 Cass civ 23.6.1879, p. 123, n. 5, above.
7 Cf the Common law maxims: *Ex turpi causa non oritur actio* and *In pari delicto potior est conditio defendentis*; Cheshire and Fifoot *Law of Contract* (10th edn) pp. 331 ff.
8 As in English law: Cheshire and Fifoot *Law of Contract* pp. 337 f.
9 Sometimes expressly, e g Colmar 4.1.1961, Gaz Pal 1961.1.304.
10 For cases see Ghestin *Contrat* ss. 929 f, Weill/Terré s. 335.

gambling, as we have seen,[11] is also included. Again, restitution has been allowed in cases involving the corruption of
officials, but refused where the purpose of the contract was to
assist the German occupation authorities.[12] The truth seems to
be that no rule will accommodate the full diversity of the
jurisprudence, which, it has been said,[13] reflects a 'conscious
empiricism' in application of the policy behind the maxim.
There is a close parallel here with English law, in which the
general rule is the same as in French law (though without any
distinction between the immoral and the simply illicit), but is
subject to exceptions which, it has been said,[14] bring the law
close to asking simply whether recovery or non-recovery is the
more likely to promote the purpose of the invalidating rule.
The difference is that the detailed nature of the English judgment makes it possible, at least to some extent, to identify the
types of situation in which recovery will be allowed, whereas
the abstract character of the French *arrêt*, as we have noted
before, is not favourable to the evolution of detailed rules.

It remains to consider the general policy of the law in this
matter. It has sometimes been said to be an expression of
revulsion from any contact with 'turpitude', but, as we have
noticed, if this were so, the courts would refuse even to declare
a contract null on this ground. It is agreed, however, that the
policy does express an essentially moral attitude[15] and that this
accounts for the broad distinction between the immoral and
the simply illicit. This has the consequence, surprising to an
English lawyer, that a party seeking restitution will usually be
more harshly dealt with where the purpose of the contract was
lawful but immoral (as was the position in the many cases
concerning brothels before they were made illegal in 1946),
than where the purpose was unlawful but morally indifferent
(e g a breach of exchange control regulations[16] or a black

11 P. 126, above.
12 See p. 125, above.
13 Weill/Terré p. 365; cf Planiol and Ripert *Traité de droit civil* vol VII,
s. 749, Flour and Aubert *Droit civil - Les obligations* vol 1, s. 368.
14 Treitel *Contract* p. 368.
15 Ripert *La règle morale dans les obligations civiles* (4th edn, 1949)
ss. 104 ff, esp. 108.
16 Douai 29,7,1926, S 1926.2.94.

market transaction).[17] Subject to ths limitation, the policy can be said to be to deter by uncertainty.[18] For when the contract is wholly executory neither party can enforce it, and when it is executory only on one side the party who has performed is at the mercy of the one who has not. The purchaser of a house used as a brothel, for example, who has entered into possession without paying the price can have the contract declared null and thereby avoid paying the price, but at the same time he cannot be required to return the house. The same policy of deterrence by uncertainty accounts also for the at first sight inconsistent rule, mentioned above, that in a gratuitous contract the benefit can always (within the limitation period of thirty years) be reclaimed. Thus a gift made to a mistress to secure the continuation of the relationship may be reclaimed years later.[19]

e Utility of the concept of cause

We have seen that in the context of illicitness cause bears sometimes an objective and sometimes a subjective meaning. It is objective when, as in the case of an undertaking to commit a crime in return for a reward, cause is the correlative of *objet* and the contract is null whatever the purpose of the parties. It is subjective when, as in the majority of cases, cause has no relation to *objet* and the nullity of the contract is determined by the purpose of the parties. Here therefore, as in the context of absence of cause,[20] the first part of the anti-causalist argument (that cause is unworkable) is justified, in that the consequences attributed to the concept can only be accommodated by allowing a shift of meaning. The second part of the argument (that cause is unnecessary) can also be sustained. The distinction between the two senses in which a contract may be illicit serves no purpose. We have seen[1] that the treatment of *ordre public* as a restriction on freedom of contract is at present divided between article 6 on the one hand and the doctrine of *objet illicite* and *cause illicite* on the other. This

17 Cass civ 25.10.1949, Gaz Pal 1950.1.27; cf Hemard RT (1950) 100.
18 Weill/Terré p. 361; see Caen 29.7.1874, D 1875.2.128.
19 See p. 125, above.
20 Pp. 120 ff, above.
 1 Pp. 123 ff, above.

division of treatment could be eliminated and the doctrine of illicitness of contract could be simplified by enlarging article 6 to include both aspects of *ordre public*.[2] An agreement, or a clause in an agreement, would then be null if it offended against *ordre public* either by derogating from a *loi impérative* or by pursuing an illicit end.

E Restrictions on the content of contracts

It follows, as we have seen, from the doctrine of the autonomy of the will that the parties are in principle free to make what contracts they wish, provided that they comply with the four requirements laid down in article 1108 Cc.[3] In particular, the law is not concerned with the balance of advantage which is struck between the parties or with questions of inequality of bargaining powers. To this there are a few exceptions. As we have seen,[4] the rules relating to *violence* have been extended to provide a limited, but possibly expanding, protection against abuse of a dominant position. The extension of *dol* to include *dol par réticence*[5] may require the party with superior resources of information to communicate that information. And in extreme cases of disparity between the *prestations* required of the parties the contract may be declared void for lack of *cause*.[6] These exceptions are the result of judicial interpretation. The Code itself, however, provides a remedy for disparity between *prestations* (*lésion*) in three cases, and in this century legislation has intervened, at first to regulate various specific contracts and very recently to limit the consequences of inequality of bargaining power in general.

1 *Lésion*

a Meaning and scope

The term *lésion* (literally 'injury') denotes in general the pecuniary disadvantage or loss resulting from disparity

2 Cf Ghestin *Contrat* pp. 616 f; Zweigert/Kötz vol 2, p. 54.
3 P. 108, above.
4 Pp. 103 ff, above.
5 See pp. 98 ff, above.
6 See p. 144 f, above.

between the *prestations* required of the parties. It is concerned with the principal *objet* of each *prestation* (e g in a sale, the thing and the price) and not with collateral terms. In accordance with its underlying philosophy the Code[7] lays down that *lésion* does not affect a contract except in three contexts. With two of these we need not be concerned. *Lésion* is a general ground for the rescission of contracts entered into by minors;[8] and in the case of an agreement between heirs for the partition of the inheritance (*partage*) it is a ground for rescission if the value of the share actually received is less by more than a quarter than the value of a fair share.[9] The third exception is that of *lésion* in sale.

Articles 1674 ss Cc provide for one case only: where, in a sale of an immovable, the price received by the seller is less than five-twelfths of the 'just price' (or, to use the correct terminology, where there has been a *lésion* of more than seven-twelfths). In such a case the seller can claim *rescision* of the contract. This differs from *résolution* in that there is a limitation period of two years, but much more importantly in that the buyer has an option. He may either return the thing and get back the price, or keep the thing and pay a *supplément* consisting of the difference between the contract price and the 'just price' less one-tenth.[10]

Where the contract is aleatory, there can, on the accepted view, be no *rescision pour lésion*, on the ground either that the parties accepted the *aléa* or that the 'just price' cannot be calculated. In the context of sales of land the most obvious contracts of this kind occur in sales in return for a *rente viagère*.[11] It can indeed be said that actuarial calculations remove the aleatory element, but the *Cour de cassation* has taken the view[12] that though this is true where (as with annuities issued by an insurance company) a large number of lives are concerned, it is not so in the case of an individual contract.

7 Art 1118.
8 Arts 1305 ss Cc.
9 Arts 887 ff Cc.
10 Art 1681 Cc.
11 See pp. 44, 115, above; cf Weill/Terré s. 211.
12 Cass civ 27.12.1938, DP 1939.1.81 3e espèce, note Savatier. *Lésion* is inapplicable to a *bail à nourriture* because it is not in law a sale, but see p. 115, above.

The courts have refused to extend *rescision pour lésion* to any other case. Nor, quite apart from the categorical nature of article 1674, is this surprising. For intervention of this particular kind is consistent neither with the dominant *laissez-faire* philosophy of the last century nor with the more recent policy of restraining the abuse of a dominant position. One may therefore ask why and on what basis the *Code civil* intervened in this case.

b Basis

Historically speaking, the remedy for *lésion* in the sale of immovables goes back to legislation of the later Roman empire, which allowed rescission at the suit of the seller on almost exactly the same conditions as those in the *Code civil*. The underlying policy was probably that of keeping on the land a population from which taxes and, particularly in the frontier areas, soldiers could be drawn. In the Middle Ages *lésion* was seen as expressing the wider idea of the just price, but before the Revolution, during which the whole institution was abolished, French law had returned to the narrow Roman limits. Napoleon, who during the debates[13] on the drafting of the *Code civil* vigorously supported its re-introduction, justified it on the ground of the importance to the family (and therefore to the state) of retaining within it the land which was the guarantee of its continuing existence. (This is the same policy as justified the requirement of form for the gratuitous alienation of immovables.)[14]

In terms of legal theory Portalis, in the same debates, justified the re-introduction of *lésion* within its Roman limits both on the objective basis that where the *lésion* was so extreme there was no *cause* and on the subjective basis (argued also by Tronchet) that the *lésion* raised a presumption of a *vice du consentement*. The latter basis is echoed in the Code itself by the placing of the general article on *lésion* (article 1118) immediately after the articles on the *vices*, but there is no further reference to such a basis in the detailed articles (1674–1685) on the subject. Nevertheless, the subjective basis

13 For what follows see the passages excerpted in Mazeaud/Mazeaud pp. 187 ff and the note by Torat to Cass req 28.12.1932 (n. 15, below).
14 See p. 140, below.

was more in accord with nineteenth century views and it was not until 1932 that it was categorically rejected by the *Cour de cassation*[15] in an *arrêt* which declared that *lésion* is a ground for *rescision* 'in itself and by itself, independently of the circumstances which may have accompanied or given rise to it'. The *Cour* had, however, already in 1916 implicitly adopted the objective approach in a case[16] concerning a *promesse de vente*. A landlord had agreed, in a lease made in 1905, that the tenant should have the option of purchasing at a named price. The tenant sought to exercise this option in 1912 and the landlord pleaded *lésion* on the ground that the named price, though reasonable in 1905, was less than five-twelfths of the value of the land in 1912. The case turned on the interpretation of article 1675 Cc, which provides that the value of the immovable is to be calculated 'at the moment of the sale'. The *Cour de cassation* held that though the agreement was made in 1905, it could not ripen into a sale, which involves a transfer of property, until the exercise of the option. And yet, from the subjective point of view, if there had been a *vice du consentement*, it could only have related to the moment when the agreement was made. Moreover, the decision can be said to stray over the line between *lésion*, which is concerned with a bargain which was bad when it was made, and *imprévision*, which is concerned with a bargain which turns out, in the light of subsequent events, to be bad. As we shall see,[17] the civil courts have resolutely refused to admit a doctrine of *imprévision*.

The effect of the decision of 1916 was incorporated in the Code in 1949 in the shape of a second *alinéa* for article 1675.[18] A related question, also made crucial by inflation, arises in the calculation of the *supplément* which the buyer must pay if he is to retain the immovable. If there is a substantial delay between the sale and the calculation of the *supplément* (and though the seller can only initiate his action within a two-year period, the

15 Cass req 28.12.1932, S 1933.1.377 note Torat, D 1933.1.87 rapport Dumas, *Source-book* p. 388.
16 Cass civ 14.11.1916, DP 1921.1.34.
17 Pp. 202 ff, below.
18 'In the case of a *promesse unilatérale de vente*, *lésion* is calculated at the moment when the sale takes effect.'

buyer can offer the *supplément* at any time up to judgment) there is likely to be an important difference between valuations made at one date and at the other. The courts have held that the existence of *lésion* and its extent (i e the proportion which the contract price bears to the value), is calculated as at the date of sale, but that the date at which the *supplément* is fixed determines the figure to which that proportion is applied. This in turn gives rise to some problems.[19]

The objective character of *lésion* is therefore established, but in terms of current policy a subjective approach would be more acceptable. It is difficult to see why in sales of immovables alone, and in favour only of sellers, the law should impose the rules of the just price, but there are nowadays well-accepted arguments for a general intervention where there has been abuse of a dominant position. Thus the Italian Civil Code provides generally (article 1448) for rescission where there is a lesion of at least a half and this results from one party's having taken advantage of the 'state of need' of another.[20] And the draft of the new Civil Code of Quebec provides (Obligations article 38): 'Lesion vitiates consent when there is a serious disproportion between the prestations of the contract, resulting from the exploitation of one of the parties. Serious disproportion creates a presumption of exploitation.'[1] In the light of provisions such as these we should look at French legislation since the *Code civil*.

2 Legislative interventions

An approach in terms of *lésion* has been adopted on occasion in specific instances. A *loi* of 1907[2] allows buyers of fertiliser and some other agricultural supplies who can show *lésion* of more than a quarter to obtain a reduction of price and damages. A similar provision was made at one time for buyers of businesses (*lésion* of a third). Since 1957 the creators of literary and artistic works who assign their copyrights for a lump sum

19 See Ghestin *Contrat* s. 563.
20 The German Civil Code, art 138, is even wider.
1 Cf Swiss Code of Obligations, art 21.
2 8.7.1907, amended by *loi* of 10.3.1937; the text is printed in the *Petit Code Dalloz* after art 1683 Cc.

can obtain rescission if subsequent exploitation by the assignee of the assignor's works as a whole reveals a *lésion* of more than seven-twelfths. In other instances (e g maritime salvage, domestic rents, moneylending) legislation has either fixed maximum prices or given the courts discretion to reduce excessive charges.[3] The courts themselves control, on grounds of *ordre public*, the price at which *offices ministériels* (i e those offices connected with the courts, the right of presentation to which is alienable) change hands, and, on grounds which are debated, the remuneration of business agents, lawyers and bankers, and possibly other professional men.[4] In this case, as in the case of the assignment of copyright, the fairness of the sum paid is judged in the light of subsequent events, an approach which is open to the same criticism as has been made above[5] of the rule as to *lésion* in *promesses de vente*.

These are all piecemeal interventions, without any underlying general policy. More recent legislation has been, as in England, on the whole more general in character and motivated by a policy of protecting the consumer against abuses resulting from the large scale of modern commerce. And not surprisingly, since the problems to be solved are the same as in this country, the French solutions have usually been broadly similar to our own, but, so far, less extensive and, in accordance with the general French approach to legislation, less detailed.[6] Apart from the regulation of aggressive selling methods such as doorstep sales and the supply of unsolicited goods, a cooling-off period before the contract takes effect has been imposed on some contracts and a right of withdrawal within a period in others. Again, there has been regulation of the information which must be provided, particularly in matters of consumer credit. More generally, a *loi* of 10 January 1978 (sometimes referred to as *la loi Scrivener*,[7] after Mme Scrivener, the Minister for Consumer Affairs who promoted it)

3 See Weill/Terré s. 202.
4 See Ghestin *Contrat* ss. 550 ff.
5 P. 134, above.
6 See Ghestin *Contrat* ss. 455 ff; Françon; Travaux de l'Assoc H Capitant vol 24 (1973) pp. 117 ff; Calais-Auloy D 1970 Chr 37; Malinvaud D 1981 Chr 49.
7 See Ghestin *Contrat* ss 314 ff, 587 ff.

provided (by article 35) for the setting-up of a *Commission des clauses abusives*, broadly representative of suppliers, consumers, lawyers and the Government, and empowered the Government, on the advice of the Commission, to 'forbid, limit or regulate' a wide range of clauses in contracts between 'professionals' on the one hand and 'non-professionals or consumers' on the other, 'when such clauses seem to have been imposed on the non-professionals or consumers by an abuse of economic power by the other party and when they confer on that party an excessive advantage'. In exercise of the power thus conferred upon it, the Government made a decree on 24 March 1978. Article 2 and article 4 concern exemption clauses in sales and are dealt with below.[8] Article 3 prohibits any clause having as its purpose or effect to reserve to the 'professional' party the right to modify unilaterally the characteristics of the goods or services to be provided (subject to a qualification in favour of technical developments). Article 1 purported to outlaw any clause having as its purpose or effect to make the 'non-professional or consumer' party adhere to contractual provisions 'which do not appear in the document which he signs'. The exact effect of this provision (which seemed to pre-suppose that all contracts were signed) was very far from clear, but speculation was cut short by a successful challenge before the *Conseil d'Etat* to the legality of this article of the decree.[9] A group of insurance companies contended that the article was void for *excès de pouvoir* (i e in English legal terms that it was *ultra vires*) as being too wide, in that the type of clause which it prohibited did not necessarily involve 'an abuse of economic power' nor did it necessarily 'confer an excessive economic advantage', as required by the *loi Scrivener*..It remains to be seen what further interventions the *Commission des clauses abusives* may initiate.

The English lawyer, it may be added in parenthesis, may think that both the *loi* and the decree reveal the shortcomings of the simplicity of French legislative drafting. Apart from the obvious difficulties in interpreting article 1 of the decree, the meaning of 'non-professional or consumer' is far from clear.

8 P. 229, below.
9 CE 3.12.1980, 1981 JCP II.19502 concl Hagelsteen.

F The absence of a requirement of consideration

Before leaving the subject of formation of contract we should try to determine how far there is any fundamental difference between the French and the English idea of contract.

We have seen[10] that whereas in French law a contract consists of an agreement, it can more nearly in English law be said to be a promise given in return for good consideration. Where the consideration is itself a promise, there is no practical difference between the two approaches, but where the consideration is the performance of an act (i e in unilateral contracts in the English sense of the term), we have seen[11] that the French approach requires that there shall be an act of the will to constitute acceptance. In the ordinary case this can be implied from the performance of the act indicated in the offer, but it is clear (though the matter gives rise to no discussion by the writers and there appear to have been no decided cases) that an offer of a reward could not be accepted merely by the doing of the indicated act, in ignorance of the offer.[12] And it is likely that even where, as in *Williams v Carwardine*,[13] the act was done with knowledge of the offer but without any intention of claiming the reward, there would be held to have been no agreement. (The other question traditionally mooted in connexion with unilateral contracts, viz whether the offeror can withdraw his offer before the performance of the act is completed, would present less difficulty in French law, which would hold, if the view taken above is correct, that the revocation was effective, but that the other party's reliance interest should be protected in delict.)

On the other hand, the conception of contract as agreement accounts for the French unease in dealing with the real contracts,[14] which are a survival of a more primitive idea of obligation deriving from receiving a thing[15] (or from the reliance placed in the receiver).[16]

10 Pp. 37 ff, 63, 72, above; cf Zweigert/Kötz vol 2, p. 6.
11 P. 63, above.
12 Cf Schlesinger (ed) *Formation of Contracts* pp. 667,1255.
13 (1833) 5 C & P 566, 4 B & Ad 621.
14 Pp. 39 ff, above.
15 Nicholas *Roman Law* pp. 159 f, 167 f.
16 Atiyah *The Rise and Fall of Freedom of Contract* p. 187.

It is obvious, however, that the difference between the two systems lies much more in the requirement of consideration. What, if anything, takes its place in French law? It has been usual to cast *cause* in this role, but, though, as we have seen, it sometimes coincides with consideration, the only functions which it can be said to perform do not include that of determining which agreements should be enforceable, which is the main function of consideration.[17] Still less is it concerned with the subsidiary functions of consideration. These may be briefly considered first.

For the discharge or modification of contracts French law requires only agreement. The Common law resort to ideas of promissory estoppel or injurious reliance is necessary only to escape from the extension of consideration into this area. It is generally agreed[18] that this extension is justified only in so far as it protects creditors who are in financial difficulty and therefore vulnerable to improper pressure, and that this would be better dealt with in terms of the taking of advantage by one party of the other's state of need.[19]

That an offer, even though expressed to be irrevocable, should (unless accompanied by consideration) be revocable with impunity, is peculiar to the Common law. Even there it has been rejected, with safeguards, for contracts of sale by merchants under the Uniform Commercial Code[20] (USA); and it has been rejected also for international contracts of sale in both the recent conventions.[1] As we have seen, however, though there is no doubt as to the existence of a sanction in French law for wrongful revocation of offers of this kind, there is uncertainty as to its foundation.[2]

These two subsidiary applications of the doctrine of consideration have therefore no counterpart in French law and cannot be said to need one. A third subsidiary application is the requirement of 'mutuality', or the rule that an illusory

17 J P Dawson *Gifts and Promises* (1980) pp. 113 ff. The rest of this section draws heavily on this perceptive book.
18 Dawson, above, p. 210; Treitel *Contract* p. 96; cf the Law Revision Committee's 6th Interim Report of 1937.
19 Pp. 103 f, above.
20 §2-205.
1 Uniform Law on the Formation of Contracts for the International Sale of Goods 1964, s. 5 (2); Vienna Convention on Contracts for the International Sale of Goods 1980, art 16(2).
2 Pp. 63 ff, above.

promise is no consideration. This finds its counterpart to some extent in the French rule as to 'potestative conditions', which is discussed below.[3] Finally, the rule that past consideration is bad is an aspect of the main function of consideration, i e the identification of those promises which are enforceable. To this we must now turn.

It might be thought that the counterpart of the rule that a gratuitous promise is without effect unless under seal could be found in the rule that a *donation* is null unless made before a notary.[4] This would, however, be doubly erroneous. First, the rule is confined to *donations*, i e to gratuitous agreements to transfer property (in movables or immovables); it does not apply to any other gratuitous agreements. Secondly, the policy underlying the rule is quite different from that of the doctrine of consideration. Moreover, the courts have largely deprived the rule of practical effect. These points need further elaboration.

We have referred above[5] to the policy in the *Code civil* of preserving the patrimony of the family for subsequent generations. This is principally expressed in the rule which denies freedom of testation in respect of a portion of the inheritance (*réserve héréditaire*), a portion which increases with the number of descendants.[6] For a man who leaves three or more children (or their descendants) the *réserve* amounts to three-quarters, i e he is free to dispose by will of only one quarter (the *quotité disponible*). The inheritance on which these fractions are based is taken to include all the gifts which the testator has made in his lifetime. If these gifts, together with any legacies provided for in the will, exceed the *quotité disponible*, a process of reduction must be undertaken, first of the legacies and then of the gifts *inter vivos*, beginning with the most recent. It is into this system that the rule requiring notarisation of *donations* fits. Its aim is to ensure, on pain of nullity, that *donations* are recorded. (A notarised gift may be subject to reduction; an unnotarised gift is null from the beginning.) On the other hand, the restriction to (in a crude sense) capital

3 Pp. 154 ff, below.
4 Arts 931, 932, 1339 Cc.
5 Pp. 43, 133.
6 See Amos and Walton pp. 338 ff.

leaves to the present generation some freedom of management and use.[7]

The courts, however, very soon after the enactment of the Code, allowed the opening of three wide avenues of escape from the requirement of notarisation. (i) A distinction is made between a *donation*, which is an agreement, and a *don manuel*,[8] which is what a Common lawyer would call a perfected gift, i e the actual delivery (literally, by hand) of a movable. A *don manuel* does not require notarisation. This is justified either on the tenuous ground that the requirement of delivery supplies an element of visibility to the transaction which can take the place of notarisation, or by invoking the counsel of despair that such transactions cannot be controlled in any case. The first ground is made even more unconvincing in that the *don manuel* has been extended to intangibles by treating as a delivery of the intangible the handing over of the document needed for its enforcement, and in that any gift has been allowed to be subject to a life interest (usufruct) if it leaves the thing in the possession and enjoyment of the donor. (ii) The rule does not apply to a *donation indirecte*, i e to the gratuitous conferring of a pecuniary benefit, not directly by an agreement to give or a perfected gift, but indirectly through another juridical act. A waiver of debt (*remise de dette*),[9] for example, will have this effect, or a *stipulation pour autrui*,[10] by which the benefit of a contract between the donor and another person is transferred to the donee. In either case there has been no passage of assets through the donor's patrimony. (iii) Even more surprisingly, the rule does not apply to a *donation déguisée*,[11] i e to a transaction which is intended as a gift, but is disguised as an onerous transaction (e g a sale in which it is not intended that the price shall be paid). This escape from the requirement of notarisation was justified *e contrario* from the fact that in two instances such gifts are expressly declared

7 See Dawson *Gifts and Promises* pp. 67 f. For the Roman antecedents of the rule see Dawson ch 1.
8 See Dawson *Gifts and Promises* pp. 70 ff.
9 Arts 1282-1288 Cc; see Starck ss. 2465 ff. The Code makes a confusion between the transaction and the document which records it.
10 See pp. 175 ff, below.
11 See Dawson, above, pp. 74 ff; and see pp. 188 ff; below on *simulation*.

by the Code to be null; they are therefore, ran this unconvincing argument, in other cases by implication valid.

The practical result therefore is that anyone who is prepared to take a little care can escape from the expense (and perhaps from the visibility to the tax authorities) involved in notarisation. It must be emphasised, however, that the result is only to ensure the initial validity of the gift. All forms of gift are equally subject to reduction if in the event the *quotité disponible* is exceeded.

It is, however, the question of validity which makes the matter relevant in our present context. Since an unnotarised *donation* is (subject to the three exceptions just discussed) null, it will on occasion be necessary to determine whether a particular transaction is a *donation* or a *contrat à titre onéreux*. This will usually occur when the supposed donor (or his heir) has thought better of his generosity. In one case,[12] for example, a successful man had promised (in writing, but without notarisation) to pay for a bell, to be made to his specifications, for the tower of the church of his native village. His widow refused to pay, contending that the agreement was a *donation*. This contention was rejected by the *Cour de cassation* on the ground of the satisfaction to the donor's 'caprice, fantasy or vanity', which had been the purpose of the transaction. This line of reasoning has been followed in the few similar subsequent cases[13] in which the question has arisen, but it suffers from the obvious defect that it makes almost any gift into an onerous contract. It draws attention in fact to the incompatibility between the definition in the Code of gratuitous contracts,[14] which is in terms of the conferring of an unrequited advantage, and the definition of onerous contracts,[15] which is in terms of each party's conveying or doing something. The courts in these cases have asked whether the agreement is gratuitous and have said that the advantage conferred by the benefactor is not unrequited. This approach applies (to adopt the terminology of discussions of consideration) the test of benefit; but if the courts had asked whether the

---

12 Cass req 14.4.1863, DP 1863.1.402; Dawson *Gifts and Promises* pp. 87 f.
13 See Dawson, above, pp. 88 ff; Zweigert/Kötz vol 2, p. 67.
14 Art 1105; see p. 42, n. 10, above.
15 Art 1106.

agreement was onerous, they would have looked to detriment. In the case of the church bell this could have yielded the same result, since the church managers had made considerable changes in their plans in order to accommodate the benefactor's wishes.[16] There had, in other words, been an injurious reliance.

Here, then, there is a distinction which does echo one of the problems to which consideration gives rise, but it is far from being a central issue. It belongs in a small corner of the law and is little discussed. It in no way is the expression of the policy underlying the requirement of consideration. A gratuitous contract is in principle as valid as an onerous one, though, as we have seen, it may be more easily terminated and the burdens which it imposes may be less.

In short, it can be said that in French law any seriously intended[17] agreement which is not contrary to *ordre public* is a contract, provided that, in the case of a *donation* it satisfies or circumvents the requirement of notarisation.

---

16 Cf Dawson, above, p. 88, n. 9.
17 This may be said to beg the question, but it is an accepted, though little discussed (see Weill/Terré ss. 30 f), element in the French conception of contract, and one which is not related to the requirement of cause.

Chapter four
Effects of the contract

A Effects between the parties

1 Introductory

As has been said already, an unsatisfactory feature of the *Code civil* is its arrangement. Contract is but one of the sources of obligation and one might therefore expect the Code to treat first of obligations in general and then proceed to the different sources, but in fact it plunges straight into 'Contracts or conventional obligations in general' and treats of the nature of obligations as part of its treatment of the general principles of contract. Obligations for the Code are contractual obligations and it is left to the reader to make what adaptations are necessary in order to accommodate those which arise from quasi-contract or, with greater difficulty, those which arise from delict or quasi-delict.[1]

Having dealt, as we have done, with the essential requirements for the validity of a contract, the Code moves on to a chapter on 'The effect of obligations',[2] and under this heading places what to the Common lawyer seems to be a heterogeneous group of topics. The chapter deals first with the binding character of a contract and the obligation of good faith. It then goes on to the division of obligations according to their content (either *donner* or *faire ou ne pas faire*).[3] This is followed by sections on damages for the non-performance

1 This arrangement goes back to Gaius; see de Zulueta *The Institutes of Gaius* Part II, pp. 140 ff.
2 Arts 1134–1167.
3 See pp. 149 ff, below.

(*inexécution*) of an obligation, on the interpretation of contracts and finally on the effect of contracts on third parties.
The explanation of this grouping of topics is that the chapter
combines and confuses the question of the effect of an obligation with the logically prior question of the effect of a contract.
A contract has as its principal effect the creation, modification
or extinction of obligations (though it may also result in a
transfer of rights – real rights in the case of contracts such as
sale, exchange or *donation*,[4] personal rights in the case of
cession de créance).[5] When the chapter deals with the binding
character or the interpretation of contracts or, subject to the
exception mentioned immediately below, with the content of
obligations, it is concerned with the effect of a contract, rather
than with the effect of obligations. (This is indeed expressly
stated to be so in the heading of the section[6] dealing with the
effect on third parties.) It is only in fact in the section dealing
with damages for *inexécution*[7] and in those parts of the sections
on the content of obligations which deal with their enforcement[8] that the chapter deals with the effect of obligations. For
the Common lawyer these matters of enforcement and of
damages belong in a chapter on remedies, but this is not the
approach of the French lawyer.[9] For him the effect of an
obligation is to constrain the debtor to perform what he has
undertaken (or, in the case of non-contractual obligations,
what the law imposes on him) and to give to the creditor the
means of making that constraint effective. Or, to put the
matter in another way,[10] the effect of a contract is to create (or
modify or extinguish) an obligation, and the effect of an
obligation is either that it is performed, whether voluntarily or
under legal compulsion, or that a substitute for performance is
provided by way of damages.

French writers broadly follow the approach of the Code,
though with considerable variations in detail. For Common
law readers, however, clarity is better served by dealing with

4 Art 1138.
5 See p. 172, below.
6 Beginning at art 1165.
7 Arts 1146–1155.
8 Arts 1142–1145.
9 See further, pp. 205 ff, below.
10 Carbonnier p. 185.

remedies separately. Here therefore we shall be concerned only with the effects of contracts, as opposed to the effects of obliga-tions. Moreover, even among the effects of contracts, some have, because of their importance for an understanding by a Common lawyer of the French approach, been taken out of their due order in the usual French arrangement and placed in the Introduction.

2 Obligatory force of the contract as between the parties

We have already met the clause which embodies the pure doctrine of the autonomy of the will (article 1134 al 1):

> Agreements legally formed [sc in that they comply with the rules as to formation of contract discussed above] have the force of *loi* for those who made them.

This is a striking affirmation of the legislative power of the parties as far as they themselves are concerned, but the equation 'contract = *loi* ' is a rhetorical exaggeration. That a contract does not have all the effects of a *loi*, even for the parties themselves, is easily shown. (i) The terms of a contract are a matter of fact and not of law and therefore, unlike legal rules, they have to be proved. For the same reason the inter-pretation of a contract is within the *pouvoir souverain du juge du fond* and therefore escapes the control of the *Cour de cassa-tion*. (ii) While a contract will prevail over a *loi supplétive*, it obviously cannot override a *loi impérative*, and the interven-tionism of the modern legislator has, as we have seen,[11] greatly eroded the foundations of the doctrine of the autonomy of the will.

The conventional treatment of the obligatory force of the contract deals with it first as between the parties and then as regards the judge. The latter heading accommodates matters of interpretation, which, as we have seen, are placed at this point by the *Code civil*, but which we have already dealt with in the Introduction. As between the parties the consequences of the obligatory force of the contract do not differ significantly from

11 Pp. 135 ff, above.

those found in the Common law. Article 1134 al 2 specifies that '[Contracts] can be revoked only by mutual consent or on grounds authorised by *la loi* '. Where the Code itself[12] recognises such grounds, for example in contracts for continuing performance over an indefinite period, it can reasonably be said that *la loi* expresses what would have been the parties' intention had they given thought to the matter and therefore that there is no significant departure from the principle of the parties' autonomy, but recent legislation for the protection of the economically weak or the ill-advised (e g the buyer in a doorstep sale)[13] has had the professed purpose, like its counterpart in England, of restricting that autonomy.

3 Requirement of good faith in performance[14]

Article 1134 al 3 provides that '[Contracts] must be executed in good faith'. We have seen that good faith is introduced indirectly into the requirements for the formation of contracts under cover of the concepts of *erreur* and *dol* (particularly *dol par réticence*) and that it plays a part in pre-contractual liability, but it is only here that the Code makes any explicit reference to it.

The example of German law shows how fertile such a provision can be. The famous 'general clause' of article 242 of the German Civil Code, which is to the same effect as the French article, has been used by the German courts with remarkable freedom to adapt the law of contract to changed economic and social circumstances and attitudes, by, for example, requiring the revision of agreements in the light of the inflation and revaluation of the currency after the First World War and again after the Second, or, more recently, by policing exemption clauses. The French courts however, have made very little express use of article 1134[15], though there are indeed a considerable number of decisions which are seen by *doctrine* as applica-

12 Arts 1736, 1780, 1869.
13 P. 136, above.
14 See Zweigert/Kötz vol 1, p. 150; vol 2, pp. 187 ff; Dawson (1934) 33 Mich L Rev 171; Cohn (1946) 28 Jo Comp Legisl 115; von Mehren *The Civil Law System* (2nd edn) pp. 1066 ff.
15 See Weill/Terré ss. 356 f.

tions of the requirement of good faith in the performance of the contract. Many of these (e g requiring a tenant of a building to inform his landlord of repairs which are needed, or a transporter of goods to send them by the route which is most advantageous to the consignor, or a supplier of equipment to explain its use and warn of its dangers)[16] would in English law be dealt with by implied terms and are treated by French courts in a similar way, as applications of the *pouvoir souverain* to interpret the contract. In others (e g denying to a landlord the right to invoke a forfeiture clause in a lease because he waited before giving notice until the tenant was likely to be on holiday, or denying to the client of a builder the right to require correction of defects when the cost of correction was out of all proportion to the seriousness of the defects)[17] an English court would arrive at the same conclusion on the ground that remedies other than damages, being equitable, are discretionary. Although some writers see all such cases as applications of the principle of good faith, it is only very rarely that in deciding them the French courts expressly invoke article 1134 al 3. It may be that, like the English courts, they are reluctant to set loose such a wide-ranging principle.[18] If one leaves aside certain contracts, such as partnership (*société*) and agency (*mandat*), in which a convergence of interest is essential, or those which an English lawyer characterizes as *uberrimae fidei*, the interests of contracting parties are commonly to some extent at least opposed and to yoke them together under a general requirement of good faith may impose too great a strain on the relationship. Carbonnier has said,[19] 'It is surprising that at a time when marriage has perhaps been too much converted into a contract, some should have dreamt of converting every contract into a marriage.'

---

16 Paris 28.3.1939, DH 1939.231; Cass civ 28.11.1905, D 1909.1.193, S 1909.1.269; Cass com 25.11.1963, Gaz Pal 1964.1.281.
17 Cass civ 29.6.1976, 15.12.1976, RT (1977) 340.
18 Cass req 23.3.1909, S 1909.1.552.
19 Carbonnier p. 191.

4 Content of the obligation created by the contract

As has been said above, the Code here adopts the traditional classification into (a) *donner*, (b) *faire ou ne pas faire*. It is important to notice that *donner* in the technical legal sense means neither to make a gift nor to deliver (*livrer*), but to convey, to pass ownership or some other real right. (The Latin word *dare* has the same technical meaning.)

In Roman law and in principle in the *ancien droit*[20] the obligation was executed by delivery of the thing. Article 1136 Cc still says that the obligation of *donner* imports the obligation of delivery, but article 1138 provides that

> The obligation of delivering the thing is completed by the mere agreement of the contracting parties. It makes the creditor owner and puts the thing at his risk from the moment when it should have been delivered, even though the handing over has not been effected.

Provided therefore that the thing is specific,[1] the obligation of *donner* is self-executing: property passes by agreement. The effect of this must not, however, be exaggerated. In most cases the property will pass only as between the parties.[2] For as against third parties a transfer of property in immovables is, as we have seen, ineffective without registration. And movables are governed by the famous provision of article 2279 Cc: 'As far as movables are concerned, possession is equivalent to title.' As we have seen,[3] this maxim, though not as sweeping as it appears, nevertheless has the effect, broadly, of enabling a *bona fide* possessor to obtain title immediately if he acquires the thing from a bailee (to use the Common law term), and after three years if the owner has parted with the thing involuntarily.

---

20 See Amos and Walton pp. 105 f.
1 Cf art 1583 Cc.
2 Cf Lawson (1949) 65 LQR 352.
3 P. 78, above.

In the ordinary case therefore of an obligation of *donner* relating to a specific thing, the obligation is no sooner created than it is executed. There remains, of course, the obligation of actual delivery, but this is an obligation of *faire*. Similarly, where the obligation of *donner* relates to generic things, the obligation to identify the thing and make it specific is also an obligation of *faire*. The distinction, therefore, between the two categories of obligation is not of great practical significance.

5 'Modalities' of the obligation

It is convenient in connexion with the content of the obligation to deal with what French writers call 'modalities', i e provisions in the contract[4] which modify or qualify either the existence or the enforceability of the obligation.[5] Such a provision is either a *condition* or a *terme*.

a Suspensive and resolutive conditions

The term 'condition' is notoriously fluid in English law. In French technical language, which derives from the common Romanistic tradition of the Civil law, it has a precise meaning. The Romanistic tradition has had some influence also on English law and its terminology is therefore to some extent familiar to Common lawyers, but it may be useful briefly to set out the essentials of the French law. For the matter is dealt with systematically and at some length in the *Code civil*,[6] by contrast with the fragmentary treatment in the English books.

A condition is a provision which makes the existence of a juridical act – in the present context a contract – and therefore the existence of the obligation resulting from it dependent on a future uncertain event. The condition may be either suspensive, in that the obligation will not exist unless and until the

4 Or imposed by law, especially in non-contractual contexts, e g arts 455, 1660 Cc.
5 We omit plurality of creditors and debtors and plurality of *objets* (alternative obligations), which are commonly included under this heading. The complexity of these topics bears, as in English law, no relation to their practical importance.
6 Arts 1168-1184.

event occurs, or resolutive (*résolutoire*), in that the obligation will cease to exist if the event occurs. (The corresponding English terms are 'condition precedent' and 'condition subsequent'.) A promise to pay on the promisee's marriage, for example, or (in an insurance contract) to pay if it rains on a particular day, is subject to a suspensive condition; a *donation* of a house until such time as the donor marries is subject to a resolutive condition. Whether a particular condition is suspensive or resolutive is a matter of construction. In a sale on approval, for example, article 1588 Cc establishes a presumption that the condition is suspensive,[7] but the presumption is rebuttable.

On a strict analysis both types of condition are suspensive. In the one case it is the coming into existence of the obligation which is suspended and in the other case its disappearance. The Romans spoke only of *condicio*, by which they meant a suspensive condition. In the one case, they said, it is the contract which is conditional, in the other the contract is absolute and it is its resolution which is conditional. The modern distinction is, however, useful, since the effects of the one and the other are different.

We may take first the position pending the occurrence of the event. In the case of a resolutive condition the obligation is, for the moment at least, fully effective and enforceable. In the example given above, the donee of the house has full ownership; the donor has only a potential right in the event of his marriage. In the case of a suspensive condition the matter is more complex. The obligation is for the most part without effect. It cannot be enforced, no property passes and if money is paid in the mistaken belief that the condition has been fulfilled (e g because the promisee's supposed marriage is void), the money can be recovered back. But the obligation has a partial existence for other purposes.[8] The debtor cannot withdraw; the creditor can alienate his right and transmit it on death; and he can take what steps (*actes conservatoires*) are necessary to protect his right, e g, where applicable, by registration.

---

7 Contrast *Head v Tattersall* (1871) LR 7 Exch 7.
8 Arts 1179, 1180 Cc.

On the occurrence of the event the effect of both types of condition is for most purposes retrospective.[9] If, for example, S agrees to sell his computer to B provided that S receives within the next six months the new one which he has ordered, B's ownership will, if the condition is satisfied, relate back to the date of the agreement and any intervening alienation or creation of real rights in favour of a third party will be without effect. And similarly in the case of a resolutive condition, as in the example of a *donation* of a house until such time as the donor marries, any intervening alienation or burdening of the property will be invalidated.[10]

These effects can obviously be inconvenient and the parties may in making the conditional agreement provide otherwise. The articles in the Code are only *lois supplétives*. Moreover, normal acts of administration by the interim owner in relation to any property involved are binding on the eventual owner.[11] And the principle of retroactivity does not apply to the incidence of risk. In the case of a suspensive condition there is express provision in article 1182 Cc. In the case, for example, of a sale, if the thing perishes between the making of the contract and the fulfilment of the condition, the risk is on the seller in the sense that, though he is released by supervening impossibility from the obligation to deliver the thing, he cannot claim the price from the buyer. The same solution is generally given for the case of a resolutive condition, though there is no text. If the thing perishes in the intervening period, the buyer must nevertheless pay the price (or, since he is likely to have paid the price, will not be able to recover it back).

Whether, and when, a condition is fulfilled is of course a question of fact, though the Code provides some suppletive rules.[12] In one case, however, there is a fiction. The condition is deemed to have been fulfilled if the person who would have been bound prevents its fulfilment.[13] (This will not, of course, apply if he was not at fault or if he had an independent reason for doing so, e g, in the example above of the promise to sell a

9 Art 1179 Cc.
10 Arts 952, 1673 al 2 Cc.
11 And the interim owner may keep the fruits: Paris 28.10.1893, DP 1894.2.104.
12 Arts 1176, 1177 Cc.
13 Art 1178 Cc.

computer on the seller's receiving a new one, if the seller refuses to accept the new one because it is unsatisfactory).

b **Termes**[14]

A *terme* is like a condition in that the event to which it refers is in the future, but it differs in that the event is certain to occur (though the moment at which it will occur may not be certain). A promise to pay at the end of next month or a *donation* of a house on the death of X is subject to a *terme*, whereas a promise to pay if X dies before the end of next month is conditional. A *terme* differs in its consequences from a (suspensive) condition in that, pending the occurrence of the event, the contract is effective for all purposes (including the passing of risk) save that of enforcement. The promisor cannot be required to pay before the end of the month or to hand over the house before the death of X (nor can the promisee set off the unenforceable debt against a claim by the promisor), but if for any reason (e g because he mistakenly believes X to be dead) he discharges his obligation prematurely, he cannot claim restitution. As we have seen, the rule is otherwise in the case of a condition. One can see the rational basis for this distinction (which is Roman), in that in the case of a condition the debt may turn out not to be owed, whereas in the case of a *terme* there is no possibility of its not being owed. The only question is as to when. But the practical result (which may be to penalise the debtor heavily for his mistake if X lives on for a long time) is not easy to defend.

We have been considering so far those *termes* which delay the enforceability of an obligation until the event occurs, and it is only *termes* in this sense which are mentioned in the Code. But in common legal parlance the word is also used of a provision which terminates an obligation on the occurrence of a future and certain event, as in a tenancy agreement which comes to an end after two years or a promise to pay a *rente viagère*.[15] Such a provision is referred to as a *terme extinctif*, as opposed to a *terme suspensif*. A *terme extinctif* can hardly, however, be said to be a 'modality' in that so long as the obligation exists it is fully effective and unmodified. The *terme* simply brings it to an end. There is no retroactive effect.

14 Arts 1185–1188 Cc.
15 P. 44, above.

c Potestative conditions[16]

The *Code civil*[17] makes a threefold distinction between conditions which are 'casual', 'mixed' and 'potestative' (*condition casuelle, mixte, potestative*). This subject is for the Common lawyer doubly confusing. It is confusing in the first place (and even for French lawyers) both because the threefold distinction is unworkable and fails to give effect to what was evidently the intention of the draftsmen[18] and because the fourfold distinction which the classical writers of the nineteenth century substituted for that of the Code is itself unsatisfactory. (It is, however, still universally used by the writers and we shall therefore adopt it here.) The subject is confusing in the second place for the Common lawyer because the problems dealt with by French law in terms of potestative conditions are obviously similar to those dealt with by the Common law in terms of discretionary promises and illusory consideration, but they turn out on analysis not to be identical, and the transition from one method of thought to the other is not easily made. It is, however, for that reason a subject which from the comparative point of view deserves more attention than its practical importance by itself might justify. Moreover, the French rule gives rise to far more litigation than does its analogue in the Common law.

The rule is stated in article 1174 Cc:

> Any obligation is null if it is contracted under a condition which is potestative on the part of the person obliged.

A potestative condition in this sense, which, for reasons which will appear, is called 'purely potestative', is one which depends for its fulfilment purely on the will of one of the parties.[19] A promise by B to buy a house from A for 300,000

---

16 See Taisne J-Cl Civ arts 1168-1174, fasc 40-43, ss. 25-64; Wood Brown (1931) 5 Tulane L Rev 306.

17 Arts 1169-1171 Cc.

18 See p. 156, n. 4, below.

19 Cf art 944 Cc: 'Any *donation* between living persons, if made on a condition the fulfilment of which depends purely on the will of the donor, is null.' In this case, however, *doctrine* includes also simply potestative conditions (see text, below). The purpose of this forced interpretation is to ensure that the policy that *donations* should be irrevocable is not circumvented. *Jurisprudence* has, however, held that a *condition mixte* (see text, below) does not nullify a *donation*.

francs 'if I feel like it' is null because it is subject to a purely potestative condition on the part of the person obliged, i e B. (It should be noticed that it is the obligation which is invalidated, not the condition.)[20] In terms of the will theory the reason for the rule is that there can be no obligation if the promisor's will is unrestricted. On the other hand, in the familiar and more practical example of the option (A agrees to sell a house to B for 300,000 francs if B notifies A within ten days that he has decided to buy) the condition is indeed potestative, but on the part of the person entitled, (i e B) and the contract is therefore valid.

Not many promises are cast in a form as simple as this and the difficulty lies in determining the limit within which a condition is purely potestative in this sense. The polar opposite of the purely potestative condition is the 'casual condition', which is adequately defined in the Code (article 1169):

> A casual condition is one which depends on chance and is in no way within the control of either the creditor or the debtor.

The contract of insurance against rain, considered above, provides an example: the condition 'if it rains' is casual in this sense. Here there can be no question but that the contract is valid. It is in the area between the casual and the purely potestative that the difficulty lies. Traditional *doctrine* distinguishes from the purely potestative condition what it confusingly calls a 'simply potestative' condition and what (following in this respect the Code) it calls a 'mixed' condition. A simply potestative condition is one which depends for its fulfilment partly on the will of one of the parties and partly on an external event, or, to put it in another way, one which depends for its fulfilment on the will of one of the parties expressed in the accomplishment of an act or a fact. (A gives B the option of buying A's furniture if A sells his flat; A, a publisher, undertakes to pay a royalty to B, an author, when A has sold 15,000 copies of B's book.[1] In both cases there is a valid contract.) A 'mixed condition' is defined by the Code (article 1171) as being dependent on the will of one of the parties and the will of

---

20 But even French lawyers confuse the two. See e g the *pourvoi* in Cass req 20.2.1905, S 1905.1.508, *Source-book* p. 322.
1 Paris 6.12.1969, JCP 1971.II.16796 note Ghestin.

a third party. This definition does not, however, serve to differentiate a mixed from a simply potestative condition. For very few of the latter type can be fulfilled without the participation to some extent of a third party. In the examples given above, A's selling his furniture or 15,000 copies of B's book both obviously involve third parties as buyers. In order therefore to maintain the separate existence of the two categories, nineteenth century *doctrine* defined a mixed condition as one which was dependent on the will of one of the parties and of a *determinate* third party. Thus, 'if I marry' was classified as simply potestative, but 'if I marry X was mixed. This distinction is still stated in the books, but, with one exception,[2] no practical consequences attach to it and discussion centres on the simply potestative condition. Recent *jurisprudence*[3] indeed tends to use the term 'mixed' to cover both kinds of condition, thereby implicitly adopting a threefold distinction (purely potestative, mixed and casual).[4]

A simply potestative condition does not invalidate the obligation, whereas a purely potestative condition on the part of the debtor does. The distinction is therefore vital, but the line between a condition which depends on the will alone and one which depends on the will and an event is not sharp. If a condition in the form 'if I sell my flat' is simply potestative,

2 See p. 154, n. 19, above.
3 Cass civ 28.5.1974, D 1975.144 note Poussard, JCP 1975.II.17911 note Thuillier; Cass com 22.11.1976, JCP 1978.II.18903.
4 The distinction in the Code between casual, potestative and mixed conditions is defective in three ways. (1) The potestative condition to which art 1174 attaches the consequence of nullity of the obligation so conditioned is obviously not that which is defined in art 1170: 'A potestative condition is one which makes the performance of the agreement depend on an event which it is in the power of one or other of the parties to cause to happen or prevent from happening.' To go no further, art 1178 (p. 152, above) provides that if a party does prevent such a condition from happening, the condition is deemed to have been fulfilled (sc and the obligation therefore to be unconditionally valid). (2) Potestative conditions as defined in art 1170 and mixed conditions as defined in art 1171 do not exhaust the possible types of condition; they leave out precisely that type of condition which is referred to in the text as purely potestative; it is evidently to this type of condition that art 1174 should have referred. (3) A mixed condition (art 1171) cannot be clearly distinguished from a potestative condition as defined in art 1170; see text above.

what of (to take the traditional example) 'if I wear my grey hat'? And if it is satisfactory that a promise to sell my furniture 'if I sell my flat' should be enforceable, is it also satisfactory that a promise to pay off a loan 'if I sell my flat' should enable me to put off repayment indefinitely?[5] The attempt to apply the distinction mechanically led to inconsistent and unsatisfactory decisions and in recent years the courts and some of the writers[6] have looked more to the underlying policy. The importance of the rule obviously does not lie in preventing the enforcement of purely potestative debts. Even if the condition were effective, the result would be the same: a promise to pay 'if I feel like it' is, as a straightforward matter of interpretation, unenforceable. The effect of the rule is to protect the creditor. For example, in the case of the promise to pay off a loan 'if I sell my flat',[7] it was the creditor who invoked the rule in order to have the obligation to repay declared null so that he could then claim immediate repayment in quasi-contract. And in the case of the publisher's promise to pay a royalty after he had sold 15,000 copies,[8] it was the author who (unsuccessfully) contended that this promise was null, in order to be free of his own side of the contract. Similarly, where a prospective borrower from a finance company was required, as a preliminary to an eventual loan, to make an initial deposit and to produce security, and yet the finance company reserved an unrestricted discretion to delay or to refuse a loan after all, it was the prospective borrower who contended that the finance company's obligation was subject to a purely potestative condition, in order to be able to recover back his deposit in the finance company's supervening insolvency.[9] Again, where the active partner in a partnership had made a *donation* to a charity of the income for the next five years of certain shares in the partnership, it was one of the donor's heirs, after his death, who sought to have the *donation* declared void on the ground that, as the law then stood, the donor had had the power to

5 Paris 15.3.1974, JCP 1974.II.17786 note Goubeaux.
6 See esp. Ghestin D 1973 Chr 293; Goubeaux, n. 5, above; Taisne J-Cl Civ, arts 1168–1174, fasc 40–43, ss. 25–64, cf Carbonnier p. 230.
7 N. 5, above.
8 P. 155, n. 1, above.
9 Paris 22.12.1953, Gaz Pal 1954.1.268, D 1954 Somm 48.

provoke the dissolution of the partnership and therefore the cessation of the income.[10]

It is therefore the creditor who is in practice protected by the rule, and it is against the arbitrary economic power of the debtor that he is protected. Hence the same condition may, it seems, be differently interpreted according to the relative positions of the parties. The promise to sell my furniture to X if I sell my house, seen as an executory promise, is from the point of view of this policy unobjectionable, but the promise to repay a loan subject to the same condition enables the borrower to keep the lender out of his money indefinitely.[11] The position was the same where a buyer had entered into possession in pursuance of a contract which required him to pay the price when he re-sold.[12]

The same consideration influences the drawing of the line by the courts between the purely and the simply potestative. The line cannot be drawn mechanically in terms of the condition's fulfilment being dependent on the will alone or the will together with an act. It would be absurd to draw the line between 'I will sell if I feel like it' and 'I will sell if I wear my grey hat'. The question is, in traditional terms, whether there is a significant external restriction on the debtor's freedom of will, or, more realistically, whether he is economically free to escape from his debt. For example, where an agent was employed on terms which made his commission depend on the profit made by his principal's business, the agent contended that the principal's obligation was subject to a purely potestative condition, since he was free so to arrange matters that no profit was made; but in economic terms he had no such freedom and the court ruled against the agent.[13] The same was true in the case of the publisher and the royalty after 15,000 copies,[14] or in another case in which it was contended that a

10 Cass civ 28.5.1974, p. 156, n. 3, above.
11 Paris 15.3.1974, p. 157, n. 5, above. It is, however, an extreme case. Moreover, a promise qualified by 'when', as opposed to 'if', has usually been regarded as valid: Cass civ 9.11.1846, D 1850.1.346; Wood Brown (1931) 5 Tulane L Rev 410.
12 Cass civ 8.10.1980, JCP 1980.IV.417.
13 Cass req 21.7.1926, S 1926.1.297.
14 P. 155, n. 1, above.

contract of employment was void because it was open to the employer (a company) to bring the contract to an end by securing a winding up.[15] A freedom to ruin oneself is not a freedom which the law can take into account in this context.

Another factor which the courts evidently take into account is the extent to which the debtor's freedom to escape from his obligation is subject to any external check. Thus, where it was contended that a gift of partnership income was subject to a purely potestative condition because the donor could have terminated the gift by provoking the dissolution of the partnership, the court held[16] that the condition was not purely potestative because the law required that the dissolution be initiated 'in good faith and not inopportunely' and this requirement was a circumstance outside the partner's control (sc in that it was subject to verification by the courts). Similarly, where a buyer had made his purchase of a house conditional on his getting a loan within three months, the court held that he was under a duty to try to get a loan and therefore that the condition was not purely potestative.[17] In this connexion the provision in article 1178 Cc should be remembered, that the condition will be deemed to have been fulfilled if the debtor has prevented its fulfilment.

The paradigm cases with which we began were of unilateral contracts, such as the granting of an option (potestative on the part of the creditor) or a promise to sell if the buyer feels like it (potestative on the part of the debtor) and it is usually said in the books and has many times been declared in the decisions of the courts that the rule applies only to such contracts. Synallagmatic contracts, it is said, are not invalidated by a purely potestative condition on the part of the debtor, because the debtor is also a creditor.[18] If, for example, wine is sold subject to the buyer's tasting and approving it,[19] the sale is valid. The

15 Cass soc 9.11.1961, D 1962 Somm 84.
16 Cass civ 28.5.1974, p. 156, n. 3, above.
17 Cass com 22.11.1976, JCP 1978.II.18903. Contrast Cass civ 8.10.1980, p. 158, n. 12, above.
18 See e g Marty/Raynaud s. 751 (p. 762).
19 Art 1587 Cc. The condition is potestative, since it depends on the subjective opinion of the taster, by contrast with the condition in a sale on approval (art 1588), which is regarded as being objective.

buyer's duty to pay the price is subject to a purely potestative condition, but so also is his right to the delivery of the wine. The buyer cannot be compelled to accept the wine, but the seller cannot refuse to tender it and complete the sale if the buyer approves; on the other hand, the buyer cannot claim delivery without being prepared to pay the price. In this case the proposition is obviously correct and the justification offered in terms of policy is that the seller is not subjected to the arbitrary power of the buyer, because the buyer can only exercise that power at the cost of losing his rights under the contract. Moreover, the Common lawyer has to remember that if one side of a synallagmatic contract is null the result can be seen as a unilateral contract, and in French law unilateral contracts are valid. Thus, where A gave B for 25,000 francs an exclusive concession to dig for phosphates on A's land, but B did not bind himself to exploit the concession, the court held in effect that the contract was unilateral and the purely potestative condition was on the part of the creditor only.[20] And it would indeed be strange if a valid unilateral concession by A to B could become null because there was appended to it a purely potestative promise by B. On the other hand there are cases[1] in which a synallagmatic contract has been declared void because of a purely potestative condition on one side, and it can be argued that since in such a contract the obligation of one party is the *cause* of the other, if one obligation is void the other must be void also. This was expressly the reasoning, for example, in the case in which an agreement for a loan was declared void because of a purely potestative condition on the part of the prospective lender.[2] Moreover where, as in that case or the case in which the repayment of a loan was conditional on the borrower's selling his flat,[3] the creditor has already performed his part of the bargain, the argument of policy that the debtor can only exercise his power over the creditor at the cost of losing his rights under the contract is deprived of its force. The truth seems to be that the courts will follow the latter route when it is necessary to do so in order to give effect to the policy

20 Toulouse 21.5.1885, D 1886.2.187; cf Cass req 11.3.1879, D 1881.1.34.
1 See Taisne J-Cl Civ, arts 1168-1174, fasc 40-43, ss. 46f.
2 Paris 22.12.1953, p. 157, n. 9, above.
3 Paris 15.3.1974, p. 157, n. 5, above.

of protecting one party against the arbitrary power of the other.[4]

It is also usually said that the rule applies only to suspensive and not to resolutive conditions. This conclusion is based on two arguments. On the one hand, article 1174 says: 'Any obligation is null if it is *contracted* under a condition etc', whereas in the case of a resolutive condition the obligation is not conditionally contracted, but conditionally resolved.[5] On the other hand, there are several particular instances in the *Code civil*[6] in which obligations contracted under a resolutive condition are valid. Against this it can be said that, since resolutive conditions operate retrospectively and are therefore no less effective than suspensive conditions in enabling the debtor arbitrarily to throw off his obligation, the policy argument would lead one to expect them to be treated in the same way. In fact the cases commonly cited in this connexion are instances not of resolutively conditioned obligations in the strict sense but of a power in one party arbitrarily to terminate a contract, usually a contract for successive performances, e g by a theatre manager with an actor, the manager having the right to terminate the contract at specified intervals.[7] Such terminative conditions are indeed effective if, as in the example just given, there is a restriction on the freedom to terminate, but where there is no such restriction the obligation has been declared void.[8]

If we turn to the Common law,[9] the most nearly corresponding rule is that a discretionary and therefore illusory promise is no consideration. A promise by a buyer to pay the price 'if he feels like it' cannot be consideration for the promise of the seller. The question is no longer one of the nature of the condition which qualifies a promise, nor, formally, of whether

4 This policy should lead to the conclusion that the nullity resulting from a purely potestative condition is relative, but though this question has been discussed by some writers, there has been no support for it in the *jurisprudence*.

5 See p. 151, above.

6 Arts 1096, 1659, 1780 al 2.

7 Cass civ 2.5.1900, D 1900.1.392.

8 Wood Brown (1931) 5 Tulane L Rev 405 ff.

9 Treitel *Contract* p. 65; *Restatement, Contracts* s. 79; *Williston on Contracts* (3rd edn) s. 104; *Corbin on Contracts* s. 152; Wood Brown, above, 424 ff.

one party can freely escape from his obligation, but of whether the promise of one party (in French terms the conditional debtor) constitutes consideration for the promise of the other (the creditor). We have seen that in French law, although the rule is formulated in terms of the promise of the debtor (in the example given above, the buyer), it has the effect of protecting the creditor (the seller) from the arbitrary power of the debtor. In the Common law the rule can hardly be said to have a policy; it is a particular consequence of the doctrine of consideration. It is, moreover, a rule of no great practical importance, whereas, as we remarked above, the French rule has given rise to a considerable body of case law and at any rate on occasion is used to correct an unequal bargain.

We may begin by asking the reason for this difference. The answer lies partly in the absence from the Common law of the unilateral contract (in the French sense) and the presence of the requirement of consideration, and partly in the greater readiness of English law to give to ostensibly subjective terms an objective meaning.

We have seen that many of the French cases concern unilateral agreements, which the doctrine of consideration excludes from the Common law, and indeed that the dominant view both in *doctrine* and in *jurisprudence* is that the rule has no application to synallagmatic agreements, a view which is the easier to maintain in that an executory synallagmatic agreement which is subject to a purely potestative condition can be seen as a unilateral agreement and therefore valid. It is only exceptionally, and then in cases where the creditor (as defined above) has performed his part of the agreement, that we find French courts declaring a synallagmatic agreement to be null on the ground that one party's obligation is subject to a potestative condition. If, for example, A agrees to sell a book to B for 100 francs 'if A feels like it' and B pays the 100 francs before he has received the book, a French court may adopt the analysis that since A's obligation is null as being subject to a purely potestative condition and since A's obligation is the *cause* of B's obligation, B's obligation is also null and B is entitled to the return of his 100 francs. Except in cases such as this, in which *cause* plays a part which is close to that of consideration, the problems which are dealt with in French law in terms of potestative conditions cannot arise in that form in English law because they are excluded by the requirement of consideration.

Conversely, the problems which present themselves in the Common law in terms of the discretionary and therefore illusory character of a promise (and they are in practice few) usually concern the enforceability of the other party's promise. The party who promises 'if I feel like it' or who effectively attaches to his promise a clause exempting himself from all liability for its breach, gives no consideration for the other party's promise. The example of the 'requirements' contract[10] illustrates the difference in the ways in which the two systems operate. A agrees to sell to B for £100 a ton as much coal as B may order in the next six months, up to a maximum of 1,000 tons. In the French analysis there is a potestative condition, but B can nevertheless, as explained above, enforce the contract, though A cannot do so (except of course to the extent of requiring payment for whatever B may in fact order) and cannot even withdraw from the contract. In the Common law there is no consideration for A's promise, which is therefore usually regarded as a mere offer. If B places an order he *pro tanto* accepts A's offer, but A can at any time before such acceptance revoke his offer.

It can thus be seen that the French doctrine of the potestative condition and the Common law doctrine of the discretionary promise set out to answer different questions and in the outcome produce different practical results. What the two systems have to a considerable extent in common are the criteria by which they determine whether or not a condition is purely potestative or a promise is discretionary. We saw that the French criteria can be said to be (i) Is the promisor economically free to escape from his promise? (ii) Is his freedom subject to any external check and in particular to control by the courts? The Common law can be seen as adopting the same criteria, but in regard to the second the Common law, with its tradition of invoking the criterion of what is reasonable, is more likely to hold that an apparently subjective discretion is to be objectively construed. This difference of approach can be

10 See Adams (1978) 94 LQR 73.

illustrated by the attitude of the two systems to the requirement that there should in a contract of sale be a price. The *Code civil* (article 1591), following in the Roman law tradition, requires that the price should be 'fixed and specified by the parties' and though interpretation allows this to include determination by reference to external criteria, such as market prices, it does not go as far as to permit the reasonable price of the Common law, still less to accept as valid a sale which leaves the price to be fixed by one of the parties. In the Common law, by contrast, it seems clear that such a contract would be valid,[11] the fixing to be done in good faith and therefore under the ultimate control of the courts. This readiness of Common law courts to interpret objectively provisions which French courts would regard as being left to the discretion of the parties still further reduces the area within which the rule as to purely potestative conditions has a counterpart in the rule as to illusory consideration. Moreover, it is unlikely that a Common law court would be as ready as French courts, as we have seen, have sometimes been recently to intervene to protect a party who, without inequality of bargaining power, has committed himself economically to the discretion of the other party. In the cases, for example, of the loan repayable on the borrower's selling his flat or of the purchase price of land repayable on the buyer's reselling,[12] a Common law court would be likely to go no further than to interpret the condition objectively, so as to require reasonable steps to be taken for its fulfilment.

B Effects on third parties[13]

1 General principle of relative effect

This is the French counterpart of the doctrine of privity. Article 1165 Cc provides that:

11 *Benjamin's Sale of Goods* (2nd edn) s. 183; cf Uniform Commercial Code (USA) 2-305(2). This matter presents difficulties in connexion with 'solus' agreements. For the French treatment of this and other aspects of such agreement see Ghestin D 1973 Chr 293.
12 Paris 15.3.1974 (p. 157, n. 5, above) and Cass civ 8.10.1980 (p. 158, n. 12, above).
13 Zweigert/Kötz vol 2, pp. 134 ff.

Agreements have effect only between the parties to them; they impose no burdens on third parties and confer benefits on them only in the case provided for in article 1121 [which deals with the *stipulation pour autrui*].[14]

Both systems therefore start from the same principle, and for the same reasons. Both systems, however, have been driven by the demands of justice and convenience to admit exceptions to the general principle, and it is with those exceptions in French law, and particularly with the *stipulation pour autrui*, that we are here principally concerned. But before we come to the exceptions the French approach to the principle itself needs some elucidation.

a *Opposabilité*
The first sentence of article 1165 is not precisely accurate. An agreement may have an effect on a third party in that he cannot ignore its legal consequences or that its existence enables him to found a claim.

'The doctrine of privity', it has been said[15] of English law,

means that a person cannot acquire rights or be subjected to liabilities *arising under* a contract to which he is not a party. It does not mean that a contract cannot legally . . . affect third parties. Thus. . . a contract may affect third parties by creating proprietary or quasi proprietary rights . . . or by giving rise to a duty of care to a third party . . . Also more generally it may be said that although a contract primarily creates rights and duties enforceable by the contracting parties against each other, it also incidentally imposes on third parties the duty not to interfere with the contracting parties in performing the contract.

The same is in substance true of French law, but the language used is different. The fact of the contract and its consequences, it is said, are 'opposable' to and by third parties, i e they may be invoked against third parties and by them.

A contract may be opposable *to* a third party either in that it creates a proprietary right which can be set up against him if he makes a claim of ownership (*revendication*), or in that it creates a relationship interference with which, if culpable, is

14 On art 1119 see p. 170, below.
15 Treitel *Contract* p. 477.

an actionable wrong. This interference may take the form of inducing a breach of the contract[16] or even knowingly collaborating in its breach (e g by agreeing to buy a thing over which the plaintiff had a prior option).[17]

Conversely a contract may be opposable *by* a third party when he suffers damage as a result of the non-performance or misperformance of the contract by one of the parties to it. The defective performance constitutes a fault which is sufficient to found an action in delict. For example, where the defendant had entered into a contract with the state to incarcerate German prisoners of war, and some of the prisoners had been enabled by his negligence to escape and then while at large had stolen three of the plaintiff's sheep, the plaintiff obtained damages in delict. On a strict analysis, of course, the plaintiff's action was not based on the defendant's failure to perform his contractual duty, but on the fault which was involved in that failure.[18] And so the *Cour de cassation*, in a formula which recurs in cases such as this, said:

> A failure to discharge a contractual obligation can constitute in relation to a third party a fault which entails liability, when this fault has an existence which is independent of the contract.

The same is, of course, true of English law (the tort in *Donoghue v Stevenson*[19] arose out of, but was nevertheless independent of, a breach of contract with the person who bought the ginger-beer), but we do not express it in these terms. This is mainly because the basis of the action in tort is negligence and negligence is irrelevant to an action for breach of contract, whereas in French law fault is ordinarily the basis of both actions.[20] Moreover, the French law of delict has no requirement of a duty of care owed to the plaintiff. The plaintiff has simply to show that the defendant was at fault and that the damage resulted from that fault. The problem posed for

16 Cass civ 27.5.1908, DP 1908.1.459, S 1910.1.118, *Source-book* p. 483.
17 Cass civ 13.11.1927, D 1929.1.131.
18 Cass civ 3.12.1953, JCP 1954.II.8025 note Savatier.
19 [1932] AC 562.
20 Actions in delict have, however, been admitted even where fault is not the basis of the contractual action, as in the case of the *garantie* against latent defects (p. 54, above) Cass req 8.3.1937, DH 1937.217; Cass civ 8.6.1948, JCP 1949.II.4778; Cass req 5.5.1924, DH 1924.433.

English law by the 'unforeseeable plaintiff' presents itself in French law, if it presents itself at all, in the guise of a problem of causation.

The independence of the two faults, on which the *Cour de cassation* insists, is nevertheless important. A contractual exemption clause, for example, will be no bar to the action in delict.

b Who is a third party?

What constitutes from the English point of view the first exception to the principle of relative effect is found in the interpretation which French law puts on the term 'third party' (*tiers*). Like other Civil law systems, French law expresses the acquisition of rights or duties by one person from another in terms of succession, and the succession may be either universal or singular. Universal succession occurs on death, when the dead man's *patrimoine*,[1] comprising both rights and liabilities, passes as a whole to his heir (or to his heirs, if more than one, jointly). Singular succession, on the other hand, occurs when there is a transfer from one person to another of one or more particular rights, whether they are real rights, as in a sale of immovable or movable property, or personal rights, as in an assignment (*cession de creance*). Universal succession presents no problem in the present context. The universal successor (*ayant cause à titre universal*) stands in the place of the dead man and succeeds to his 'patrimonial' rights and liabilities. He is not a third party. And although English law does not have the concept of universal succession, we have no difficulty in accepting that in general a dead man's rights and, to the extent of his assets, his liabilities pass to his personal representatives. In both systems one must make exceptions for contractual rights and duties which are personal to the deceased either because the parties so agreed[2] or because of the nature of the *prestation* involved (e g a contract by a painter to paint a picture).[3]

It is in relation to the singular successor (*ayant cause à titre particulier*) that the two systems diverge. In both of course it is

1 See p. 28, above.
2 Art 1122 Cc.
3 See also arts 1795, 2003 Cc.

obvious, on the one hand, that in the case of acquisitions of a proprietary character the singular successor takes, along with the property and subject to requirements of notice or registration, those benefits or burdens of a 'real' character, such as servitudes (easements), which attach to it and modify its content; and, on the other hand, that in the case of assignments he takes, as English law puts it, subject to the equities.[4] But as far as benefits are concerned French law goes further and allows the singular successor to enforce rights which, while having in general no 'real' character, can be said to be accessory to the thing acquired. For example, it has long been established that the purchaser of a movable can sue the original supplier or an earlier vendor on the statutory warranty against latent defects[5] or that the purchaser of a house can claim for defects under the guarantee in his vendor's contract with the architect or builder,[6] or that a purchaser of a business can sue on an undertaking not to compete given by an earlier vendor.[7]

French law's readiness to allow the transmission of such accessory rights was made easier by the very wide scope which, as we shall see,[8] has been given to the *stipulation pour autrui*. Some writers have indeed been prepared to see this as the basis for the transmission of accessory rights and to argue for a much wider extension. There would on this view (which finds some support in article 1122 Cc) be a presumption of an intention to benefit the singular successor unless the contrary were proved. The *jurisprudence* has, however, on the whole adhered to the requirement that the right transmitted should be accessory. But the criterion is not always easy to apply. On the one hand it is clear, for example, that the purchaser of a tenanted building cannot claim rent due before the purchase was made or that the purchaser of a business cannot enforce trading debts incurred to the vendor before the sale.[9] It is less obvious that a purchaser of land which is held by a tenant under a lease

4 Arts 1615, 1692, 2112 Cc.
5 Cass civ 12.11.1884, DP 1885.1.357.
6 Paris 14.1.1906, DP 1907.2.391; Cass civ 4.2.1963, S 1963.193.
7 Cass req 18.5.1868, DP 1869.1.366, S 1868.1.246.
8 Pp. 175 ff, below.
9 Cass req 16.7.1889, D 1890.1.440, S 1892.1.119. (It is assumed in this discussion that there is no assignment or subrogation.)

made by the vendor cannot claim resolution of the lease on the ground of a breach by the tenant before the purchase was made,[10] and still less perhaps that the purchaser of defective goods, although he can sue the original vendor for damages under the guarantee against latent defects, cannot claim resolution of the contract.[11] The *rationale*, however, in all these cases is that the claim for damages is part of the thing in that it compensates for the defects and brings the value of the thing up to what it should have been, whereas the claim for resolution is more specifically related to the contract between the original parties. Even so, however, it is difficult to justify the decision[12] which, after the sale of a plot of land subject to a covenant to use it only for residential purposes, denied to purchasers of adjoining plots the protection of the covenant. It has to be said, however, that, by contrast with the English law of easements, French law does not limit the categories of servitude which can be created by grant[13] and therefore that the restriction in question could have been, but was not, embodied in a servitude.

What has been said so far relates only to the transmission of benefits. As far as burdens are concerned, while a singular successor may expressly or implicitly accept his predecessor's duties or liabilities and while he cannot of course succeed to the rights arising under a synallagmatic contract without also accepting the burdens, there is in general no succession. This exclusion of succession to accessory burdens would be readily explicable if the succession to accessory rights were seen as founded on an implied *stipulation pour autrui* or an implied assignment. For neither of these institutions allows the transmission of burdens. But, apart from other difficulties, such a foundation cannot, as we have seen, explain the emphasis on the accessory character of the rights transmitted, a feature which has no place in either the *stipulation pour autrui* or assignment. The exclusion of the transmission of accessory

10 Cass civ. 8.5.1917, D 1917.1.99, S 1921.1.25; cf Carbonnier RT (1958) 421.
11 Cass com 27.2.1973, D 1974 note Malinvaud, JCP 1973.II.17445 note Savatier; cf Cornu RT (1973) 582.
12 Cass civ 29.3.1933, DH 1933.282.
13 This is not, however, universally admitted: see Weill *Droit civil - Les biens* s. 10.

burdens is presumably founded on the general repugnance to the imposition of burdens without notice and without the consent of the person to be burdened, a repugnance which itself underlies the restriction of the *stipulation pour autrui* and assignment to the transmission of rights.

To the general exclusion of the transmission of accessory burdens there are some statutory exceptions. Thus the *Code civil* itself provides[14] for the continuation of tenancies when an immovable is sold and more recent legislation has provided, for example, for the continuation of contracts of employment entered into by a business when that business is sold or otherwise changes its legal character.[15]

2 Exceptions to the principle of relative effect

a Agency (*représentation*)

Although in English treatments of privity this is usually presented as an exception, it is not so seen in French law. And there is good reason for this. For even in English law it can be argued that in the ordinary case where the agent contracts for a named principal and within the limits of his authority there is no departure from the principle of privity since the agent is an instrument or extension of the principal, who is himself the real contracting party.[16] And so article 1119 Cc says: 'One cannot in general enter into an engagement or make a stipulation in *one's own name* except for oneself.'[17] In English law, however, the principal may be entitled or bound in a number of situations which go beyond this ordinary case and are not compatible with the principle of privity.[18] The French law of agency, on the other hand, is more restrictive and does not recognise most of these situations. In particular, the doctrine of the undisclosed principal is unknown. The agent must con-

14 Art 1743, al 1.
15 *Code du travail* art L 122-12, al 2.
16 But it can be objected that this imports a fiction, since the agent, unlike a mere messenger has discretion and it is his intention and conduct which are relevant. It is also inconsistent with the admission of agency on behalf of an incapable principal.
17 Italics added. 'Oneself' includes one's *ayants cause*.
18 Treitel *Contract* pp. 482 ff.

tract as agent and not in his own name. There is also no doctrine of agency of necessity, though the institution of *gestion d'affaires*[19] does allow an unauthorised person (the *gérant*) to intervene in the affairs of another (the *maître*) where such intervention is urgent and necessary in the interest of the *maître*. If in these conditions the *gérant* makes a contract with a third party in the name of the *maître*, the *maître* is liable and entitled on that contract.

Apart from *gestion d'affaires*, the clearest exception in the area of agency to the principle of relative effect is found in cases of apparent authority. The Code itself[20] protects the third party who is unaware that the agent's authority has been terminated, whether by revocation or by the death of the principal, and the courts have done likewise in other cases in which the third party has justifiably relied on the agent's apparent authority. But they have had difficulty in finding a satisfactory theoretical basis for these exceptions to the consensual principle. In English law the cases of apparent authority can be accommodated within the principle of estoppel, which debars the supposed principal from denying what can be construed as a representation, made to the third party and relied on by him, that the agent has authority. But French law, in common with other Civil law systems, has nothing to correspond to the rules of evidence of Common law systems and therefore no doctrine of estoppel. At first the liability of the supposed principal was founded on his fault in allowing the third party to think that the agent had the authority which he appeared to have, the most appropriate remedy being found not in damages but in a *réparation en nature* consisting in allowing the third party to 'oppose' the contract to the supposed principal. But in many such cases the finding of fault will be very artificial and in any event this approach through quasi-delict places the emphasis on the misconduct of the principal, whereas it should lie, as it does in the Common law approach through estoppel, on the justifiable reliance of the third party. Recent decisions have accordingly abandoned the approach through fault and have based the liability simply on the doctrine of the *acte apparent*, i e in this case on the third

19 Arts 1372–1375 Cc; Amos and Walton pp. 192 ff.
20 Arts 2005, 2009.

party's legitimate reliance on the 'apparent mandate'. The question of when reliance is legitimate has been answered either by requiring that the circumstances be such as to dispense the third party from verifying the existence of the agent's authority or by applying the maxim that 'common error makes law' (*communis error facit ius*) and requiring that the third party's error should be a 'common' one, or, as the Common lawyer would say, that it should be one which the reasonable man would make.[1]

b Assignment (*cession de créance*)

This also is not presented in French law as an exception to the principle of relative effect, though writers on English law usually treat it in the context of privity. For French law, as we have seen, it is an instance of singular succession or of the transmission of an obligation seen as a thing (as indeed in English law assignment is the transfer of a chose in action). The Code[2] places it in the context of the contract of sale under the heading of 'the transmission of *créances* and other incorporeal rights'. The main features of *cession de créance* are the same as those of assignment in English law (but without of course the complexities of the distinction between equitable and statutory assignment) and do not justify detailed exposition here.[3]

c *Promesse pour autrui*

The true exceptions to the principle of relative effect occur when the parties to a contract which they have made in their own names intend that rights or duties created by that contract should attach to a third party. Following the order of the Code, we deal first with the creation of duties, i e with a promise intended to bind the third party. Article 1165 Cc[4] excludes the imposition of burdens on third parties, and there are obvious reasons of policy for this, but article 1120 appears to make an

1 On this development see Starck, ss. 1207-1216; Weill/Terré s. 82.
2 Arts 1689-1701.
3 See Starck ss. 2317-2347; Weill/Terré ss. 956-977.
4 P. 165, above.

exception in the form of a qualification of the proposition, already quoted,[5] in article 1119.

Art 1120 Nevertheless one can make oneself a *porte-fort* for a third party by promising that he will do something; but if the third party refuses to maintain the undertaking, an indemnity will be required from the person who has made himself a *porte-fort* or has promised that the third party will ratify.

The *porte-fort* is someone who undertakes that a third party will do something. If the third party ratifies the promise (or a fortiori if he does the promised thing), the *porte-fort* is released; if the third party does not ratify, the *porte-fort* must indemnify the promisee. A *porte-fort* therefore differs from a surety (*caution*) in that the latter's promise is accessory to a simultaneous or pre-existing promise made by the principal debtor, whereas the promise of the *porte-fort* is never accessory, but on the contrary is fulfilled and discharged by the making of the principal debtor's promise (i e by the ratification). If that promise is subsequently broken, the *porte-fort*, unlike the surety, incurs no liability.

Now it is obvious that since the third party is entirely free to ratify or not,[6] the promise of the *porte-fort* constitutes no exception to the principle of relative effect. Some writers[7] do indeed find a tenuous exception in the fact that if the third party does ratify, the ratification relates back to the moment when the *porte-fort* gave his undertaking and the third party is therefore bound by the undertaking before he has acceded to it, but the truth is, as we shall see[8] in more detail when we consider the parallel but more important case of the *stipulation pour autrui*, that the proposition in article 1119, though nowadays it is treated as premonitorily enunciating the principle of relative effect (which is set out in article 1165), was intended, at least in the context from which the draftsmen took it, to set out a different, though related, principle.

5 P. 170, above.
6 Except where the intervention of the *porte-fort* constitutes a *gestion d'affaires* (see art 1375 Cc); but this exception derives from the institution of *gestion d'affaires* (p. 171, above), not from that of the *porte-fort*.
7 E g Carbonnier s. 56.
8 Pp. 175–177, below.

Article 1165 declares that a promise which purports to benefit or burden a third party has no effect on that party; article 1119 says that such a promise (unless made by an agent) is without effect even on the parties themselves. This is an echo of Roman law which, like many other such echoes, comes into the Code through Pothier. The Roman lawyers had argued that the content of a contractual obligation must be some act or forbearance by the party obliged. A promise that someone else will act or forbear must either be empty, as being impossible of fulfilment, or be construed as a promise that the promisor will ensure that the other acts or forbears.[9] Similarly, a promise by a seller that the thing sold is free from defects or has certain qualities was said to be without effect. For if the statement was true it was superfluous, and if it was false it was the promise of an impossibility. To be effective the promise must be construed as one to ensure that the thing should be free from defects etc.[10] Accordingly it is under the heading of the *objet* of the obligation that Pothier[11] places the principle which was to appear in article 1119. And the *porte-fort* is accommodated without any difficulty, since his promise is precisely that envisaged in the Roman argument, viz to ensure that the third party does the thing promised. In the Code itself article 1119 appears, less happily, under the heading of 'consent', and subsequent commentators had to justify the principle on the ground that one who intends to confer a benefit or burden on a third party (an intention which article 1165 declares for other reasons to be ineffective) cannot intend to confer a benefit or burden on himself. This explanation, of course, leaves the *porte-fort* unaccounted for and leads to the forced attempt, mentioned above, to make him an exception to the principle of relativity.

There is in fact no exception in the *Code civil* unless agency or assignment are seen as exceptions) to the principle that a contract cannot impose a burden on a third party. Modern legislation has, however, by-passed the principle in the case of collective labour contracts.[12]

9 *Inst Just* III.193; *Dig* 45.1.38 pr.
10 *Dig* 21.2.31.
11 *Obligations* s. 56.
12 Aubry and Rau *Cours de droit civil français* vol IV (6th edn) s. 343 ter; Baudry-Lacantinerie *Droit civil-Obligations* (3rd edn) vol 1, ss. 128, 129, 145.

d *Stipulation pour autrui*

We now come to the main exception to the principle of relative effect. Article 1165 Cc provides, we have seen, that contracts can confer benefits on third parties 'only in the case provided for in article 1121'. That article, which follows immediately on the treatment of the *porte-fort*, runs as follows:

> One can likewise stipulate for the benefit of a third party when this is the condition of a stipulation which one makes for oneself or of a gift which one makes to another. The person who made the stipulation cannot revoke it if the third party has declared that he wishes to take advantage of it.

One must distinguish between the meaning which the draftsmen may have intended that this rather obscurely framed provision should bear and the meaning which the courts have given to it.

i *Historical background*

As in the case of the *promesse pour autrui*, the intended[13] meaning of the text can only be understood in the light of its Roman origins and again they are set out by Pothier. As with the preceding articles, we are primarily concerned, not with the principle of relativity, but with the principle that a promise for the benefit of a third party is without effect even as between the parties to it. If the promisor, P, promises the stipulator,[14] S, to pay the third party beneficiary, T, it is for the Roman lawyer[15] and for Pothier[16] self-evident that the principle of relativity (to use the modern French term) prevents T from suing P, but in the ordinary case the law also denies any action to S. For S will have no interest, unless, for example, he is indebted to T and the purpose of the agreement is that P shall pay that debt. It is, however, possible for S to create such an interest by so framing the stipulation that P promises to pay T or, in default of such payment, to pay a penalty to S.[17] The

---

13 We are left here to inference, since there was no discussion of arts 1119 and 1121 when the text was approved.

14 French law uses the language of Roman law, in which the stipulator is the promisee; Nicholas *Roman Law* p. 193.

15 *Inst Just* III.19.19.

16 *Obligations* ss. 53–60.

17 *Obligations* s. 70. Until recently French law, like Roman law, placed no restriction on penalty clauses as such; see pp. 226, 229 ff, below.

effective promise is then to pay the penalty; the payment to T (or rather the non-payment) is the condition of this promise. This is the first case set out in article 1121, and Pothier, following the Roman texts, makes no mention of enforcement by T.

The second exception in article 1121 is made for the case where the stipulation for the third party is 'the condition of a gift which one makes to another'. This is the *donatio sub modo* of Roman law (the French term is *donation avec charges*), which Pothier discusses immediately after the penal stipulation.[18] In its essentials this is a gift by S to P, subject to a limit (which article 1121 treats as a stipulation) on the use to which the gift is to be put. In the Roman examples the limit might require P to erect a monument or to build a public bath, or it might require him to transfer the gift to T, perhaps after a certain time, or to use it in some way for the benefit of T. (The similarity to this extent to a trust is obvious.) If for any reason the purpose failed, S could obtain restitution from P, but in the classical Roman law T could not require performance. In this case however, unlike that of the penal stipulation, T's right had been recognized by the time of Justinian, perhaps because a *donatio* had more affinity with the law of succession or of property, where third party rights are familiar, than with the law of contract.

Pothier thus, following Roman law, gives different answers in the two cases included in article 1121. (i) In general, where P promises S to pay T, T has no action against P. Whether S has such an action depends on whether he has an interest, and S can create such an interest by stipulating for a penalty. (ii) Where S makes a *donation* to P, subject to a *charge* or stipulation in favour of T, T has an action against P to enforce the stipulation. Article 1121 reproduces Pothier's two cases, but without making any distinction between them. It seems, however, that long before Pothier's time T had been allowed an action outside the limits of case (ii), though it is not clear how far this extension went,[19] and Pothier makes no reference to it.

18 *Obligations* ss. 71 f.
19 Charondas *Responses de droict françois* (Paris, 1605) deals with the case where S, when selling land to P, exacts an undertaking from P that he will discharge debts in relation to the land which S owes T. He rejects the Roman refusal of an action by T against P as pedantry (*subtilité*) and

Article 1121 also, however, says that S cannot revoke the stipulation if T has declared that he wishes to take advantage of it. In Pothier, as in the Roman texts, the question of revocation is discussed only in relation to the *donation avec charges*, and this is not surprising since, as we have seen, it is only in this connexion that there is any mention of a right in T which could be affected by revocation. Article 1121 seems, however, to treat the restriction on revocation as applying both to the conditional stipulation and to the *donation avec charges* and therefore by implication to recognise a right in T in both cases. This is consistent also with article 1165, which treats the two cases as one ('Agreements . . . confer benefits on [third parties] only in *the case* provided for in article 1121'). In any event, as we shall see in the next section, any distinction between the two cases disappeared in the course of the interpretation of the article by the courts.

Article 1121, therefore, like article 1120, sets out to state an exception to the principle in article 1119, that an agreement between S and P which is intended to benefit or burden T, is of no effect even between S and P. The two instances which it gives are, unlike the one in article 1120, genuine exceptions to the principle, but they are also, more importantly, intended to be exceptions to the principle of relative effect, which is stated only later, in article 1165. This ambivalence of article 1121 leads modern writers, as we have seen, to read back the principle of relative effect into article 1119.

ii *Development by the courts*
For some fifty years after the enactment of the Code there seems to have been little interest in going beyond the instances

cites in support of this opinion two decisions, dating from 1536 and 1542, which were made in order to avoid the circuitousness which resulted from the Roman rule. It is not clear whether Charondas means to allow an action to T generally (case (i) in the text) or only where the stipulation relates to property which S conveys to T (i e an extension of case (ii) to any transfer of property, gratuitous or not, an extension for which there was authority in the glossators; Ripert/Boulanger p. 238). Modern writers (apparently following Ripert/Boulanger) erroneously relate the opinion of Charondas to the case of the *solutionis causa adiectus* (i e where P promises S to pay either S or T, T being added as an alternative payee).

in article 1121. Such decisions as are reported fall within the classical limits of the *donation avec charges* or are closely analogous to it.[20] The pressure for development came from the need to provide a legal framework for life assurance. The view, which had been strongly held,[1] that it was a moral evil was giving way to an appreciation of its merits in making provision for dependants,[2] but the principle of relativity stood in the way of allowing the benefit of the assurance to be enforceably conferred on anyone but the heir of the person assured; and if it were conferred on the heir it would be open to the claims of the creditors of the inheritance. The matter of life assurance is now regulated by a *loi* of 13 July 1930[3] and the actual decisions are therefore obsolete, but since they largely determined the character of the modern *stipulation pour autrui*, they are still significant.

The earliest reported case seems to be one in 1863[4] in which the *Cour d'appel* of Lyons declared flatly that life assurance contracts came within article 1121 and that the beneficiary's right, though not enforceable until the death of the assured, never entered the *patrimoine* of the dead man. This approach was consecrated by the *Cour de cassation* in 1884[5] in a decision which rejected the claim of creditors of the inheritance. There was still, however, the difficulty that article 1121 envisaged the stipulation in favour of the third party as being accessory to a principal stipulation in favour of the stipulator himself. The approach of the courts, which recognised a right created directly in the third party, seemed to overlook this. The difficulty was resolved by looking to what lay behind the device

---

20 See Ripert/Boulanger s. 637, with references.

 1 See the quotation from Portalis in *Source-book* p. 457.

 2 But even in 1864, in a criminal case in which the accused had been convicted of murdering a woman whose life he had assured, the *Procureur-général*, after an impassioned recital of famous cases of poisoning from Roman times onwards, had questioned the lawfulness of life assurance (but more with an eye on the legislator than on the courts); Cass crim 4.6.1864, D 1864.1.497 concl Dupin.

 3 Now embodied in the *Code des Assurances*, printed after art 1983 Cc in the *Petit Code Dalloz*.

 4 Lyon 2.6.1863, S 1863.2.202 concl Onofrio, *Source-book* p. 457.

 5 Cass civ 2.7.1884, S 1885.1.5 note Labbé, rapport Crépon, D 1885.1.150, *Source-book* p. 459.

of the principal and the accessory stipulation. As we saw, the device was adopted in order to overcome the objection that the stipulation was void for lack of an interest in the stipulator. Pothier had emphasised that the interest must be a pecuniary one and the device supplied such an interest in the shape of the penalty to be paid for non-performance of the accessory promise. The *Cour de cassation*, however, in a decision of 16 January 1888, blandly declared that a moral interest (in the case of life assurance, the assured's 'moral profit' from the advantage conferred on the beneficiaries) was sufficient.[6] It could indeed be said that in the parallel case of the *donation avec charges* the 'stipulator' had no more than an interest of this kind (and as far as life assurance is concerned the policy will normally give the assured a right to revoke during his life and this will give him a pecuniary interest), but the decision effectively neutralised the principle of relativity as far as it concerns the conferring of benefits. For it both by-passed the requirement of a principal and an accessory stipulation, and also reduced to nothing the underlying requirement of an interest in the stipulator. For no-one in his right mind will contract for a benefit to be conferred on a third party in whose welfare he does not have even a moral interest.

The total abandonment of the requirement of a principal stipulation is strikingly illustrated by a decision in 1934.[7] The life assurance policy in this case provided that the sum assured should be payable 'exclusively to the designated beneficiary or in default of such beneficiary to the wife of the assured'. The assured, having designated no beneficiary, died unmarried and without children and his father and sister, as heirs, claimed the sum assured. Under the *loi* of 13 July 1930 (article 66) their claim was expressly provided for, but the policy had been taken out before the *loi* came into effect. They relied therefore on article 1122 Cc, which provides that:

> One is deemed to have stipulated for oneself and one's heirs and *ayants cause* unless the contrary is expressly stated or results from the nature of the agreement.

6 Cass civ 16.1.1888, D 1888.1.77, S 1888.1.121, *Source-book* p. 461.
7 Cass req 15.5.1934, D 1934.1.141 rapport Pilon, Gaz Pal 1934.2.252, *Source-book* p. 464; see Mazeaud/Mazeaud pp. 760 ff.

But the court had no difficulty in finding that the clause quoted above did state the contrary by excluding everyone except the designated beneficiary or the wife. No attempt was made to argue that if article 1122 did not apply and there was therefore no principal stipulation at all, the whole transaction must be void according to article 1121 and the heirs must be entitled to restitution. And this is not surprising nearly 50 years after the decision of 16 January 1888, but the plaintiffs could also have argued that even the stipulation for the third party was void for lack of a beneficiary. But to this the court could have replied that there could have been beneficiaries and that, since all insurance contracts are aleatory, a potential beneficiary is sufficient.[8]

In sum therefore the effect of these developments[9] was to establish that wherever it could be shown that an agreement[10] between S and P was intended to confer a benefit on T, T could claim the benefit from P. (In order to do so T must evidence an intention to accept the benefit, but since the making of the claim will be sufficient evidence, the practical importance of this requirement is that it preserves in the meantime S's power to revoke.)[11] T's right vests in him directly and retrospectively from the moment of the agreement between S and P and it does not therefore pass through the *patrimoine* of S, but it is nevertheless S's right to the extent that P can set up against T any defences which would have been available against S. Moreover, it is S's right in the sense also that S can proceed against P if P fails to perform the contract. S has all the remedies normally available to the plaintiff in a contractual action. Since in the ordinary case his interest will be no more than a moral one, the action for damages will be empty, but his interest is nevertheless sufficient to enable him, where

8 See Mazeaud/Mazeaud p. 761; a point made also by the *rapport*, in answer to a contention in the *pourvoi* that the defendant was unjustifiably enriched.

9 See also the five decisions reported in S 1888.1.121; cf *Source-book* pp. 463 f.

10 Which could be implied; see pp. 183 ff, below.

11 Since S's power can be exercised by his heirs and T might not know of his right until after S's death, this could produce injustice. The *loi* of 13.7.1930 therefore required notice to be given to T (now *Code des assurances* L 132-9).

T himself takes no steps, to claim either *résolution* of the contract or, as was laid down in an *arrêt de principe* in 1956,[12] its specific enforcement.

Once it was established that T's right vested in him immediately and retrospectively at the moment when the contract was made, the courts had to consider the effect of a contract in favour of persons who were either not yet in existence (as in the common case of a life insurance policy in favour of children as yet unborn) or not yet identified (as where goods which are likely to be sold while in transit are insured in favour of the eventual owner). To meet the objection that rights could only vest in determinate persons, such contracts were construed as conditional upon the beneficiary's being subsequently identified.[13] In the case of a beneficiary not yet in existence, however, this interpretation came up against a specific text. Article 906 Cc provides that the beneficiary of a *donation* must be conceived at the moment when it is made. Rather surprisingly, in view of their boldness elsewhere in this context, the courts felt bound to apply this provision to gratuitous (but not to onerous) *stipulations pour autrui* and policies in favour of unborn children were made valid only by the *loi* of 13 July 1930.

iii *Theoretical basis*
Before the end of the nineteenth century therefore the courts had in effect transformed what had originated as apparently a limited exception for 'the case provided for in article 1121' into a general principle of third party contractual rights. Such a breach with traditional doctrine did, however, cause misgivings and, before considering the uses to which the new-found principle was put, we may consider briefly the attempts which were made to find a theoretical foundation for it within the traditional system.

(a) *Theory of offer* In the early years of the development the accepted explanation was that S must be taken to have made an offer to T of the benefit of S's contract with P and that the

---

12 Cass civ 12.7.1956, D 1956.749 note Radouant, *Source-book* p. 465; cf *Beswick v Beswick* [1968] AC 58.
13 As to heirs see *Code des assurances* L 132-8; cf Weill/Terré pp. 609 f.

effect of T's acceptance of that offer was to substitute him for S. This explanation did the minimum damage to the principle of relative effect and also explained S's power of revocation. But it presented two difficulties. T would acquire his right from S and therefore would be vulnerable to the claims of S's creditors; and since an offer lapses with the death of the offeror, T would not be able to make his acceptance after S's death (as he would need to in the normal case of life assurance, where the beneficiary learns of his entitlement only after the assured's death). This theory was made finally untenable by a decision of the *Cour de cassation* on 8 February 1888,[14] which confirmed that the benefit vested directly in T at the moment of the making of the contract between S and P and rejected the suggestion that T's acceptance was governed by the principles which regulate the formation of contracts. There was no need, said the court, to go outside article 1121 itself.

(b) *Theory of* gestion d'affaires[15]   This explanation, favoured by the great *arrêtiste* Labbé, saw S's making of the contract with P as constituting a *gestion* of the *affaire* of T. T was therefore in a position by ratifying S's act to acquire retrospectively[16] a right against P. This accounted satisfactorily for the now clearly established rules (i) that T's right existed from the moment of S's agreement with P and (ii) that it was unaffected by the death of S or T. It could not, however, account for S's power, by revocation before T had accepted to destroy T's right, and it involved a considerable distortion of the concept of *gestion d'affaires*. For in the normal situation the *gérant* (i e in this case, S) acts on behalf of the *maître* (T) and not on his own account, and he expects, and is entitled, to be indemnified by the *maître* for any expenses which he 'usefully' incurs, whereas in the usual *stipulation pour autrui* S acts in his own name, as well as for the benefit of T (and hence has the power of revocation) and he is entitled to no indemnity.

(c) *Theory of unilateral juridical act*[17]   Some writers have attempted to apply here the idea that a man may be bound by

14 Cass civ 8.2.1888, S 1888.1.121, D 1888.1.193, *Source-book* p. 463; cf p. 18 n. 9, above.
15 See p. 171, above.
16 See p. 173, above.
17 See p. 35, above.

a unilateral act of his will. On this analysis there would be a contract between S and P and a unilateral act of P's will which binds him to confer the benefit on T. Apart from the general objections to the theory of the unilateral juridical act, this particular application encounters the obvious difficulty that it does not explain how S can have the right to revoke the benefit conferred on T or why P can set up against a claim by T the defences which would be available against S.

It is now accepted that, as the *Cour de cassation* indicated in its *arrêt* of 16 January 1888,[18] attempts such as these to fit the *stipulation pour autrui* into the traditional framework are unnecessary and misleading and that it is an independent institution resting on its own foundations.

iv *Applications other than life assurance*
As we have said, once the *stipulation pour autrui* is freed from the restrictions of the two instances given in article 1121 and from the requirement that S should have a pecuniary interest, it becomes of universal application and one can proceed only by way of illustration. Thus, as has already been remarked,[19] it was used to make effective insurance policies on goods in transit, the benefits of which attach to whoever is the owner of the goods at the time when the loss occurs. Again, where a public authority has made stipulations in its agreement with a contractor as to the conditions of service of the persons to be employed, those persons have been held entitled to enforce these stipulations. Or again, if the vendor of an immovable sells it on terms that the purchaser will pay off the mortgage debt, the mortgagee will be able to claim the debt from the purchaser. The *stipulation pour autrui* can also be used in the case of sales of goods to successive purchasers to make the original purchaser's rights against the original vendor run with the goods.[20]

A less predictable development came from the possibility of an implied stipulation. In a case decided by the *Cour de*

18 See p. 179, n. 6, above.
19 P. 181, above; Cass civ 2.12.1891, DP 1892.1.161.
20 For these and other instances see Amos and Walton p. 176; Weill/Terré s. 533.

cassation on 6 December 1932,[1] the plaintiff's husband had been killed while travelling as a passenger on the railway. There was no evidence of negligence and therefore no action in quasi-delict under article 1382 Cc would lie. In accordance with the settled rule governing passenger transport[2] the railway was under an *obligation de sécurité* to the dead man, but if the plaintiff sued as his heir, she could be met by the contention that since his death had been instantaneous he had suffered no damage. The court, however, held that she was entitled to sue, in her own name and in respect of her own damage, in virtue of a *stipulation pour autrui* impliedly made by her husband when he bought his ticket. The governing principle was said to be that 'in case of a fatal accident occurring in the course of the performance of the contract, the right to obtain compensation, in virtue of article 1147 Cc, is open to the relict and the children of the dead person, who made a stipulation in their favour to the extent of their interest, there being no need for the stipulation to be express'.

A problem presents itself, however, if an implied stipulation is allowed to arise merely from the making of a contract the non-performance of which will cause loss to a third party. In the United States, where (outside Massachusetts) there is no general rule against third party rights arising by way of contract, it is known as the problem of the 'incidental beneficiary'.[3] If, for example, A agrees with B to erect an expensive building on B's land and if the erection of such a building would enhance the value of C's adjoining land, the non-performance of the contract by A will cause loss to C but it would obviously be undesirable to allow such an incidental beneficiary to bring an action. Any such extension of the implied stipulation is excluded, in the statement of principle by the *Cour de cassation* which is set out above, by the restriction to the relict and the children of the contracting party.

1 Cass civ 6.12.1932, S 1934.1.81 note Esmein, D 1933.1.137 note Josserand, *Source-book* p. 467.
2 See p. 49, above.
3 See *Williston on Contracts* (3rd edn) s. 402; Calamari and Perillo *Contracts* 17-2; *Restatement-Contracts* s. 147.

That the stipulation would not be freely implied was emphasised by a decision in a similar case in the next year.[4] The plaintiff in this case was the dead man's sister, who was entirely supported by him. The *Cour de cassation* ruled that 'while a traveller who is the victim of a fatal accident must be presumed to have made a stipulation for the benefit of the persons to whom he owes a duty of support by virtue of a legal bond, such a presumption cannot be extended to the case in which the plaintiff cannot, as in the present instance, adduce any duty of this kind'. Since the legal duty of support does not extend to brothers and sisters, the plaintiff's claim was rejected.

On the other hand, where a hospital asked the defendant, a blood transfusion centre, to provide a donor of blood for the plaintiff, a patient in the hospital, and the centre, without fault on its part, provided a donor who had syphilis, which was transmitted to the plaintiff, the *Cour de cassation* found a *stipulation pour autrui* in favour of the plaintiff to be implicit in the contract between the hospital and the defendant centre and the plaintiff was therefore entitled to damages under article 1147 Cc for breach of the *obligation de sécurité* which was inherent in the contract.[5]

There has been little discussion of the criterion to be applied in determining whether or not a *stipulation pour autrui* should be implied in favour of a particular plaintiff. The question of intention is now clearly irrelevant (except in the unlikely event of there being evidence of an intention *not* to benefit the plaintiff). In his note[6] to the decisions of 6 December 1932 and 24 May 1933 Esmein took the view that the reference to the stipulation was no more than a manner of speaking, expressing the conclusion that the third party's right attached to the contract. No-one doubted, he said, that what the *Cour de cassation* intended was to establish a legal rule that the relatives of persons carried by the railway had a right in their

4 Cass civ 24.5.1933 (reported with Cass civ 6.12.1932, above).
5 Cass civ 17.12.1954, D 1955.269 note Rodière, JCP 1955.II.8490 note Savatier, *Source-book* p. 472. The claim had been framed in delict, but the *Cour de cassation* chose to treat it as contractual. In view of this it can be objected (see the note by Rodière) that there had never been an acceptance by the plaintiff.
6 P. 164, nn. 1 and 4, above.

own names to an indemnity in case of accident. And it is consistent with this that in the decision in the blood transfusion case the court said simply that since the purpose of the contract was to get a donor for the plaintiff, it followed that the contract was accompanied by a stipulation in the plaintiff's favour. The criterion to be applied is presumably the imprecise one of remoteness or foreseeability. It seems that in the blood transfusion case the request for the donor was made for a particular patient, who was the plaintiff. It is not clear whether the stipulation would have been implied at large for all patients in the hospital, but it presumably would not have been implied in favour of a fourth party who caught the syphilis from the plaintiff.

v *Conclusion*

The developments which we have considered, coupled with the doctrine of accessory rights,[7] have given to French law a flexible general principle of third party rights arising by way of contract. Nor is it easy (subject to what has been said about the implied stipulation) to make an objection of policy to the institution when it is contained within the limits set out above. English law is indeed an exception among western systems in not having a general principle of third party rights. It is true that for a Common law system the doctrine of consideration creates a difficulty but, as has already been said, United States jurisdictions, except for Massachusetts, recognise the general principle. The Law Revision Committee's proposal of 1937[8] would have brought English law close to the French position. The Committee recommended that:

> Where a contract by its express terms purports to confer a benefit directly on a third party, the third party shall be entitled to enforce the provision in his own name, provided that the promisor shall be entitled to raise as against the third party any defence that would have been valid against the promisee. The rights of the third party shall be subject to cancellation of the contract by the mutual consent of the contracting parties at any time before the third party has adopted it either expressly or by conduct.

7 Pp. 168 f, above. The two doctrines are complementary.
8 On which see Treitel *Contract* pp. 495 f.

The chief difference lies in the words 'express terms' and 'directly' which were evidently intended to deal with the problem posed by the 'incidental beneficiary'[9] and which would, of course, exclude the implied stipulation. There is also the difference that 'cancellation' requires the consent of both contracting parties, whereas in French law 'revocation' is the act of the stipulator alone, but this reflects rather a difference in the conceptual background than any important divergence in practice. For, as we have seen, the *stipulation pour autrui* originates as a unilateral transaction in which S is creditor and P debtor, whereas the Common law background of consideration pre-supposes a bilateral transaction.

e *Action oblique, action Paulienne, action directe*

Following the statement of the principle of relative effect and the reference to the exception for the *stipulation pour autrui* in article 1165, the Code goes on in the next two articles to what it presents as two further exceptions or qualifications. These are two remedies available to creditors which go under the names of *action oblique* or *indirecte* and *action Paulienne* or *révocatoire* (derived from but not identical with the Roman *actio Paulianna*).[10] The first enables a creditor of an insolvent debtor to bring the debtor's actions ('except those which are purely personal') and the second enables a creditor to revoke the effects, as far as that creditor is concerned, of a transaction entered into by the debtor to the prejudice of the creditor ('in fraud of his rights').

Neither action in fact constitutes an exception to the principle of relative effect. The oblique action is brought in the name of the debtor and the purpose of the Paulian is to assert rather than to deny the principle, since it protects the creditor (i e the third party) from being affected by the transaction into which the debtor has entered. They are in fact an aspect of the French treatment of insolvency, a treatment which is radically different from that of English law. For French law has a system of bankruptcy (i e the orderly administration of the insolvent's affairs as a whole for the benefit of all his creditors) only in the

9 P. 184, above.
10 Buckland *Textbook of Roman Law* (3rd edn) p. 596.

case of merchants. If a non-merchant becomes insolvent, each creditor is left to protect his interests as best he can. The details of these two actions and of other methods of protection open to creditors are complicated and fall outside the scope of this book.[11]

The oblique action is in fact of little interest to the creditor because any benefit which he derives from bringing it will have to be shared with the other creditors. In a few cases legislation has provided 'direct actions' which are free of this disadvantage. We may mention two in the Code and one outside. Where a tenant who has sub-let fails to pay his rent, the landlord may claim against the sub-tenants to the extent of the rent which they owe to the tenant.[12] Building workers may claim their wages from the person who has commissioned the building to the extent to which he is indebted to their employer.[13] And the *loi* of 13 July 1930 has been interpreted as giving an injured third party a direct action against the insurer to the extent of the sum assured in a third party accident policy.[14] These actions are true exceptions to the principle of relative effect.[15]

f Simulation

i Nature
For one reason or another the parties may agree to conceal the true nature of their agreement behind the facade of a sham transaction. In French terminology the act of concealment is termed *simulation* and the hidden agreement, whether written or oral, is referred to as a *contre-lettre*. (Scots law uses the terms 'back-letter' or 'back-bond'.) The problems which arise from such transactions do of course come before English courts, but we are not accustomed to their being treated under a single heading. We see them, according to the context in which they arise, as questions either of the proof of the true

11 See Amos and Walton ch XI; Weill/Terré ss. 849 ff.
12 Art 1759 Cc.
13 Art 1798 Cc. For another case see art 1994.
14 *Code des assurances* L 124-3; the interpretation was necessary because on its face the text says only that the insurer may not pay to anyone else.
15 As are comparable legislative interventions in English law, such as Road Traffic Act 1970, s. 148(4).

content of the contract, or of illegality or, as far as third parties are concerned, of estoppel. The French courts and *doctrine*, however, starting from a single article in the *Code civil*,[16] have elaborated a set of rules. One might expect these rules to be treated in connexion with the formation and validity of contracts, but that would lay the emphasis on the effect of the transaction as between the parties to it, whereas the more difficult question is that of the effect on third parties. The matter is therefore commonly treated in connexion with the principle of relative effect, to which *simulation* is seen as offering an exception.

Simulation may take various forms and have various motives, both licit and (much more commonly) illicit. (a) The sham transaction may be entirely illusory, the parties intending their relationship to remain unaltered. For example where a debtor wishes to put an asset out of the reach of his creditors he may make an ostensible sale accompanied by a secret agreement with the buyer that the transaction shall have no effect. Here the motive is obviously illicit. (b) The secretly intended transaction may be different in its legal character from the ostensible one, as in the case of a *donation déguisée*.[17] The motive will usually again be illicit. The 'seller' may wish to defeat one of the legal restrictions on gifts, such as the rule which reserves to certain heirs a 'reserved share'.[18] Or he may wish to make a gift to his mistress which would, unless concealed, be null for *cause illicite*.[19] But he may have a perfectly licit and even laudable reason for wishing to hide his generosity. (c) The two transactions may differ only in some term, as where the price or the rent to be paid is understated in the ostensible transaction, the motive being usually to evade tax. (d) The ostensible transaction may conceal the identity of one of the parties, as where the intention is to make a gift to a person who is legally disabled from receiving gifts;[20] the gift is made to another person who secretly undertakes to make it over to the disabled person.

16 Art 1321; see below.
17 P. 141, above.
18 Discussed above, pp. 140 ff.
19 See p. 125, above.
20 Art 911 Cc; cf art 1099 al 2.

The case of the undisclosed principal is superficially similar to the case in (d), but it is better analysed as the converse of (a). When the agent (who in this instance is called a *prête-nom*) makes his contract with the third party, he conceals the existence of the contract of mandate between himself and his principal. There is ostensibly no contract between them,[1] but secretly there is a contract of mandate. We have already said that in French law the agent in this case is liable to the third party, but that the third party is not liable to the undisclosed principal. We shall find that the rules of *simulation* entitle the third party to prove the existence of the *contre-lettre* constituted by the secret contract of mandate and therefore to sue the undisclosed principal. The motives of the undisclosed principal and the *préte-nom* are, of course, licit.

ii *Effects*

Article 1321 Cc provides that:

> *Contre-lettres* can have effect only between the parties to them; they have no effect on third parties.[2]

(a) *Between the parties* Article 1321 applies in this respect the general principle, expressed in article 1134,[3] that the parties are bound by what they have agreed. The will of the parties is the foundation of a contract and effect must be given to it, provided that it can be proved in accordance with the ordinary rules. If the ostensible transaction was oral, there is no obstacle to oral proof of the *contre-lettre*, unless of course its content is such as to require writing.[4] But (commercial transactions apart) if the ostensible transaction was in writing,

---

1 It is therefore perhaps not strictly a case of *simulation*, since there is no simulated transaction; see Marty/Raynaud s. 273; Perrot & Wiederkehr J-Cl Civ art 1321, fasc 138, s. 2.

2 Art 1321 is placed in the context of the rules governing the proof of obligations and in particular written proof. The reason for this lies in a confusion between two meanings of *contre-lettre*. In a wide sense it denotes, as has been said above, the hidden agreement, which, though it may be in writing, need not be so. But in a narrow sense it may denote the written document, if there is one. Cf the similar confusion in the case of *remise de dette*, p. 141, n. 9, above.

3 P. 31, above.

4 See art 1341 Cc; cf pp. 56 ff, above.

the *contre-lettre* must also be in writing,[5] or there must be 'a commencement of written proof'.[6] (A strict application of the parol evidence rule in English law would produce the same result, but by treating the ostensible act and its secret variation not, as French law does, as two separate acts, but as a single transaction, the courts have been able to say that the parties did not intend that transaction to be wholly in writing and have therefore accepted extrinsic evidence to establish the secret element.)[7] All this is subject to the overriding rule that if the purpose of the transaction was illicit, the *contre-lettre* may be freely proved.

In general therefore the law gives effect, as between the parties, to a properly evidenced *contre-lettre*. But we have seen that the purpose of the parties will commonly be illicit and this might be thought to vitiate the entire transaction. For the English lawyer, who looks at the two agreements as a single transaction, the legal effect will depend on whether, in the particular circumstances in which the case comes before the court, the party relying on the transaction can do so without revealing the illicit element.[8] The French lawyer, however, does not see the matter in this relative way. The two acts are separate. Prima facie, as between the parties, the *contre-lettre* is valid, but only, obviously, on the same terms as it would be if it were not secret. In particular, if its cause is illicit it will be null and the question will then shift to the validity of the sham transaction, in the same way as it would if the *contre-lettre*, though licit, were not provable. The illicitness of the *contre-lettre* will not taint the sham transaction. This can be seen in two particular instances in which *contre-lettres* are declared by *loi* to be null.

Certain public offices (*offices ministériels*), such as those of *notaire* or of *avocat* before the *Conseil d'Etat* and the *Cour de cassation*, are heritable and assignable, but the state seeks to control the price which is exacted from the assignee.[9] A *contre-*

---

5 To this the *donation déguisée* p. 189, above, provides a surprising exception; see Weill/Terré s. 572 and, more fully, Mazeaud/Mazeaud vol 4.2, ss. 1479 ff.

6 See p. 58, above.

7 See Treitel *Contract* pp. 140 f; Law Commission Working Paper No. 70.

8 *Chettiar v Chettiar* [1962] 1 All ER 494.

9 See p. 136, above.

lettre fixing a price higher than that in the ostensible agreement is therefore declared void.[10] The same applies to concealment (for purposes of tax evasion) of the full price paid on sales of immovables or businesses or assignment of leases. The fact that the ostensible transaction in these cases is valid encourages the purchaser to reveal the illegality because he can do so without destroying the whole transaction.[11]

Doubts have been expressed[12] as to the desirability of this approach where the determining purpose of the whole transaction is tax evasion. On ordinary principles the transaction would be null for *cause illicite*, but the result of this, since the nullity would necessarily be absolute, would be to make a very large inroad on the principle, implicit in article 1321, that third parties can rely on the simulated transaction. To this we now turn.

(b) *As regards third parties*   We are not here concerned with third parties in the ordinary sense. It would be superfluous for article 1321 to say that against them *contre-lettres* have no effect, since this is already laid down in article 1165. The third parties envisaged in article 1321 are those persons who would otherwise be affected, i e the *ayants cause à titre particulier* and the creditors, to whom the *contre-lettre* would otherwise be *opposable*. If therefore A sells his house to B with a *contre-lettre* which deprives the sale of any effect, B's creditor, C, is entitled to treat the house as part of B's assets. Or if A lets his house to B at a secret rent which is lower than the ostensible one and if A then sells the house to C, C is entitled to claim the ostensible rent. In English law such transactions would raise questions of estoppel, with similar results. The English approach is in one respect, however, conceptually tidier. If C

10 See Weill/Terré s. 571.
11 In another instance, however, both the *contre-lettre* and the sham transaction are void. Gifts between husband and wife, if openly made, are valid, but art 1099 al 2 Cc declares them void if hidden behind a simulated transaction. The purpose of this rule seems to be a deterrent one. The purpose of the donor will usually be, as we have seen, to evade the rules which protect the reserved share of his future heirs by entitling them to have gifts reduced or cancelled. The price of a detected evasion will be total nullity, whereas an openly made gift will be null only to the extent that the inheritance is insufficient to meet the claims of the heirs.
12 Marty/Raynaud s. 282; Weill/Terré s. 570 n.

in either of these examples was aware of the secret transaction he would be unable to set up an estoppel because he would not have relied on the ostensible transaction. The French rule, declaring the *contre-lettre* to be without effect against C, has to be qualified by importing a requirement of good faith.

Article 1321 says that *contre-lettres* have no effect *against* third parties and this is to be taken strictly. A third party may, if he wishes, assert the validity of the *contre-lettre* against the parties to it. (He does so, as does one of the parties who invokes the *contre-lettre* against the other party, by an *action en déclaration de simulation*.) In the first example given above, where A makes a purely fictitious sale to B, A's creditors may wish to invoke the *contre-lettre*. There is clearly here a possibility of conflict with B's creditors, who are entitled to rely on the simulated sale. For this conflict article 1321 provides no resolution and for a long time there was no consistency in the decisions of the courts. The matter is usually regarded as having been settled by a decision of the *Cour de cassation* in 1939[13] in favour of the creditor who relied on the simulated transaction. The court referred to 'error which the invincible force of appearances had provoked in the mind' of this creditor. This is seen as an expression of the wider doctrine of the *acte apparent*.[14] The ordinary person assumes the *acte apparent* (in this context the simulated transaction) to be genuine and this 'common error' makes law. In terms of policy this principle, like that of estoppel, allows the preservation of the security of transactions to prevail.

C Limits of contractual obligation - effect of supervening obstacle to performance

1 General

In the traditional Common law view, as we have remarked already,[15] contractual liability is in principle absolute: a party is bound to perform what he has promised. The fact that

---

13 Cass civ 25.4.1939, D 1940.1.12, Gaz Pal 1939.2.57, *Source-book* p. 477.
14 Cf pp. 171 f, above.
15 Pp. 53, 110, above.

performance was impossible when the agreement was made or
has subsequently become impossible is in principle irrelevant.
The rigidity of this approach is of course mitigated by the
courts' power to construe the contract and by the growth of
implied terms, and in particular by the development via the
device of the implied term of the doctrine of frustration, but
the starting-point remains. The starting-point of French law,
on the other hand, as of all Civil law systems, is the principle
that a promise of the impossible is null (*impossibilium nulla
obligatio*). The principle is not indeed expressly stated in the
Code civil, but is implicit in a number of articles[16] and is
universally accepted. If performance is impossible from the
beginning, the *objet* is impossible and therefore, as we have
seen,[17] there can be no contract. In the case of supervening
impossibility a contract has of course come into existence, but
the debtor is freed from his obligation to perform. French
law, however, distinguishes between performance (and its
enforcement) and the payment of damages in substitution for
performance.[18] The debtor cannot be required to perform the
impossible, but the question of damages is distinct and is
separately provided for in article 1147 Cc:[19]

> The debtor is condemned, where appropriate, to the payment
> of damages, either on account of the non-performance of the
> obligation or on account of delay in its performance, whenever
> he does not show that the non-performance is due to a an external
> cause (*cause étrangère*) which cannot be imputed to him, even if
> there is no bad faith on his part.

This is amplified by article 1148:

> There is no occasion for damages where, in consequence of *force
> majeure* or *cas fortuit*, the debtor has been prevented from
> conveying or doing (*donner ou faire*) that to which he was obliged
> or has done what he was debarred from doing.

Where therefore the impossibility is due to the fault of the
debtor or, more precisely, where the debtor cannot show that
the non-performance is attributable to a *cause étrangère*,

16 E g arts 1108, 1126–1130, 1172, 1302, 1601.
17 P. 110 f, above.
18 See p. 145, above and p. 205, below.
19 Cf p. 50, above.

defined as *force majeure* or *cas fortuit*, a claim for damages
will lie, even though a claim for performance will not.

We are concerned here, of course, with *obligations de
résultat*.[20] The question of impossibility as such cannot arise in
the case of an *obligation de moyens*, since the debtor is there
only obliged to exercise the diligence of a *bon père de famille*.
He will therefore only be liable if the creditor can show that
such diligence would have enabled him to provide against the
event which has made the performance impossible, i e that he
was at fault. (In the case of an *obligation de résultat* the
burden is on the debtor to show a *cause étrangère* and this,
as we shall see, he cannot do if he could have provided against
the event.)

We should note that what is in question is the non-
performance of *an obligation*, whereas the Common law thinks
of impossibility of performance (or frustration) of *a contract*.
Most commonly, of course, the two will coincide, in that the
obligation (or obligations) which the debtor has not performed
will be substantially the whole of those created by the contract,
but it may be otherwise. An exporter who has sold goods may
have undertaken to pack them in a certain type of plastic
container, the export of which has subsequently been forbidden. The main part of the contract is still capable of
performance, other containers being substituted, and the seller
will not be liable for his failure to use those specified. Or a
shipowner who has contracted to call at ten ports will not be
liable for failing to call at one of them which has become an
enemy port. And the same is true of temporary impossibility.[1]
The debtor is exempted from liability for any damage caused
by the delay, but the contract remains and can be enforced
when the impossibility ceases.[2] The Common law, on the other
hand, has allowed impossibility of performance to be absorbed
into the category of frustration, and in consequence it thinks
only of the whole contract and attributes to impossibility

20 See pp. 48 ff, above.
 1 Cf Treitel *Contract* p. 654. Cases on partial impossiblity are rare, even in
   French law, and the issue tends to be blurred by the use of the remedy of
   résolution under art 1184 Cc; see pp. 199 ff, below.
 2 There may remain the difficulty that by then the character of the obligation has changed, but, as we shall see (pp. 196 ff, below) French law
   refuses to take account of this kind of change of circumstance.

the single catastrophic consequence of termination of the contract. It therefore has difficulty in knowing how to deal with partial or temporary impossibility. This can be seen in the English textbooks, which either do not discuss the question or (while recognising that this is a faulty analysis) treat it tentatively as an aspect of frustration.[3]

The primary consequence of impossibility of performance in French law is therefore to exempt the debtor from liability for his non-performance. There remains the question of whether the non-performance entitles one or other party to avoid the contract and of the consequences of such avoidance. Before considering this question, however, we must examine the scope of the defence of impossibility or *force majeure*.

2 Scope of *force majeure*

We have seen that article 1148 Cc replaces the term *cause étrangère* by *force majeure*[4] and *cas fortuit*. Attempts have been made to distinguish between these two terms, but without success. They occur in a number of places in the *Code civil*, usually together, but even where they are found separately, no difference seems to be intended and none is to be found in the *jurisprudence*. We shall therefore follow the common practice of speaking of *force majeure* alone.[5]

The scope allowed to *force majeure* is far narrower than that of frustration in English law (which itself is markedly more restrictive than its counterpart in German law).[6] The decisions of the *Cour de cassation* reiterate the proposition that '*force majeure* refers to events which make performance impossible, not to those which only make it onerous'. No doctrine of change of circumstances or economic impossibility or disappearance of the foundation of the contract or frustration of

3 *Chitty on Contracts* (24th edn) s. 1414; Treitel *Contract* p. 654; *Williston on Contracts* (3rd edn) s. 1956. See also Nicholas (1979) 27 Amer J Comp Law 231, 235–237.
4 The term *force majeure* occurs in English law as one of the commonly excepted risks in shipping contracts, but it plays no part in the general law.
5 Zweigert/Kötz vol 2, pp. 188 ff.
6 See e g Cass civ 4.8.1915, S 1916.1.17 note Wahl, D 1916.1.22, *Sourcebook* p. 441.

the adventure has been admitted by the civil courts, even in the aftermath of two catastrophic wars. (The legislator intervened to rectify some of the least acceptable consequences.)[7] The impossibility must be absolute. To this the only exception is for contracts involving personal performance. Thus an author who had contracted to write a play by a certain date was exempted from liability when a dental operation prevented him from writing for three weeks.[8] On the other hand, where there was no element of personal performance a stroke was no defence to the forfeiture of a policy of insurance for failure to pay the premium on the due date.[9] This is not to say, of course, that on occasion actual decisions are not less rigorous than might be expected. A finding of *force majeure* was upheld, for example when a vendor who had contracted to deliver wine 'by the end of February' found, on attempting to do so in the last three days of the month, that all roads were impassable owing to 'diluvian rain'.[10] Moreover, the question whether in any particular case performance is impossible is one of fact and it is therefore open to the lower courts, provided that they express their decision in the appropriate words, to modify in practice the rigour of the rule.[11]

In addition to making performance impossible, the impediment must have been unforeseeable and irresistible. The latter term imports also the idea that it should be unavoidable and insurmountable. Thus administrative delay in granting a building permit has been held to be foreseeable,[12] but the order to evacuate in 1940 which caused a garage owner to leave behind the plaintiff's car was not.[13] Again, the failure of telephone communication which prevented the placing of a bet was unforeseeable but not irresistible (other steps could have been taken).[14] The question of unforeseeability and

7 See Marty/Raynaud s. 229.
8 Paris 17.1.1910, D 1910.2.292.
9 Cass req 1.6.1911, D 1912.1.181.
10 Cass req 28.11.1934, S 1935.1.105, *Source-book* p. 447.
11 David *English Law and French Law* p. 121; for examples see pp. 200 ff, below.
12 Cass com 26.10.1954, D 1955.213.
13 Cass civ 22.12.1954, D 1955.252.
14 Paris 30.6.1958, D 1958.578.

irresistibility, unlike that of impossibility, is subject to the control of the *Cour de cassation*.[15]

Where *cause étrangère* is invoked as a defence to quasi-delictual liability under article 1384 al 1 for things under one's control (*sous sa garde*), the courts insist that the impediment should be external to the thing. The defendant cannot therefore plead that the damage was due to a defect in the thing of which he was unaware and could not have foreseen. To allow him to do so would drastically curtail the scope of the liability. The same is true of the defence of *force majeure* to contractual liability, in so far as the cause is located in the thing used in the performance of the contract. Thus the *restaurateur* who served a dish of infected turbot[16] was not allowed to plead that the bacillus could not have been foreseen or surmounted. But there is no general requirement that the cause should be external in a wider sense (e g the author prostrated by a dental operation).[17] Indeed a strike by the debtor's employees may constitute a *force majeure* if, exceptionally, it can be shown to be unforeseeable and irresistible.[18] The *Cour de cassation* has even suggested that unemployment might be a *force majeure* preventing a participant in a building co-operative from expulsion for non-payment of contributions.[19]

The act of a third party may, of course, on the same conditions constitute a *force majeure*, as where a passenger in a train was injured by a stone thrown from outside the train.[20] And so also may the act of the creditor himself, if it is the exclusive cause. (If it is not the exclusive cause, but the creditor is at fault, the debtor may be partially exonerated;[1] in this case, of

15 Cass civ 5.2.1957, D 1957.178.
16 Poitiers 16.12.1970, p. 50, above.
17 Paris 17.1.1910, p. 197, above.
18 Cass civ 7.3.1966 and Cass com 28.2.1966, JCP 1966.II.14878 (in both of which, however, the plea failed); see further Weill/Terré p. 466, n. 2.
19 Cass civ 14.4.1972, D 1973.205 note Souleau; when the case was re-heard (Orléans 25.10.1973, D 1974.66), the court below decided, however, that it had not been shown that the strike (i) was not imputable to the debtor, either in its origin or in its continuance, (ii) was unforeseeable, (iii) had made performance absolutely impossible.
20 Cass civ 21.1.1946, D 1946.131; but the railway is usually liable for what goes on within its own premises.
 1 Cass civ 31.1.1973, D 1973.149 note Schmelck, JCP 1973.II.17450 note Starck.

course, there is no need for the act to be unforeseeable or irresistible, since the ground for the partial exoneration is not *force majeure*, but what a Common lawyer, if he thought in terms of fault in this context, would call contributory negligence.) We have already remarked that if the impediment is due to the act of the debtor himself, there is no exemption. So where an employer was refused renewal of a work permit for an employee, but the reason for the refusal was that the employer already had too many foreign employees, the employee was entitled to damages for wrongful dismissal.[2]

3 Consequences of impossibility

In the case of total impossibility, as we have seen, the debtor is released from his obligation.[3] If the contract is unilateral, this presents no problem. If the contract is synallagmatic, the question is one of risk (*théorie des risques*). If one party is released by *force majeure*, is the other also released? The principle of interdependence, which, as we have seen, is embodied in the doctrine of *cause*, answers this question in the affirmative. Since each obligation is the *cause* of the other, the extinction of one entails the extinction of the other. The risk is on the debtor of the obligation which has been extinguished by *force majeure*, in the sense that, though he is not liable for his non-performance, he cannot claim the counterperformance, and if the counterperformance has already been made, he will be bound to make restitution. So when at the beginning of this century the religious orders were dissolved by the legislature, it was held that since the orders could no longer discharge their obligation of support to their members, those members were entitled to the return of the endowment or 'dowry' which they had brought with them when they joined.[4]

2 Cass soc 30.12.1954, D 1954 Somm 77.
3 The *Code civil* contains no express general statement of the rule but there are various particular applications (arts 1722, 1741, 1788, 1790, 1867). It is of course suppletive.
4 Cass civ 13.3.1907, D 4.6.1907, S 1907.1.321; Cass req 8.1.1906, D 1906.1.262.

The preceding paragraph has expressed the consequence of impossibility in terms of the *théorie des risques* and the doctrine of *cause*, entailing necessarily the nullity of both obligations without the need for recourse to a court to rescind the contract. Restitution follows, where this is applicable. This is in accord with principle and is the approach adopted by *doctrine*. *Jurisprudence*, however, habitually applies article 1184, which provides for rescission of the contract by a court (with damages where appropriate) in case of non-performance. This is the article under which rescission is sought where the non-performance is imputable to the defendant (i e where it constitutes in Common law terms a breach of contract)[5] and according to the dominant view among the writers it is appropriate only in this case. (It is certain that it is only then that damages can be given.) The wording of the article itself (apart from the reference to damages) is, however, compatible with the approach of the courts. It speaks simply of 'the case in which one party does not fulfil his obligation'. The leading decision,[6] indeed, justifies the application of the article in terms of *cause* ('the obligation of one party has as its *cause* the obligation of the other and vice versa, so that, if the obligation of one is not fulfilled, for whatever reason, the obligation of the other becomes without *cause*'), but the objection of *doctrine*[7] is that this should lead to absolute nullity, not to a claim for rescission under article 1184.

The *jurisprudence* is, however, well settled. And, inelegant though it may be, it has considerable advantages in introducing a large element of flexibility. If the approach of *doctrine* were adopted there would, in principle, be no need for recourse to a court, and even if a court were seised of the matter it would have no discretion: it would have to declare the contract either null or not. In applying article 1184, however, the court has a discretion. It need not grant rescission if the non-performance is partial or temporary, and whether it is partial or temporary or not is a matter of fact. Where therefore the contract has been performed in part before the *force majeure* supervened, or where the *force majeure* does not

5 See further, pp. 236 ff, below.
6 Cass civ 14.4.1891, S 1894.1.391, D 1891.1.329 note Planiol, *Source-book* p. 496.
7 See e g Planiol's note to the case.

wholly or permanently prevent performance, the court may indeed rescind the contract and order restitution, but it may also refuse to do so. It cannot, of course, award damages, but it can reduce or vary the creditor's obligation in order to take account of the reduced performance of the debtor. This is a remarkable qualification of the otherwise rather rigid attitude of French law to questions of *force majeure*.[8]

For example, where the plaintiff had taken advertising space on an illuminated pillar in the *Gare St Lazare* under a long-term contract and on the outbreak of war in 1939 the pillar had to be blacked out at night, the *Cour d'appel* of Paris held that performance had become partially impossible owing to *force majeure* and ordered a 20 per cent reduction in the amount paid by the plaintiff.[9]

The power to vary can, however, be more extensive than this. In a recent case[10] the plaintiffs, a married couple, had 'sold' their house and land to the defendants in return for a *rente viagère* coupled with an undertaking both to allow the plaintiffs to continue to live in part of the house and to take care of them. In the event this last obligation became, the court held, impossible of performance because of friction between the parties. The court refused the plaintiffs' claim for rescission and substituted for the defendants' obligation of care an increase in the amount of the *rente viagère*. A similar earlier case[11] differed only in that the impossibility of discharging the obligation of care arose from the plaintiff's going into an old people's home. In these last two cases the flexibility of the remedy is matched by that of the meaning given to 'impossibility'.

A further consequence of proceeding under article 1184 is that the rescission, if ordered, is retrospective to the beginning of the contract. And a corollary of this is that restitution, in kind or in money, must be made of benefits received by each party.[12] This remedy, which is primarily, of course, adapted

8 It is not confined to cases of *force majeure*; see pp. 237 ff, below.
9 Paris 13.11.1943, Gaz Pal 1943.2.260.
10 Cass civ 8.1.1980 (noted in J-Cl Civ art 1184, fasc I, s. 84 suppl.).
11 Cass civ 18.5.1978, JCP 1978.IV.217; see further, Weill/Terré s. 487 (p. 544); Culioli J-Cl Civ art 1184, fasc I, ss. 85 ff.
12 Cass civ 4.5.1898, S 1898.1.281, D 1898.1.457 note Planiol, *Source-book* p. 450.

r

to the case of rescission for breach (with damages in addition), is not necessarily adequate for cases of (total) non-performance because of *force majeure*. If, for example, one party has incurred expense when impossibility supervenes, but the other has not yet received any benefit, a restitutionary remedy plainly does not yield an equitable result. Problems such as this are familiar to English lawyers because they are, to some extent, provided for in the Law Reform (Frustrated Contracts) Act 1943, but there seems to be no discussion of them in French law. The narrower scope of the doctrine of impossibility does, of course, reduce their practical importance.

4 *Imprévision*

We have seen that the civil courts have refused to countenance anything akin to the English doctrine of frustration or the German doctrine of the disappearance of the foundation of the contract. The last judicial attempt before the war of 1914 to introduce such a doctrine seems to have been that quashed by the *Cour de cassation* in its decision in the case of the *Canal de Craponne*.[13] By agreements dating from 1560 and 1567 landowners agreed to pay a fixed annual sum for irrigation water to be supplied by a then projected canal. By the nineteenth century the sum had become derisory and the *Cour d'appel* of Aix had held that in the case of contracts for successive performances article 1134 Cc[14] was qualified by a power in the courts, when there was no longer an equitable relationship between the payments of one party and the expense of the other, to restore the original balance. The *Cour de cassation*, however, categorically re-affirmed the full rigour of article 1134, which the court said, was general and absolute and governed contracts of all kinds. 'In no case is it open to the courts, no matter how equitable their decision may seem to them to be, to take time and circumstances into account in

13 Cass civ 6.3.1876, S 1876.1.161, D 1876.1.193 note Giboulot, *Source-book* p. 430. There were some further attempts (e g Cass civ 6.6.1921, D 1921.1.193 note Hugueney, D 1921.1.73 rapport Colin, note X, *Source-book* p. 432) after the decision of the *Conseil d'Etat* in 1916 (see text, below), but to no avail.

14 P. 31, above.

order to modify the agreement of the parties and substitute new terms for those which have been freely acepted by those parties.'

In regard to public law contracts, however, the *Conseil d'Etat* developed a different approach. In general, as has been said above,[15] the *Conseil* applies to contracts the ordinary principles of the *Code civil*, but it does not necessarily confine itself to those principles. The leading case[16] in this context was decided in 1916, but there was already then a line of cases dating back three decades concerning public works contracts for excavation in which the nature of the ground had proved to be very different from what had been forecast by experts and the work in consequence had been so far more expensive as altogether to exceed the risk which the contractor could reasonably have been expected to undertake. The remuneration to the contractor had accordingly been increased. The case decided in 1916 canonised this development and clearly established the general principle of *imprévision*. The facts were that in 1904 the City of Bordeaux had given to a company the concession for the provision of gas within the city for thirty years, the price to be paid for the gas being fixed by the contract. As a result of the outbreak of war the cost of coal rose steeply (by the time of the hearing it had increased fourfold in twenty months) and the company claimed an increase in the price of gas. The case came on appeal to the *Conseil d'Etat*. The *commissaire du gouvernement*[17] argued in his *conclusions* that the previous line of cases had established that the *Conseil* would apply the doctrine of *force majeure* more widely than the civil courts and would treat as an insurmountable obstacle an event which had 'very gravely disturbed the economy of the contract'. In so doing it took account of the principle that contracts should be performed in good faith and of the needs of the public service, which demanded that the contract should continue to be carried out. 'The public power (*puissance*

15 P. 25.
16 CE 30.3.1916, S 1916.3.17 concl Chardenet, note Hauriou, D 1916.3.25 concl Chardenet.
17 Whose functions can be said to combine those of the representative of the *ministère public* and of the *rapporteur* in a civil case (pp. 10 ff, above); see Brown and Garner *French Administrative Law* (2nd edn) p. 50.

publique), which granted the concession, will have to bear the expense which the functioning of the public service demands, in so far as it exceeds the maximum which a sensible interpretation of the contract could accept as being possibly and reasonably foreseeable.' The *Conseil* followed the lines proposed (though without reference to good faith). The increase in the price of coal, it held, had exceeded all reasonable expectations and the economy of the contract had in consequence been entirely upset. A solution must be found 'which takes account both of the general interest, which demands the continuation of the company's service . . . and the special circumstances which do not allow the contract to be applied normally'. The case was remitted for assessment of an appropriate indemnity.

The foundation of the doctrine is therefore the need to protect the public interest, which in the particular case would obviously have suffered if the company had collapsed. This is a need which is not normally present in a contract governed by the civil law and which in any event a civil court would hardly be justified in meeting at the expense of one of the parties. By contrast the *Conseil d'Etat*, as an arm of the 'public power', determines what steps that power should take to protect its own interest, while taking account of what in equity is due to the contractor. Since the protection of the public interest is the primary basis of the intervention by the *Conseil*, it has usually been said that the indemnity will not be given after the contract has come to an end. A recent decision has, however, rejected this restriction.[18]

18 CE 12.3.1976, Actualité Juridique – Droit Administratif (1976) 528, 552.

Chapter five
Remedies for non-performance[1]

1 General

A French work would not have a chapter exclusively devoted to this subject. Treatments vary in detail, but they broadly reflect the arrangement of the Code. As we have seen,[2] what English law classifies as remedies for breach are classified by the French lawyer among aspects of the effect of contracts or of obligations. The effect of an obligation is to constrain the debtor to perform what he has undertaken; if the debtor does not do so voluntarily, the law, in principle, provides the means of compelling him to do so. It is only if those means are for some reason not available or not effective that a question of non-performance (*inexécution*) arises, and in that event the law provides a substitutionary relief in damages.[3] This difference between the two systems is partly a mere matter of arrangement, and as such it is of no great importance once the arrangement is understood, but it also reflects a significant difference of emphasis or approach. From the point of view of the French lawyer the creditor's primary recourse is in principle to have the contract performed, whereas for the Common lawyer the primary remedy is damages. In practice,

---

1 On this subject (apart from the *exceptio non adimpleti contractus*) see the valuable comparative monograph by Treitel in International Encyclopedia of Comparative Law, vol VII, ch 16, 'Remedies for Breach of Contract' (cited here as Treitel *Remedies*).
2 P. 145, above.
3 The sanction of nullity attaches to the conditions of the validity of a contract and has therefore been treated under that heading (pp. 74 ff, above).

it is true, as is explained in more detail below,[4] the remedy of specific enforcement is less important than principle suggests, but the attitude of mind remains.

This attitude of mind is seen more fundamentally in the contrast between the Common lawyer's emphasis on remedies and the French lawyer's emphasis (which is that of the Civil lawyer in general) on rights and duties. We have remarked before that the French lawyer sees law as a system of rules, in principle complete, for the conduct of life in society. The courts will, or should, enforce the rights and duties which these rules create, but this is a logically secondary matter. Mr Justice Holmes's well-known assertion that 'the duty to keep a contract at common law means a prediction that you must pay damages if you do not keep it – and nothing else'[5] is an exaggeration,[6] but, as well as pointing to the primacy, already noted, of the remedy of damages, it does correctly reflect the fundamental approach of the Common lawyer, which is to ask, not 'is there a duty?', but 'will a court give a remedy?'. (This is not to say, of course, that the lawyer's commercial client will have regard only to this question, but the duty which will weigh with him will be a matter of commercial practice and commercial reputation.)

There is also to be noticed a greater reluctance in French law than in the Common law to allow recourse to self-help,[7] this term being used in the wide sense, to include not only the exercise of physical force against the person or property of the debtor, as in abatement of nuisance, but any remedy which is exercised without recourse to a court. Thus, where the Common law allows one party to rescind for non-performance merely by giving notice to the other, French law normally requires a court proceeding. To this rejection of self-help the only exception in the present context is the purely defensive withholding of performance which goes under the name

4 Pp. 210 ff.
5 'The Path of the Law' (*Collected Legal Papers* p. 175; (1897) 10 Harvard L Rev 462); cf *The Common Law* p. 301.
6 Buckland (1944) 8 Camb LJ 247; *Some Reflections on Jurisprudence* pp. 97 ff.
7 On the French maxim *Nul ne peut se faire justice à soi-même* see Béguin Trav Assoc H Capitant vol XVIII (1966) 41.

of *exceptio non adimpleti contractus* (under which can be subsumed the *droit de rétention*). We therefore begin with this extra-judicial remedy.

2 Exceptio non adimpleti contractus[8]

This term, deriving from medieval Roman law (and meaning literally 'defence of unperformed contract') is still commonly in use, though the Ministry of Justice recently urged the courts not to use Latin expressions and mentioned, among others, this one.[9] The French translation is *exception d'inexécution*. The term is misleading in either language, since the word *exceptio* suggests a defence to an action, whereas an essential characteristic of this remedy is that the party exercising it need not go to court (though he may choose to do so).[10]

The remedy, which is available only in the case of a contract in which the duties of the parties are concurrent, consists in the refusal by one party to perform his duty unless the other party performs his. The remedy was well established in the *ancien droit* and there are what can be seen as specific instances of it in the *Code civil*. Thus in a contract of sale the seller can withhold delivery if the buyer does not pay the price.[11] The English parallel is the unpaid seller's lien.[12] Similarly the buyer can withhold the price if he is threatened by eviction, until the seller removes the threat or gives a surety.[13] There is, however, no general text and, in view of the firmly rooted policy against self-help, it was not until this century that the courts made bold to apply it to all synallagmatic contracts.[14] In so doing they founded it on the doctrine of *cause*: since each obligation is the cause of the other, the non-performance of one justifies the non-performance of the other. It is, however, essentially

8 See Weill/Terré ss. 463 ff; Huet J-Cl Civ, App art 1184.
9 Circular of 15.9.1977, JCP 1977.III.46255.
10 Cass soc 10.4.1959, D 1960.61. There is no need for *mise en demeure* (pp. 232 ff, below): Cass com 27.1.1970, JCP 1970.II.16554 note Huet.
11 Arts 1612, 1613.
12 Sale of Goods Act 1979, s. 39(1).
13 Art 1653 Cc; cf art 1704 (contract of exchange) and 1948 (contract of deposit).
14 Huet, above, ss. 17 ff.

a temporary and provisional non-performance. The contract and the duties under it remain and the party making use of the *exceptio* (who will be referred to here as the creditor) must be ready to perform as soon as the other (the debtor) does so. This is obviously a situation which the creditor may find inconvenient. The unpaid seller, for example, will not wish to tie up for long goods which he can sell elsewhere. But if the creditor wishes to repudiate the contract altogether and recover his freedom of action, he must bring an *action en résolution* under article 1184. The point is illustrated by a case[15] in which the creditor had given to the debtor for three years the exclusive agency for the sale of his boats, the debtor undertaking to sell nine boats a year. At the end of the first year, during which the debtor had sold none at all, the creditor gave notice that he was terminating the contract and granting the exclusive agency to a third party. It was held that the creditor was entitled to suspend performance of the obligation of exclusivity (i e to allow others as well as the debtor to sell), but that he could not give the exclusive agency to another. For this involved a total resolution of the contract, which could only be done by a court under article 1184.

The remedy is therefore a means of putting pressure on the debtor. It is, however, capable of abuse. For example, it is in principle available to a tenant whose landlord has not fulfilled one of his obligations, such as the obligation to repair. But it would obviously be inequitable if the tenant were entitled to refuse payment whenever the landlord had failed to carry out a repair, however trivial. There is no precise rule (and the matter lies in any event within the *pouvoir souverain*), but the remedy must not be disproportionate to the wrong. The payment of rent is the essential obligation of the tenant; the making of repairs may or may not be of comparable importance. The courts have accordingly denied the right to refuse payment where the landlord's failure is relatively trivial.[16] Similarly, an electricity supply company was not entitled to cut off the supply

15 Cass com 15.1.1973, D 1973.473 note Ghestin, Gaz Pal 1973.2.495.
16 Cass civ 21.2.1927, DH 1928.82; Angers 14.4.1934, S 1935.2.97 note Hebraud, DH 1934.371, *Source-book* p. 489; On the other hand the tenant was held entitled to refuse payment and was also given damages in Cass soc 10.4.1959, D 1960.61, where the tenant's flat was made uninhabitable during the winter by fumes from a leaking chimney.

where the customer had refused payment of a small part of the sum claimed by the company, which he contended was not due.[17] The obligation of which the creditor suspends performance must be correlative to an obligation of the debtor's which arises out of the same legal relationship. A shop-keeper tenant, for example, cannot refuse payment of rent in order to put pressure on his landlord to pay for goods which he has bought from the tenant. And the two obligations, as has been said already, must be concurrent. Thus, in the case of the unpaid seller's right to withhold the goods sold, the Code[18] expressly excludes the case where the seller has agreed that the buyer may pay later (but further provides that even in this case the seller can retain the goods if the buyer has subsequently become insolvent). In general it is obvious that if, expressly or by common usage, the creditor's performance is expected to precede that of the debtor, there is no place for the *exceptio*.

There is an evident relationship between the *exceptio* and the *droit de rétention* or lien. Indeed before the courts had openly reintroduced the *exceptio* they would in some cases[19] achieve the same result by invoking the *droit de rétention*,and there has been a good deal of doctrinal controversy about the limits of the two institutions.[20] Both serve the same purpose of putting pressure on a debtor by withholding that to which he is entitled, and the two are often indistinguishable. The unpaid seller's retention of the thing sold, for example, or the depositee's retention of the thing deposited with him, can be seen as instances both of the *exceptio* and of the *droit de rétention*. The *exceptio* is, however, much wider, in that the creditor is not confined to retaining a specific thing to which the debtor is entitled. The buyer's right to withhold payment of the price when threatened by eviction cannot be classified as *droit de rétention* because a sum of money is not a specific thing, and this applies a fortiori where the performance withheld is an act. On the other hand a *droit de rétention* is not confined to synallagmatic contracts (the creditor under a

17 Cass req 1.12.1897, D 1989.1.289 note Planiol, S 1899.1.174.
18 Arts 1612, 1613.
19 E g even in Cass civ 5.12.1934, S 1935.1.46, *Source-book* p. 487.
20 Mazeaud/Mazeaud vol 3, s. 111.

unilateral contract may retain a thing belonging to the debtor if he holds that thing in connection with the contract); nor indeed is it confined to contracts at all. It may arise out of *gestion d'affaires*[1] for example, or out of the relationship between joint heirs, one of whom has incurred expenditure in preserving or improving the property and is therefore entitled to retain that property until he is compensated.[2] In short, the two are distinct outside the central area in which a party to a synallagmatic contract withholds a performance consisting in the handing over a thing to which the other is entitled. And within this central area it is usually of no practical consequence to make a distinction.

3 Enforced performance[3]

As has been said above,[4] French law starts from the premise that what the creditor expects from an obligation is its performance in kind (*exécution en nature*) and that the law will if necessary enforce that performance (*exécution forcée*).

To this there is an obvious exception expressed in the maxim *impossibilium nulla obligatio*[5] and a less obvious one expressed in the maxim *nemo praecise cogi potest ad factum* (no-one can be compelled to a specific act), which expresses the libertarian repugnance to compulsion directed against the person.[6] (There is also the practical difficulty, in the absence of anything corresponding to the English machinery of imprisonment for contempt of court, of making an order for performance effective, but the courts have largely filled that gap by the device of the *astreinte*.[7] The maxim is embodied in the *Code civil* in the shape of article 1142:

> Every obligation to do or not to do (*de faire ou de ne pas faire*) resolves itself into damages in case of non-performance by the debtor.

1 P. 171, above.
2 Art 867 Cc; cf arts 555, 570, 571.
3 Zweigert/Kötz vol 2, pp. 139 ff; Treitel *Remedies* ss. 7–39.
4 P. 205.
5 See pp. 110, 193, above; cf Cass civ 30.6.1965 (p. 213, n. 16, below).
6 Pothier *Vente* s. 68; *Louage* s. 66.
7 See pp. 215 ff, below.

Since an obligation of *donner* is, as we have seen,[8] self-executing where it relates to a specific thing, and where it relates to a non-specific thing will involve an element of *faire*, this article might be thought to embody the Common law approach, as expressed by Mr Justice Holmes.[9] It is, however, subject to qualifications, some in the Code itself, some supplied by *doctrine* and the practice of the courts, which reduce it to the level of an exception.

Even where the obligation of *donner* is self-executing, there will commonly remain an obligation to deliver and this is strictly an obligation of *faire*; but since the creditor is already owner and the obligation to deliver is closely related to the obligation of *donner*, an order for possession will be specifically enforced by the court, through its officer, the *huissier*.[10] In the case of movables this enforcement will be by seizure (*saisie-revendication*)[11] and in the case of immovables by expulsion of the debtor.

The Code itself provides (article 1144) that the creditor may be authorised to obtain performance by a third party at the expense of the debtor. Thus, where a seller fails to deliver, the buyer may buy replacement goods, or a tenant may cause repairs to be carried out. It must be emphasised that this is not a form of self-help. The creditor must first get a court order, except in cases governed by commercial law, where a notice (*mise en demeure*) to the debtor is sufficient, and generally in cases of extreme urgency. Similarly, the Code provides (article 1143) that in the case of an obligation *de ne pas faire*) the creditor can be authorised to cause what has been done in breach of the obligation to be destroyed at the expense of the debtor. Such 'destruction' may include the reversal of a juridical act, such as an alienation. These two instances of performance in kind at the expense of the debtor constitute *exécution en nature*, in the sense that the creditor gets what he was promised, but for practical purposes they differ little from the award of damages: the creditor still has to obtain payment from the debtor and the risk of the debtor's insolvency is on the

8 P. 149, above.
9 P. 206, above.
10 Mazeaud/Mazeaud s. 934.
11 Code proc civ (ancien) art 826.

creditor. On the other hand, the creditor does not have to show damage (*préjudice*). So where one party to a building scheme had put up a building which exceeded the limits laid down in the scheme and the court below had refused to authorise the demolition sought by another party to the scheme, the ground for the refusal being that the plaintiff had shown no *préjudice*, the *Cour de cassation* quashed the decision.[12] This ruling is one of a series in the last twenty years which seem largely to deny any element of discretion in cases such as this. Earlier decisions[13] had conceded that it lay within the *pouvoir souverain* to award damages rather than to authorise destruction, and courts had therefore taken account of such matters as the disproportion between the benefit to the creditor and the loss to the debtor, the relation of the excess to the whole building, the shortage of housing, or the interests of the tenants of the part to be demolished. This last ground, in particular, was sharply rejected in one of the early manifestations of the new attitude (which itself, however, has not escaped criticism on social grounds).

It is obvious that 'surrogate performance'[14] of the kind discussed in the preceding paragraph is not applicable to obligations in which performance by the debtor in person is of the essence. If a painter, for example, refuses to carry out a commission which he has undertaken, it would be pointless to authorise the client to have the picture painted by someone else. It is in cases such as this that the obligation 'resolves itself into damages'. *Doctrine* therefore concludes, in accordance with the premise from which it starts, that article 1142 is badly formulated. It takes the form of a general rule, but it applies only to the limited category of 'personal' contracts. What is in substance the rule is contained in articles 1143 and 1144, to which article 1142 is the exception.[15]

12 Cass civ 17.12.1963, JCP 1964.II.13609 note Blaevoelt, Gaz Pal 1964.1. 158, *Source-book* p. 518.

13 See Deprez J-Cl Civ, arts 1136–1145, fasc 1, s. 56.

14 Term used by Zweigert/Kötz vol 2, pp. 139 ff.

15 See Tunc, note to Lyon 30.7.1946, D 1947.377 (*Source-book* p. 494); Weill/Terré s. 833; Mazeaud/Tunc vol 3, s. 2308. The note to Cass civ 19.2.1970, Gaz Pal 1970.1.282, says: 'The least that one can say of art 1142 is that it was very badly drafted. It presents as an imperative rule what is no more than an option, though, it is true, the statistically predominant one.'

This conclusion is then further generalised. A judgment for *exécution en nature*, whether under article 1143 or 1144 or otherwise, will be given in respect of all obligations except those positive obligations which require personal performance and those negative obligations the enforcement of which would result in such an interference with personal liberty as would be offensive to current morality. The *Cour de cassation*, in accordance with this view, declares that article 1142 is applicable 'only in the case of a personal obligation of *faire* or *ne pas faire*'.[16]

This limited application of article 1142 is commonly illustrated by reference to a *cause célèbre* of the end of the last century. Sir William Eden claimed delivery of a portrait of his wife which he had commissioned from James McNeill Whistler, Sir William had approved the picture and tendered payment for it, and Whistler had shown it at an exhibition, but, relations between them having turned sour, Whistler had not only refused to hand it over, but had replaced Lady Eden's head by that of another woman. The legal issue which came before the *Cour de cassation*[17] was as to whether the agreement between the parties was sufficient to constitute a sale or other similar contract which would have the effect of transferring property in the painting when it was finished (or when Sir William approved it). If so, as we have seen, delivery could be enforced. The *Cour de cassation* held that a contract for the painting of a portrait had a special character and that property in the painting remained in the painter until he had handed it over and the client had approved it. In the *arrêt* itself there is no reference to the personal character of the artist's under-

16 Cass civ 20.1.1953, D 1953.222, JCP 1953.II.7677 note Esmein, *Source-book* p. 515. There are occasional cases in which the courts appear to give art 1142 its face value e g Cass civ 30.6.1965 (Gaz Pal 1965.2.329, *Source-book* p. 515; cf Mazeaud/Tunc vol 3, s. 2308, n. 4), but in that case the plaintiff had conceded that performance was impossible.
17 Cass civ 14.3.1900, D 1900.1.497 rapport Rau, concl Desjardins. Whistler (who had earlier published a collection of his writings under the title *The Gentle Art of Making Enemies*) published a markedly *ex parte* selection of materials relating to the case (but including the speeches of the *avocats* on both sides in the Paris *Cour d'appel* and the *conclusions* of the *avocat-général* of that court - less fully reported in D 1898.2.465) under the title *Eden versus Whistler - The Baronet and the Butterfly* (Paris, nd (1899)).

taking, but it is plain from the *rapport* of the *conseiller rapporteur* and the conclusions of the *avocat-général* that this consideration and its relation to the nature of the contract and the consequent possibility or not of obtaining *exécution forcée* were before the court. The decision was regarded as a vindication of an artist's right to decide when his work was complete.

In 'impersonal' contracts judgment may be given for *exécution en nature*, but it should in principle be execution of the particular obligation which the debtor has undertaken, and not some substitute. So where furniture consigned by rail had been damaged, the *Cour de cassation*[18] quashed an order by the court below that the railway company should repair the furniture. The courts, the *arrêt* said, had no power to order a party to perform an act to which it was not obliged either by a contract or by *loi*. This is the strict rule, but it was not always followed during and after the Second World War when the scarcity of goods made damages an inadequate remedy. Where, for example, wheels had disappeared from a car deposited at a garage, the garage-owner was condemned, with an *astreinte*,[19] to supply the plaintiff with other identical wheels.[20] Similarly, where the court below had evidently doubted the defendant's assertion that he could not return the plaintiff's goods, it was held to have been entitled to decide that the best method of repairing the damage to the plaintiff was to require the defendant to provide him with goods of the same kind.[1]

The practical outcome is therefore that a judgment for *exécution en nature* may be given except where the obligation is personal in character.[2] The judge must give such a judgment if the plaintiff asks for it or if the defendant offers to perform; he may do so even if the plaintiff asks for damages. This is not to say, however, that *exécution en nature* is the normal outcome of an action.[3] In most circumstances plaintiffs are likely to prefer the remedy of damages, as being both more

18 Cass civ 4.6.1924, S 1925.1.97, DH 1924.469, *Source-book* p. 514; cf Cass civ 19.1.1926, DH 1926.115.
19 See below.
20 Paris 21.6.1945, Gaz Pal 1945.2.65; cf Lyon 30.7.1946, D 1947.377.
 1 Cass civ 20.1.1953, D 1953.222, JCP 1953.II.7677 note Esmein. For other cases see Marty/Raynaud p. 557, n. 6.
 2 Mazeaud/Tunc vol 3 (6th edn) s. 2306.
 3 See p. 212, n. 15, above.

expeditious and more certain. Moreover, except in the cases of *saisie-revendication* and expulsion from an immovable,[4] the public authority will not apply physical force to give effect to a judgment for *exécution en nature*. (A money judgment, whether to secure payment for 'surrogate performance' under article 1143 and 1144 or otherwise, is satisfied by seizure and sale of goods.) The Codes provide no other means of specific execution.

4 *Astreintes*

In order to remedy this weakness the courts have, since early in the nineteenth century[6] developed the device of the *astreinte*. A court may attach to a judgment for *exécution en nature* an order that the debtor shall pay to the creditor a specified sum for each day (or other fixed period) that he remains in default. An *astreinte* is therefore essentially a means of putting economic pressure on the debtor to perform. It may take either of two forms. In an *astreinte provisoire* the periodic sum fixed at the beginning is only provisional and cannot be enforced until the court has 'liquidated' it at the end of the period; and in the process of liquidation the court may vary the amount.[7] In an *astreinte définitive* the sum payable is not subject to revision;[8] the final figure is arrived at simply by mathematical calculation. If the debtor has not complied at the end of the period fixed, the court may order a new *astreinte* and so on.

The use of *astreintes* is not confined to the enforcement of contractual obligations. They can be used, for example, to secure the abatement of a nuisance[9] (to use the language of the Common law) or to enforce duties arising out of family law, as when successive orders of increasing severity were made against Princess Nabisco[10] to induce her to return her children to her

4 See p. 211, above.
5 *Source-book* pp. 520 ff; Zweigert/Kötz vol 2, pp. 147 ff; Treitel *Remedies* ss. 24 ff; Chabas J-Cl Civ, arts 1146-1155, fasc VIII, cah 6.
6 Cass req 29.1.1834, D 1834.1.81, S 1834.1.139.
7 For the effect of the legislation of 1972, see p. 218, below.
8 But see p. 219, n. 3, below.
9 Cf Cass civ 26.4.1968, D 1968.526.
10 Paris 7.8.1876, D 1878.2.125 and 13.2.1877, D 1878.2.125, *Source-book* p. 523.

husband. Nor, within the area of contractual obligation, are *astreintes* confined to the enforcement of obligations of *faire* or *ne pas faire*. They are commonly used even where forced execution is available, in the cases mentioned above of delivery of a specific thing or vacation of an immovable, or where 'surrogate performance' under article 1143 or 1144 could be invoked. But the availability of *astreintes*, even though they are free of the objection made against physical compulsion, does not extend the area within which courts will order *exécution en nature*. So when Rosa Bonheur refused to carry out a commission for a painting, the creditor's application for an *astreinte* was rejected.[11] Where, however, the *Comédie Française* sought to enforce against one of its actors his contractual undertaking not to appear with another company, an *astreinte* was imposed,[12] though the court could not have ordered his physical exclusion from the rival theatre. The difficulty, which the English lawyer discusses in connexion with *Lumley v Wagner*,[13] of determining when the enforcement of a negative undertaking, as in this case, has the indirect effect of compelling the performance of a positive undertaking seems not to be discussed.

Until 1972 the *astreinte* had no basis in any legislative text.[14] The courts from the beginning attempted to present it as a variant of an order for damages, but this was self-defeating since the nearer an *astreinte* approached to damages, the less effective it was likely to be as a means of exerting pressure. (Of course, since the assessment of damages lies within the *pouvoir souverain*, the court could not be prevented from in fact introducing a coercive element while ostensibly awarding only compensation, but this provides no answer to the legal question as to the basis of the institution.) And yet if it was not an order for damages, it was difficult to see what its legal basis could be. The confusing link with damages was therefore maintained. In the case of Princess Nabisco,[15] for example, the *Cour de cassa-*

11 Paris 4.7.1865, D 1865.2.201.
12 Paris 21.4.1896, S 1897.2.9.
13 (1852) 1 De GM & G 604.
14 See the *conclusions* of the *Commissaire du gouvernement* in CE 27.1.1933, D 1934.3.68, excerpted in *Source-book* p. 525. For the *loi* of 1949 see p. 217, n. 18, below.
15 N. 13, above.

tion sat on the fence, declaring that 'in reducing to damages the sanction asked for, it is appropriate to proportion the amount awarded to the resistance to be overcome and to the damage to be made good'. A related source of confusion was the use of the term *astreinte comminatoire* as an alternative for *astreinte provisoire*, apparently on the ground that since in this case the *astreinte* might never be put into effect, it might be no more than a threat;[16] and as a correlative to this usage the *astreinte définitive* was, even more confusingly, sometimes referred to as an *astreinte non-comminatoire*, on the ground that in fixing the figure the court was attempting no more than a pre-estimate of damage.[17]

The question of the nature of the *astreinte* came to a head for the first time after the Second World War. In the prevailing shortage of housing, public authority was reluctant to give forcible effect to orders for possession in favour of landlords, and the courts therefore intervened with *astreintes*. And in order to make them effective they had necessarily to fix the amounts at a high level. This provoked the legislature into enacting[18] that in such cases the *astreinte* must always be *provisoire* and must be liquidated at a figure which did not exceed the amount of the loss suffered by the landlord and which also took account of the difficulty which the debtor had had in complying with the judgment. There followed a period in which the leading decision of the *Cour de cassation*[19] extended this to all *astreintes*, though some other decisions insisted on a clear separation from the principle of compensation. The turning-point came in 1959 in a particularly gross case of what a Common lawyer would call contempt of court. An electricity company had been ordered, at the instance of a neighbour whose rights had been infringed, to make some modifications to a building on its land. An *astreinte* had been attached to the order. At the end of the period fixed, the company having done nothing to comply with the order, the plaintiff had the *astreinte* liquidated and obtained an order

16 See e g Cass civ 14.3.1927, S 1927.1.231, *Source-book* p. 524.
17 See the note by Houlleaux to Cass civ 20.10.1959 (p. 218, n. 1, below). The difficulty is removed by the *loi* of 1972 (below).
18 Loi of 21.7.1949, No. 49–972; *Source-book* p. 526.
19 Cass com 17.4.1956, JCP 1956.9330.

for a new one. This process was repeated twice more, but it was not until the plaintiff applied for the liquidation of the fourth *astreinte* at its full figure of 900,000 francs[20] and the fixing of a fifth *astreinte* at a higher level, that the company was moved to object that an *astreinte* was nothing other than damages and therefore that it should be liquidated in terms only of the plaintiff's provable damage. The *Cour d'appel* of Riom rejected this contention, insisting that an *astreinte* was coercive in character and independent of the idea of damages. In view of the contumacy of the defendant it liquidated the *astreinte* at the full figure. The *Cour de cassation*[1] – upheld this decision, declaring emphatically that '*the astreinte provisoire*, a coercive measure entirely distinct from damages and in essence no more than a means of overcoming resistance offered to the enforcement of a judgment, is not intended to compensate for the damage arising from the delay in compliance and is normally liquidated in terms of the gravity of the recalcitrant debtor's fault and the extent of his resources'.

The sum fixed in an *astreinte définitive* remained in principle a pre-estimate of the plaintiff's damage, but the *Cour de cassation* had already ceased to require the lower courts to justify their figures. The difference in this respect between the two types of *astreinte* was therefore simply that in fixing the amount of an *astreinte définitive* a court should not *overtly* take into account coercive considerations.

The final step to the legitimation of the *astreinte* as an independent instrument for the enforcement of judgments was taken by a *loi* of 5 July 1972,[2] which expressly authorised the use of both types for that purpose and declared that they were independent of the remedy of damages. The *astreinte définitive* therefore no longer needs to conceal its coercive character under the cloak of the *pouvoir souverain* to assess damages. (The institution still, however, bears a mark of its origin in that the creditor continues to receive the full amount of the award, even though it is, in part at least, penal in

20 At that time (1956) the equivalent of about £900.
1 Cass civ 20.10.1959, S 1959.225, D 1959.537 note Houlleaux, *Source-book* p. 527.
2 No. 72-626; *Source-book* p. 531. See Chabas D 1972 Chr 271 and Lobin in *Etudes offertes à P Keyser* (1979) vol 2, pp. 131 ff.

character; the original bill provided that part of the award should go to the Treasury, but this met opposition in the Senate.) An *astreinte* is *provisoire* unless the court declares it to be *définitive*. The power of liquidation is stated to include a discretion to reduce or extinguish[3] the award altogether, even where the debtor has not complied.

5 Damages[4]

a General

The broad principles of French law and English law are here the same. In both systems the purpose of the award of damages is to compensate (and no more than compensate)[5] the plaintiff for a loss which he has suffered as a result of the non-performance of the contract. Obviously all the elements in this proposition require further elaboration. What constitutes a loss which the law will recognise? What causal link is sufficient to make that loss a result of the non-performance? How is the amount which constitutes compensation calculated? Some differences, in particular differences of formulation, emerge when these questions are considered, but what principally strikes the English lawyer is that the French analysis is relatively undeveloped. A great deal of intellectual effort has been expended in the Common law world, particularly in recent years, on the law of damages, but there has been little to correspond to this in French *doctrine*. Nor is there a rich *jurisprudence*. It is true that the actual assessment of the amount of compensation lies within the *pouvoir souverain*, but the *Cour de cassation* in principle controls the prior question of the character of the loss for which the compensation is to be paid[6] and can require the courts below to formulate their judgments in such a way as to make that control possible. One

3 There is no mention of a power to increase. An amendment to include such a power was tabled in the Senate, but rejected (without discussion). In the case of the *astreinte définitive* a power to modify is given in the case where non-compliance is due to *force majeure*.
4 Treitel *Remedies* ss. 40–142.
5 As to penalty clauses see pp. 229 ff, below.
6 Its control is directed to the matters of law identified in the next paragraph.

might therefore expect a more considerable contribution from the courts than one in fact finds.

French law starts from the proposition that compensation should be given for all loss (*dommage*, *préjudice*) resulting from the non-performance,[7] but limits this proposition in all cases by the requirement that the loss should be the 'immediate and direct consequence of the non-performance',[8] and, in the case of non-performance which is not attributable to *dol*, by the further requirement that the loss should have been foreseeable.[9] There is also the requirement of *mise en demeure*, or notice to perform, without which in principle no damages are due.[10]

b *Dommage* or *préjudice*

For there to be a remedy in damages (by contrast with other remedies) the plaintiff must have suffered a loss. Where, for example, in a contract for the supply of furniture to be made by the defendant, the materials used were different from (and cheaper than) those specified in the contract, but the quality of the furniture was not substantially affected, the plaintiff was not entitled to damages.[11]

i Damnum emergens, lucrum cessans

Article 1149 Cc sets out the traditional Civil law headings, under which all loss is seen as falling, of *damnum emergens* (actual loss) and *lucrum cessans* (lost gain).

> The creditor is entitled, subject to the exceptions and modifications which follow [relating to the requirements of foreseeability and directness, to penalty clauses and to interest on money debts] to damages in respect of the loss which he has suffered and the gain of which he has been deprived.

The distinction is sometimes also expressed in terms of positive and negative damage. Where, for example, the seller of goods fails to deliver, the buyer may suffer positive damage

---

7 Art 1149 Cc.
8 Art 1151 Cc.
9 Art 1150 Cc.
10 Art 1146 Cc; see pp. 232 ff, below.
11 Cass civ 11.4.1918, S 1918.1.171, *Source-book* p. 511.

or *damnum emergens* if the price at which he can buy
replacement goods is higher than the contract price,[12] and
negative damage or *lucrum cessans* if he is deprived of a
profitable re-sale. The distinction is not usually made in the
Common law (and indeed no consequences are attributed to it
by the *Code civil* and nothing is made of it by the French
writers, though it may in practice be relevant to the question
of remoteness). On the other hand French law does not make
the distinction, now familiar to Common lawyers, between the
expectation loss and the reliance loss, i e between the loss of
the benefits which would have accrued to the creditor if the
contract had been performed and the loss incurred by the
creditor in reliance on the debtor's promise to perform. The
two distinctions overlap, but are not co-extensive. *Lucrum
cessans* is necessarily an expectation loss, but *damnum
emergens*, as the French understand it, may be either an
expectation or a reliance loss. Thus, in the example given
above of the seller who fails to deliver, the difference between
the contract price and the cost of replacement goods (*damnum
emergens*) is an expectation loss, in the sense that damages of
that amount are necessary to put the buyer in the position in
which he would have been if the contract had been fulfilled. But
another example discussed in the French books is that of the
singer who breaks his contract to appear in a concert, which as
a result has to be cancelled.[13] The impresario can recover his
wasted expenses in preparation for the concert as *damnum
emergens* and his net lost profit as *lucrum cessans*. Here the
damnum emergens is a reliance loss, in the sense that damages
of that amount are necessary to put the impresario in the
position in which he would have been if the contract had not been
made.

ii Dommage matériel, dommage moral

The loss will usually be pecuniary (*dommage matériel*), but
after some hesitation a now well-settled jurisprudence also
allows *dommage moral*, which includes a very wide range of

12 Cf Sale of Goods Act 1979, s. 51(3). For the converse case of failure by
  the buyer to take delivery see Cass req 6.2.1922 (Gaz Pal 1922.1.714,
  Source-book p. 504) and Sale of Goods Act 1979, s. 50(3).
13 See Treitel *Remedies* s. 51.

non-pecuniary loss. The courts have, for example, taken account of the sentimental loss resulting from the disappearance of a family portrait;[14] the affront to the religious sensibilities of a Jewish society caused by a breach by their butcher of his contractual undertaking not to sell non-kosher meat;[15] the damage to the reputation of an actress by the theatre's failure to put up her name in letters of the agreed size;[16] the distress caused to relatives of a dead man by breaches of contract by the undertaker;[17] even the grief caused by the death, resulting from a breach of contract, of a horse.[18] Although it can no longer be said that in the Common law damage of this kind is not actionable at all in contract,[19] it is clear that French law is far more generous. One reason for this is that *dommage moral* has always been freely actionable in delict in French law,[20] and there is as we have seen, a considerable overlap between the areas of contractual and delictual liability.

iii Dommage éventuel

The damage must also be 'certain'. This word, however, bears an elastic meaning. The damage may lie in the future, but it must be reasonably capable of being calculated. What is excluded is *dommage éventuel*, or loss depending on a hypothetical future eventuality. So where an insurance-broker had negligently advised a client to take out a policy which the insurer might be able to repudiate in the event of a loss of the kind for which the client had wanted cover, the client could not claim damages unless and until that event occured.[1] The courts have, however, generally been liberal in their assessment of what is certain. In particular there is a large number of cases (many of them in delict) concerning loss of a chance (*perte d'une chance*). A notary's negligence denies to a client the

14 Paris 2.12.1897, D 1898.2.465 note Planiol, concl Bulot.
15 Trib com Lyon 18.9.1936, Gaz Pal 1936.2.893.
16 Trib com Seine 20.2.1932, Gaz Pal 1932.1.895.
17 Trib Seine 20.12.1932, S 1933.2.44.
18 Cass civ 16.1.1962, D 1962.199 note Rodière, S 1962.281 note Foulon-Piganiol, JCP 1962.II.12447 note Esmein; cf Tunc RT (1962) 316.
19 See Treitel *Contract* pp. 731 ff; Treitel *Remedies* ss. 110 ff.
20 See Mazeaud/Tunc vol 1, ss. 301 ff.
1 Cass civ 20.1.1930, Gaz Pal 1930.1.413.

possibility of buying a house,[2] or that of an *avocat* the possibility of winning a case.[3] A carrier of a racehorse knows that it is to run in a certain race but fails to get it there in time.[4] In such cases the measure of damages is not the whole gain which the plaintiff could have made; the court has to make an estimate of the probability of success.

c Directness and foreseeability[5]

These are the two main limits imposed by the Code on the extent of the loss for which damages will be given. The requirement of directness is seen by *doctrine* as the necessary causal link between the non-performance, or the defendant's fault, and the loss. For this reason it is treated as applicable as much to delict as to contract, though the Code specifies it only in regard to contractual damages. The requirement of foreseeability, on the other hand, is confined to contract and is a mitigation of the full rigour of the requirement of directness in favour of the debtor who is not guilty of *dol*:

> 1150 When the non-performance of the obligation is not due to the *dol* of the debtor, he is liable only for such damage as was foreseen or as one could have foreseen at the time of the contract.
> 1151 Even where the non-performance of the agreement is due to the *dol* of the debtor, damages in respect of the actual loss suffered by the creditor and the gain of which he has been deprived should include only what is the immediate and direct consequence of the non-performance.

The debtor, therefore, whose fault does not amount to *dol* (and *dol* includes *faute lourde* or gross negligence) is liable for such direct damage as was foreseeable; the debtor who is guilty of *dol* is liable for all direct damage, whether foreseeable or not. Where the liability is in delict the debtor is always liable for all direct damage. The restriction in contract (*dol* apart) to foreseeable damage is justified on the ground that the parties can reasonably be supposed to have entered into the agreement on the basis of foreseeable risks.[6]

2 Cass req 26.5.1932, S 1932.1.387.
3 Paris 16.5.1963, JCP 1963.II.13372.
4 Trib com Seine 3.7.1913, Gaz Pal 1913.2.406.
5 Treitel *Remedies* ss. 82-97.
6 Mazeaud/Mazeaud s. 629.

The criterion for determining what damage is direct is, predictably, elusive. The French approach has been largely pragmatic. The recurrent illustration is taken from Pothier.[7] A man sells to a farmer a cow which he knows, but the farmer does not, to be infected. The farmer's other animals catch the infection and die; without these other animals he is unable to cultivate his land; because of this inability he cannot pay his debts, and his creditors seize and sell up his property. The loss of the cow and other animals is a direct consequence of the seller's *dol*. On the other hand the loss which he suffers by his creditors' levying execution is too remote; it has no 'necessary relation' to the seller's *dol*. On the loss resulting from lack of cultivation Pothier hesitates. It is not an 'absolutely necessary' consequence, since the farmer might have avoided it by buying or hiring other animals or by letting out the land, but since even these expedients would not have enabled him altogether to avoid loss, he is entitled to compensation in part. Here 'necessary' takes the place of 'direct', but this hardly carries the definition much further forward. Of the theories which have been invoked,[8] derived from German writers, none can be said to have achieved general acceptance. In principle the criterion of foreseeability ought to be excluded, in view of the clear distinction in the Code between foreseeability and directness, but the two are in practice often confused and the theory most commonly invoked, that of 'adequate causation',[9] comes very close to foreseeability. For there is adequate causation when the debtor's default has appreciably increased the possibility of loss of the kind that in fact occurred, and the criterion for determining whether there has been such an increase is the foresight of a reliable observer at the time of the default.

The problem is, however, of little practical importance in the law of contract, since it is only in the case of *dol* that the requirement of directness as distinct from foreseeability is relevant, and most breaches of contract do not involve *dol*. It is probably for this reason that the decided cases are mainly in delict.[10] And it may be that the courts take a wider view

7 *Obligations* ss. 166 f.
8 See Marty/Raynaud ss. 477 ff.
9 See Treitel *Remedies* ss. 92 f.
10 Marty/Raynaud s. 481.

of directness in delict than in contract.[11] It is in any event clear that there is a good deal of variation from case to case in the strictness of the criterion applied.[12] The *Cour de cassation* seems indeed in recent years to have been inclined to exercise control in the matter,[13] but pragmatically and without express commitment to any principle. There is, moreover, an uncertain borderline between the question of directness and the question of the assessment of damages. The latter is undoubtedly within the *pouvoir souverain* of the trial court, but that court's assessment may be influenced by its view of the directness of the loss.

The *Cour de cassation* also controls the requirement of foreseeability[14] and requires trial courts to state the facts sufficiently to enable that control to be exercised.[15] On two points there have been doubts. Until the earlier part of this century the *jurisprudence* required only that the type of loss, as opposed to its extent, should have been foreseen. Since it is foreseeable, for example, that goods consigned to a carrier may be lost or damaged, the carrier was held liable for the full extent of the damage, even though the goods were exceptionally valuable or exceptionally vulnerable. The modern rule is, however, fixed in the opposite sense, that both the type and the extent of the damage must have been foreseeable.[16] This is seen as reflecting the policy behind the requirement of foreseeability in article 1150, viz that a contracting party must be able to form an idea of the extent of the undertaking into which he is entering. The other matter on which the law is now settled is that the criterion of foreseeability is the 'abstract' one of the reasonable man (*bon père de famille*) rather than the 'concrete' one of the debtor himself. The debtor cannot escape liability by showing that he personally could foresee less than the reasonable man. This is in fact clear on the face of article 1150, which speaks of damage 'which *one* could have foreseen'

11 Mazeaud/Tunc vol 2, s. 1675.
12 Weill/Terré p. 469.
13 Mazeaud/Tunc vol 2, ss. 1423, 1675.
14 On the question of the influence here of French law on English law see Treitel *Remedies* s. 83.
15 Cass civ 9.7.1913, D 1915.1.35, S 1913.1.460.
16 Cass civ 7.7.1924, S 1925.1.321 note Lescot, D 1927.1.119; cf *Victoria Laundry (Windsor) Ltd v Newman Industries Ltd* [1949] 2 KB 528 (Treitel *Remedies* s. 85).

– not 'which *he* could have foreseen'. The question to be asked is what a reasonable man in the 'external circumstances', of the debtor (as opposed to his 'internal circumstances', such as intelligence, caution) of the debtor could have foreseen.[17] It is, however, less important in French law than in the Common law because it concerns the assessment of damages, which, as has been said, lies within the *pouvoir souverain*.

d Assessment of damages

Because it lies within the *pouvoir souverain* this subject is little developed. The overriding principle is that damages should compensate the creditor for the loss suffered. The expression of disapproval of the debtor's conduct has no place in the assessment of damages, though the trial court, as long as it makes no express reference to it, cannot be prevented from taking it into account. Since compensation is the aim, it is settled that whereas the moment at which the loss to be compensated is determined is the date of non-performance, the relevant moment for the calculation of damages is that of judgment, except where this will result in giving the creditor more than compensation. He may, for example, have obtained some countervailing benefit, or he may have taken steps to repair the loss at some earlier time when the cost was less, or have otherwise mitigated his damage. It must be noted, however, that French law does not think in terms of the Common law's 'duty' to mitigate.[18] The matter is considered, if at all, as an aspect of the need for a causal link.

6 Exemption clauses and penalty clauses

Since an agreement 'takes the place of *loi* for the parties',[19] it is in principle open to the parties to agree in advance what the damages in case of breach shall be.

> **Art 1152 Cc al 1:** When the agreement provides that the party who fails to perform shall pay a certain sum on account of

17 Mazeaud/Tunc vol 3, s. 2381-2.
18 Treitel *Remedies* ss. 100-106.
19 Art 1134 Cc al 1.

damages, no larger or smaller sum can be awarded to the other party.

The reference here is to a *clause pénale*, a term which may be translated as 'penalty clause' if that term is freed to its Common law implication of invalidity. French law makes no distinction between a penalty and liquidated damages.

The parties may, however, instead of agreeing on a fixed sum, agree on an upper limit (*clause limitative de responsabilité*). In this case the function of the judge in assessing damages remains, but subject to the limit. A clause of this kind must be distinguished from one which excludes liability altogether (*clause de non-responsabilité* or *d'irresponsabilité*).

a Exclusion and limitation clauses

A clause providing that one party shall not be liable for the non-performance of one or more of his obligations is now held to be in principle valid. Clauses excluding liability in delict have always been held to be invalid on the ground that delictual liability is a matter of *ordre public*. At first the courts took a similar view of such clauses in contractual contexts on the ground that liability in contract involved fault and that it was therefore contrary to *ordre public* to allow a party to stipulate for immunity. From 1874,[20] however, this rule was in form reversed, but in substance only modified. Exclusion clauses were valid, it was said, but that did not affect liability in delict for fault under article 1382 Cc. This left liability for non-performance of *obligations de moyens* unaffected, save that the defendant's liability for his fault, if proved, was in delict. As far as *obligations de résultat* were concerned, it had the effect of reversing the burden of proof. Had liability been in contract, the burden of showing a *cause étrangère* would have been on the debtor; under article 1382 it was for the creditor to prove fault. This rule was criticised on doctrinal grounds because it was in plain conflict with the ordinary rule that a delictual action will not lie in respect of a fault committed in performance of a contract between the plaintiff and the defendant (so-called rule of *non-cumul*), and on policy grounds because it severely limited the effect of exemption clauses, which were regarded as favourable to commercial

20 Cass civ 24.1.1874, D 1876.1.133; Cass civ 4.2.1874, D 1874.1.305.

enterprise. The rule survived, however, for some seventy years. The definitive *revirement* came in 1959 when the *Cour de cassation*[1] held that a *clause de non-responsabilité* was valid except in so far as the party invoking it was guilty of *dol* or *faute lourde*. The justification in terms of policy for the exclusion of *dol* (which has been held[2] to mean wilful failure to perform, whether or not accompanied by an intention to cause harm to the other party) is plain. The exclusion of *faute lourde* is less obviously justifiable. It seems to be a residue of the original dislike of exemption clauses, based on the fear that the removal of the risk of liability would encourage negligence or recklessness. This approach, which implicitly attributes a moral or deterrent function to the award of damages, is, however, more consistent with the French view of the law in terms of rights than it would be with the Common law view in terms of remedies, with damages as the price of breach.

There are other exceptions to the general validity of *clauses de non-responsabilité*. Some decisions have held that liability for injury to the person cannot be excluded, because 'the integrity of the human body cannot be the subject-matter of a contract'.[3] This is obviously correct in the sense that, in French law as in English law, one cannot without good reason (such as surgery) agree to the infliction of personal injury. The critics, however, contend that this, though correct, is irrelevant, because an exemption clause is not such an agreement, but rather an agreement that, if such injury occurs, there shall be no liability. The matter is disputed in *doctrine* and has not, it seems, reached the *Cour de cassation*.[4]

Clauses limitatives de responsabilité are in general valid to the same extent as *clauses de non-responsabilité*. An obvious problem presents itself where clauses of the latter type are excluded by *loi* and the *clause limitative* sets a very low limit. The courts have been ready to strike down what they regard as

1 Cass com 25.6.1959, D 1960.97.
2 Cass civ 4.2.1969, D 1969.601 note Mazeaud, JCP 1969.II.16030 note Prieur; cf Durry RT (1969) 798.
3 Toulouse 23.10.1934, D 1935.2.49 note Mazeaud; cf Mazeaud/Tunc vol 3, s. 2529.
4 See Weill/Terré s. 453.

derisory limits which have the effect of evading the purpose of the *loi* in question.[5]

The legislature has intervened on a number of occasions to exclude or limit exemption clauses in particular types of contract. For example, as early as 1905 it enacted[6] that contracts for the transport of goods by land might not exclude liability for loss or damage to the goods (as opposed to delay in their arrival). Such legislative interventions became more frequent as concern at the consequences of unequal bargaining power increased, but it was not until 1978 that a more general approach was attempted.

By article 2 of the decree of 24 March 1978[7] made under the authority of the *loi Scrivener*,[8] it is provided that in contracts of sale between professionals and non-professionals or consumers any clause having as its object or effect to exclude or limit the right of the non-professional or consumer to compensation for the breach of any of his obligations is forbidden (and therefore void) as being abusive in the sense of article 35 of the *loi Scrivener*. It is to be noted that although it embraces all exclusion or limitation clauses, this first intervention is confined to the contract of sale. Article 4 of the same decree provides, on pain of a fine, that the 'professional' party may not give an express guarantee without stating clearly (as follows from article 2) that such a guarantee does not exclude the normal guarantee provided by law.

b Penalty clauses[9]

As we have seen,[10] article 1152 al 1 presents what are usually called *clauses pénales* in terms of what a Common lawyer would call liquidated damages ('a certain sum on account of damages'), but excludes any power in the court to modify this sum. It is, moreover, accepted that such clauses may

---

5 Such exclusion clauses are in any case valid in maritime contracts, where regard must be had to the practice of other systems and in particular of English law; Mazeaud/Tunc vol 3, s. 2533.
6 C com art 103 al 2.
7 No. 78-464, D 1978.L.228, JCP 1978.III.47152; see Gode RT (1978) 744.
8 P. 136, above.
9 Treitel *Remedies* ss. 119 ff.
10 P. 226, above.

legitimately have any one of three purposes: to liquidate damages in advance and thereby obviate the need for possibly difficult calculations and the consequent delays; to limit the debtor's liability (or the creditor's entitlement); to exert pressure on the debtor.

The first of these purposes explains the rule in article 1150 al 1 denying any power of modification (but the third, as we shall see, accounts for the recent modification of this rule). In so far as a *clause pénale* serves the second purpose it obviously overlaps with a *clause limitative de responsabilité*, but whereas a *clause limitative* fixes a ceiling, the sum named in a *clause pénale* is at once a ceiling and a floor. It may therefore benefit either party. Where it benefits the debtor and therefore acts as a *clause limitative*, it is subject to the same limitations. It cannot, for example, in spite of the exclusion of review in article 1152 al 1, protect the debtor from the full consequences of his *dol*. This is illustrated by a case in which a contract between an actor and the *Comédie Française* required the actor, subject to a *clause pénale*, to obtain permission before acting elsewhere. The actor, in defiance of an express refusal of permission, had acted in a film. The actor's conduct was held to constitute *dol* and the *Comédie Française* was held entitled to recover the full amount of the damage which it had suffered, though this exceeded the figure in the *clause pénale*.[11] On the other hand, the fact that the damage suffered is less than the figure in the *clause pénale*, or indeed that there is no damage at all, is irrelevant.[12] But all the other elements of the debtor's liability must be present.

The existence of a *clause pénale* does not prevent the creditor from claiming *exécution en nature* if he wishes,[13] but the obligations are not alternative (as they would be if the debtor had undertaken either to perform or to pay a penalty). The debtor cannot therefore choose to pay the penalty rather than perform.

It is the third function of the *clause pénale*, that of exerting pressure on the debtor, that has occasioned difficulty. For it creates in effect a private *astreinte* without, in its original

11 Cass civ 4.2.1969, D 1969.601 note Mazeaud, JCP 1969.II.16030 note Prieur.
12 Subject to *alinéa* 2; see below.
13 Art 1228 Cc. But he cannot claim both, unless the penalty relates only to the consequences of delay (art 1229 Cc).

form, any power in the court to 'liquidate' it. (The parties can make provision for the penalty to increase, as with an *astreinte*, in proportion to the delay in performance.) Where the bargaining power of the parties is unequal, this uncontrolled power to fix penalties is obviously open to abuse. After complaints about such abuses in, for example, the French counterpart of hire-purchase, the legislature intervened in 1975 to give the courts a power to control the amount fixed. A second *alinéa* was added to article 1152:

> Nevertheless the judge can diminish or increase the agreed penalty if it is manifestly excessive or derisory. Any provision in the contract to the contrary shall be deemed not to have been made.

This plainly makes a considerable inroad on the principle of article 1134, on which, as has been said above, the first *alinéa* of article 1151 is based, but the discretion of the trial judge is not unlimited. The question of whether a particular penalty is to be modified lies within his *pouvoir souverain* (as of course, on ordinary principles, does the assessment of the damage actually suffered, which is the basis for determining whether the agreed figure is excessive or derisory) but in a series of decisions the *Cour de cassation* has laid down some of the limits within which this *pouvoir souverain* is exercised.[14] In particular, the judge may intervene only at the instance of one of the parties; if he does intervene, he must indicate in his judgment in what respect the agreed figure is excessive or derisory, so that the *Cour de cassation* can exercise control; and the requirement that the discrepancy should be 'manifest' imports the requirement that it should be not merely discernible, but considerable; and he may not reduce the amount below the level of the damage which has actually been suffered.

A corresponding alteration to article 1231 (which already gave, exceptionally, a power to the judge to modify the penalty where the debtor's failure to perform was only partial) yields the text:

> When the obligation has been performed in part, the agreed penalty can be reduced in proportion to the advantage which the part performance has given to the creditor, without prejudice to the applicability of art 1152. Any provision in the contract to the contrary shall be deemed not to have been made.

14 See Chabas RT (1981) 153.

7 *Mise en demeure*

An important different between French law and the Common law is found in the French rule that damages begin to run only from the moment at which the debtor is 'put in delay'. Article 1146 Cc provides that:

> Damages are due only when the debtor is in delay in fulfilling his obligation, except where the thing which he was bound to convey (*donner*) or do could only be conveyed or done within a certain time which he has allowed to elapse.

For the debtor to be 'in delay' the creditor must serve on him a notice, which article 1139 Cc refers to as a '*sommation* or other equivalent act'. A *sommation* is a formal notice requiring performance and served by a *huissier*. What constitutes the 'other equivalent act' is left to the *pouvoir souverain* of the trial judge.[15] It has, however, been held in particular cases to be satisfied by a wide variety of acts, ranging from the issue of a writ (*citation en justice*) to the sending of a letter.[16] This extensive interpretation is facilitated by the rule (article 1139 Cc) that the parties may agree to dispense with *mise en demeure*, an agreement which, it has been held, may be implicit.[17] The notice must, however, be sufficiently categorical to make it clear that performance is being demanded. Merely oral communications have sometimes been held sufficient, though obviously proof that they were sufficiently categorical may be difficult. Since the question whether any particular act will suffice will only be answered *ex post facto* by a judge, the wise creditor no doubt sticks to formalities, but it is clear that the original conception of *mise en demeure* as necessarily a strictly formal act has been whittled away.

The purpose of *mise en demeure* is to establish that the debtor knows that the creditor requires performance (his silence in the matter being presumed to indicate acquiescence in the delay). It is therefore in principle relevant to any remedy which may follow non-performance,[18] but its principal effects

15 Cass civ 5.6.1967, RT (1968) 144.
16 Cass civ 31.3.1971, D 1971 Somm 131. For the *jurisprudence* see Simon J-Cl Civ, arts 1146–1155, fasc VIII, cah 1, s. 42.
17 See Weill/Terré s. 423.
18 But not to the *exceptio non adimpleti contractus*; Cass com 27.1.1970, JCP 1970.II.16554 note Huet; cf Loussouarn RT (1971) 136.

are to fix the date from which damages will run[19] and to cause
the risk to pass in a sale or similar contract.[20] It is required as a
preliminary to other remedies also, but since the initiation of
the action itself constitutes a *mise en demeure* and since there
is no advantage (as there may be in the action for damages) in
establishing an earlier date, the requirement is for the most
part unimportant outside the action for damages. There are,
however, exceptions. In particular, in those cases in which
résolution is permitted without recourse to a court,[1] the
requirement of a *mise en demeure* has an independent
importance.

The wider justification of the requirement of *mise en
demeure* is said to lie in the avoidance of unnecessary litigation
by ensuring that the debtor is aware that performance is due.
It is in accordance with this policy that the *Code civil* specifies
that *mise en demeure* is not necessary (i) in the case of an
obligation *de ne pas faire*, in which the non-performance must
by its nature be manifest,[2] (ii) in the case mentioned in article
1146, above, in which the nature of the obligation is such that
it can only be performed within a certain time and that time
has elapsed, e g where a litigant's lawyer has culpably failed to
give notice of appeal within the time laid down.[3] It might be
thought to be consistent with this to exclude also the case
where the contract has specified a time for performance and
that time has passed. This is not, however, covered by the
words of article 1146 because the obligation *can* still be
performed and indeed article 1139, in providing for *mise en
demeure* to be dispensed with by agreement, envisages an
agreement relating to a fixed time for performance; where
there is no such agreement, therefore, the mere arrival of the
due date cannot be sufficient. This was indeed the Roman
rule, but it seems unjustifiably favourable to the debtor and

19 Art 1146 Cc.
20 Art 1302 Cc.
 1 See pp. 239 f, below.
 2 But Tunc (Mazeaud/Tunc vol 3 (5th edn) s. 2274, n. 4) suggests that this
    may not always be so. It may be a matter for argument whether a par-
    ticular act does constitute a contravention of the obligation.
 3 *Jurisprudence* dispenses with *mise en demeure* where the debtor has
    manifested his intention not to perform or where he has by his fault made
    performance impossible; Simon, above, ss. 71 ff.

the *ancien droit* had reversed it, adopting the maxim *dies interpellat pro homine* (the arrival of the due day takes the place of the creditor in demanding performance). This is the rule of German law and some other Civil law systems,[4] but before the enactment of the *Code civil* French law had gone back to the Roman rule. Even therefore where the contract expressly provides for performance by a fixed time, the debtor's failure to perform does not date from that time but only from the moment of *mise en demeure*, unless the contract waived the requirement (or the court is prepared to imply a waiver). This rule is widely deplored, but well-settled.

A separate *mise en demeure*, it should be emphasised, is never necessary, in that the beginning of an action will itself constitute a *mise en demeure*, but the debtor is liable only for damage occurring after that moment. For example, the tenants of a farm, after suffering for some time from the disrepair of the farm buildings, began an action. But by that time their hay had already been damaged. It was held that they were not entitled to damages in respect of the hay.[5]

Mise en demeure is not required where it would serve no purpose, either because the debtor has expressly refused to perform or because performance has become impossible by the debtor's fault.[6] These exceptions pose the wider question of whether the requirement of *mise en demeure* is confined to the situation envisaged in article 1146, where the debtor is in delay. A distinction is made between non-performance (including defective performance, which can be seen as partial non-performance) and delay in performance, and a corresponding distinction is made between the measure of damages in the one case and in the other. Where there is non-performance there are said to be *dommages-intérêts compensatoires* and where there is merely delay in performance there are said to be *dommages-intérêts moratoires*. The ine between non-

---

4 German Civil Code, s. 2842; Italian Civil Code, s. 1223; Swiss Code of Obligations, s. 102.

5 Cass civ 11.1.1892, D 1892.1.257 note Planiol, S 1892.1.117. In this case the position would not be different in English law, since a landlord is not liable on a covenant to repair unless he has notice of the need for repairs; Megarry and Wade *Law of Real Property* (4th edn) p. 700.

6 If it has become impossible without his fault there is no liability; see pp. 193 ff, above.

erformance and late performance is not sharp,[7] but the
distinction turns essentially on whether the failure to perform is
irremediable or not. In a contract for continuous performance,
for example, such as the supply of electricity, a failure of the
supply for a period can never be remedied, whereas this is not
so with, for example, the failure to complete a building on
time (unless, say, it is a pavilion for an exhibition which has
closed before the building is finished – a case which would be
covered by the second exception in article 1146). Again,
whether a failure to perform is a non-performance or a late
performance may depend on the construction of the agreement. A failure to repair will constitute late performance if the
obligation is construed as being to make repairs, but it will
constitute non-performance if the obligation is to keep in good
order (i e a continuous obligation). Reason (and the literal
meaning of the term itself) suggest that *mise en demeure* serves
a purpose only in the case of delay and therefore that it is only
in this case that it is required. The preponderance of *doctrine*
favours this view,[8] as, it would seem, does *jurisprudence*.[9] At
one time the *Cour de cassation* stated the rule in broad terms
which covered both types of damage. This was so, for example,
in the leading case, already cited, of the duty to repair.[10] But
in the last fifty years the trend of the *jurisprudence* has been in
the other direction.[11] The importance of this should not,
however, be exaggerated. Even if *mise en demeure* is not
required, the circumstances of the case may call for notice to
have been given, or at least for the debtor to have been aware
of the need for him to act. In a case decided in 1940,[12] for
example, the *Cour de cassation* ruled that *mise en demeure*
was not in principle necessary for the award of damages for a
landlord's failure to keep the building in repair 'once it is
established that the tenant has informed his landlord, in some

7 Mazeaud/Tunc vol 3, s. 2277; see also the examples of contracts for
  successive performances in *Source-book* p. 496.
8 For an early statement see Planiol's note to Cass civ 11.1.1892, n. 5,
  above.
9 See Carbonnier pp. 282 f.
10 Cass civ 11.1.1892, n. 5, above.
11 Cass civ 3.12.1930, S 1931.1.101, Gaz Pal 1931.1.78, *Source-book* p. 509;
  Cass civ 5.1.1938, S 1938.108. See also Weill/Terré s. 426.
12 Cass civ 13.11.1940, S 1941.1.11, DA 1941.2.

way or other, of the need to carry out, as a matter of urgency, the required repairs'. In such a case, if the landlord is not aware of the need for repairs, he cannot be said to be at fault in not carrying them out and there is therefore no failure to perform. Equally, the reciprocal duties of good faith and fair dealing[13] require the tenant to tell his landlord of the need for repairs.

8 *Résolution*[14]

a Character of the remedy

Where the contract is unilateral, the unsatisfied creditor has a choice between *exécution en nature*, where that is available, and damages. Where the contract is synallagmatic[15] and the creditor has not yet performed his part, he may, as we have seen, resort to the *exceptio non adimpleti contractus*, but where he has already performed, or where he wishes to obtain a definitive release from his obligation in place of the temporary bar created by the *exceptio*, he has the further option of rescission (*résolution*) of the contract, with damages where appropriate. In a contract of sale of goods, for example, the unpaid seller, if he still retains the goods, can invoke the *exceptio* in reply to the buyer's demand for delivery, but if he wishes to sell the goods elsewhere, he must obtain *résolution*.[16] If he has already made delivery, *résolution* may be advantageous if, for example, the market value of the goods is higher than the agreed price,[17] or if there is a possibility of the buyer's becoming insolvent.

There is obviously a broad similarity of function between the remedy of *résolution* and the Common law remedy of rescission or avoidance for breach, but there are two marked differences. (i) Save in certain exceptional cases, the creditor must normally apply to the court for an order resolving the contract; he may not, as in the Common law, simply treat the debtor's breach as

13 See pp. 147 ff, above.
14 Treitel *Remedies* ss. 143 ff.
15 And, it is usually assumed, where it is imperfectly synallagmatic and where it is real; as to *rentes viagèrés* see Starck ss. 2166 ff; Weill/Terré s. 484.
16 For the special case in art 1657 Cc see p. 239, below.
17 Cf Treitel *Contract* pp. 579 f.

discharging the contract. (ii) There is no legal criterion for distinguishing those breaches which are sufficiently serious to justify the termination of the contract and those which are not. The matter lies in the *pouvoir souverain* of the trial judge.

We are here concerned with the *action en résolution* as a remedy for *inexécution* which is imputable to the defendant, i e which results from a breach of contract, but we have seen[18] that the courts, in contradiction of the view held by *doctrine*, apply the remedy also where the *inexécution* is not imputable to the defendant because it results from *force majeure*. We have therefore already encountered some aspects of the remedy.

The textual basis for the remedy is in article 1184:

> A resolutive condition is always implied in synallagmatic contracts to provide for the case where one of the parties does not fulfil his undertaking (*ne satisfera point à son engagement*).
> In this case the contract is not resolved by operation of law (*de plein droit*). The party in whose favour the undertaking has not been performed has the choice either of forcing the other to perform the agreement, where that is possible, or of claiming *résolution* with damages.
> *Résolution* must be claimed by action at law and further time for performance (*un délai*) may be granted to the defendant depending on the circumstances.

This formulation presents the remedy as resting on an implied resolutive condition (and the article is placed in the section of the Code dealing with such conditions). In this the draftsmen were following Pothier[19] (and others before him), who linked the remedy to the practice in Roman law (which had no remedy of rescission) of inserting a resolutive condition (*lex commissoria*)[20] in contracts of sale. But this derivation is not well-founded as a matter of history[1] and is quite incompatible with the need for a court order and a fortiori with the discretion which the court exercises. The same objection can be made to doctrinal explanations in terms of *cause*. The courts are content to treat the *action en résolution* as an independent remedy without attempting any theoretical explanation.

18 Pp. 200 ff, above.
19 *Obligations* s. 672.
20 See de Zulueta *Roman Law of Sale* p. 57.
1 See Weill/Terré s. 481; Mazeaud/Mazeaud s. 1088.

b The judicial discretion

The option to claim the remedy is the creditor's, though the debtor can defeat the claim at any time, even during the course of appellate proceedings, by offering performance. Where the *inexécution* is total, the court will usually order *résolution* as of course, though it may accord a *délai* under article 1184 al 3, particularly if it thinks that the creditor is seeking to take advantage of a temporary difficulty in order to escape from a bad bargain. Where the *inexécution* is other than total, the *jurisprudence* has held that the court has a discretion. This discretion relates in the first place to the assessment of the gravity of the breach. Thus the *Cour de cassation* has constantly repeated that 'it is for the courts . . . in case of partial *inexécution*, to assess, according to the particular circumstances, if this *inexécution* is of such importance that *résolution* should be pronounced immediately or whether it would not be sufficiently made good by a condemnation in damages'.[2] In making this assessment the court will have regard to the question whether the creditor would have contracted had he foreseen the *inexécution*[3] (i e whether the element unperformed could be the *cause* of the creditor's obligation).[4] But it will also consider the economic circumstances in which the claim is made and the conduct of the parties, in order to achieve a proper balance between the advantage to the creditor and the disadvantage to the debtor.[5] *Résolution* may be justified even where the extent of the breach is small, if the court finds indications of bad faith on the part of the debtor; and the converse, as has been said above, is also true. Moreover, the court's discretion does not relate merely to the question whether it should grant *résolution* or not. As we have seen, the court may also order partial *résolution*, with modification of the creditor's obligation, thereby in effect setting the contract aside on terms.

2 Cass civ 14.4.1891, S 1894.1.391, D 1891.1.329 note Planiol, *Source-book* p. 496; the formula recurs in e g Cass civ 27.11.1950, Gaz Pal 1951.1.132 (Mazeaud/Mazeaud p. 973).
3 Cf arts 1636, 1638 Cc, which apply this test.
4 Cass civ 31.10.1962, D 1963.363.
5 Cass req 23.3.1909, S 1909.1.552; Cass req 4.3.1872, S 1872.1.431.

c Extra-judicial *résolution*

In three cases the creditor need not seek a court order.

(i) The contract may expressly provide for termination. Such a provision (referred to, as an echo of its Roman origin, as a *pacte commissoire*) is in general valid. (It would be difficult, in view of the formulation of article 1184, to argue otherwise.) There are, however, obvious objections, not only because of the general French hostility to self-help, but also because the specification of the circumstances in' which termination will occur is left entirely to the parties. There is therefore scope for abuse by the dominant party and such provisions have been restrained in two ways.[6] In certain types of contract (e g insurance, tenancies) the legislature has intervened to regulate or exclude them. And in all cases the courts apply a restrictive interpretation and, in the absence of an express and categorical formulation, will presume that the parties intend no more than a reminder of article 1184.[7] Moreover, even where the clause is sufficiently explicit to exclude the need for recourse to the court, the creditor must give the debtor a *mise en demeure*, unless this also is expressly excluded. This last possibility is obviously open to abuse, but the *Cour de cassation* has so far declined to regulate it, though any such clause is subject to the requirement of good faith.

(ii) In some specific instances the legislator has dispensed with the need for recourse to the court. The only such instance in the *Code civil* is the provision in article 1657 that where, in a contract for the sale of commodities or other movables, a date is specified by which the buyer must take delivery, the seller may after that date treat the contract as terminated by operation of law.[8] This provision does not extend to, for example, failure by the buyer to pay the price or failure by the seller to deliver, and, though the policy of article 1657 seems reasonable, it is not easy to see why the provision is so restricted.[9]

(iii) The *jurisprudence* also admits unilateral termination without recourse to the court in other circumstances which appear to justify it. The scope of this exception is very difficult to define. The earliest cases concern the dismissal of employees

6 See Weill/Terré ss. 495 f.
7 Cass req 3.5.1937, DH 1937.364, S 1937.1.371.
8 Cass req 29.11.1886, S 1887.1.63, D 1887.1.388, *Source-book* p. 502.
9 Cf Treitel *Remedies* s. 148 (p. 114).

for particularly gross breaches of duty, but the freedom to terminate has been extended to other cases where there is a special relationship of trust or confidence between the parties, where there is an urgent need to protect the creditor's interest, or where the breach is so destructive of trust as to make continuance of the contractual relationship intolerable.[10] In such cases, of course, as in all other cases of extra-judicial termination, the debtor may challenge the right of the creditor to act as he has, and therefore, as in the Common law where extra-judicial termination is the norm, the matter is ultimately subject to judicial control. The creditor therefore acts at his own risk, but the elasticity of the exception is criticised as undermining the whole principle that *résolution* must be ordered by a court.

d Effects of *résolution*

In general the effect is to make the contract null, subject to the retention of provisions, such as *clauses pénales*, specifically directed to the eventuality of *inexécution*. The nullity is retrospective, with consequential restitution, but in contracts for successive or continuous performances (e g leases, contracts of insurance or employment) it is obvious that accomplished facts cannot be reversed. Moreover, the nullity affects not only the parties themselves but also third parties, who may have acquired real rights under the contract. As far as movables are concerned, the disruptive consequences of this real effect are mitigated by the rule of article 2279 Cc (qualified by article 2280) that *En fait de meubles, la possession vaut titre*.[11] In the case of immovables there is a more specific mitigation provided by article 2108 Cc. Since the unpaid seller's right to seek *résolution* gives him in effect a real right to the property, which will prevail over the rights of any subsequent purchaser, the article provides that this *privilège*, if it is to be effective, must be registered within two months of the sale; and both the initiation of the *action en résolution* and the eventual judgment must be publicly notified. Finally, where *résolution* does have a real effect, it is well settled that 'acts of administration' by the interim owner are not invalidated.[12]

10 Cass civ 4.1.1910, S. 1911.1.195, *Source-book* p. 491.
11 See pp. 78 and 149, above.
12 See p. 151, above.

Index

Third party — *continued*
burden, exclusion of imposition on, 169, 172, 174
exceptions, 170, 173
contract, affected by, 164 *et seq.*
action in delict by, 166
doctrine of privity, 164, 165
opposability of contract, 165-167
principle of relative effect, 164, 165
exceptions to, 170 *et seq.*
action —
directe, 188
oblique, 187
Paulienne, 187
agency, see Agency
assignment, 172
cession de créance, 172
promesse pour autrui, see Promesse pour autrui
simulation, see Simulation
stipulation pour autrui, see Stipulation pour autrui
contre-lettre, right to prove existence of, 190
damage to, non-performance or mis-performance of contract, in case of, 166
meaning in French law 167-170
promesse pour autrui, See Promesse pour autrui
rights, French and English law compared, 186
résolution, after, 240
simulation, effect on, see Simulation
singular successor as, 167
stipulation pour autrui, see Stipulation pour autrui

Undue influence
nullity on grounds of, 103, 104
Unilateral contract
absence of cause in, 116, 117
consensual contracts, 117
real contracts, 116
bilateral, distinguished from, 37, 38
cause in case of, 117

Unilateral contracts — *continued*
consideration, absence of, 39
French and English law compared, 38
loan as, 41
meaning, 37
potentially bilateral, when, 41
potestative conditions, effect of, 155 *et seq.* 159
real contract, as, 39
synallagmatic contract, distinguished from, 37, 38
unilateral promise, distinguished from, 37
Unilateral promise
formal requirement, 58, 63
offer, distinguished from, 63
unilateral contract, distinguished from, 37

Vices du consentement. See Consent; *Dol; Erreur; Violence*
Value
fraud as to, 97
mistake as to, 87
Violence
consent extorted by, 73-78, 100-104
damages in case of, 105
dol and, blurring of distinction, 106
external circumstances of plaintiff, arising from, 103
fear, consent induced by, 100-104
fraud and, blurring of distinction, 106
illegitimate, must be, 101
legitimate, 101
limits, 101, 102
meaning, 100
nullity on grounds of, 73-78, 100 *et seq.*
objective test, 101
property, against, 101
salvage, in case of, 103
third party —
against, 102
by, 102, 103
undue influence as, 103, 104